PRAISE FOR
COLLABORATIVE PRII
BETTER SUPPLY CHAIN PRACTICE

"This is a very timely publication given the changing nature of the oil and gas industry and with the onset of the fourth industrial revolution. We need to continually reassess our supply chain practices, learning from other industries, adopting new ways of thinking, and maximizing our collaboration to ensure the sustainability and viability of our own sector. Norman McLennan's book provides some powerful insight into the latest supply chain practices and it is a great guide for supply chain professional across the energy sector." **Professor Paul de Leeuw, Director, Oil and Gas Institute, Robert Gordon University, UK**

"Against the backdrop of changing working styles, the impact of data, the quest for innovation, value and the speed of change, the importance of supply chains has never been higher. McLennan's timely publication gives private and public organizations the collateral to refresh and reframe their approach towards realizing better supply chain practice. It provides context, the why, the how, real examples and potential structures to enable positive outcomes for all parties. Now is the time to embrace change and take your business forward, and this is the guide to assist you in unleashing the power of collaboration."
Antony Faughnan MBA, FCIPS, Program Director, Arcadis, UK

"Norman has a plethora of experience to share on how to bridge both internal and external stakeholders' divides and build relationships within the supply chain which moved away from Michael Porter's 'balance of power' paradigm to one of collaboration and true win-win relationships to improve the whole, rather than favour the few. The concept of collaboration in any supply chain venture is not new, but practitioners are often stymied in their efforts to move away from more traditional (and human!) adversarial relationships. This book explains in a knowledgeable and engaging way why collaboration is of such value, what true collaborative principles look like and how to achieve them."
Dr Orietta Fioroni, Business Transformation Leader and former Operational Excellence Coach, Deloitte, UK

"Domestic and international projects across various sectors continue to over-run on original cost and schedule. The definition of insanity is 'doing the same thing over and over again and expecting a different result'. Projects across the globe that focused on collaborative relationships have broken that mould and delivered step change results in terms of cost and schedule which traditional execution models have not. Norman, based on his extensive practitioner experience, leading and creating collaborative relationships, has provided insights and clarity on how such relationships can be achieved and the benefits this can bring to all participants." **Peter A Jessup, Former Group VP SCM and CEO Proactive Change LLC, USA**

"Collaboration is increasingly being applied by supply chain companies as the fastest and most effective means to enact strategic change – whether to grow faster, to diversify, to apply new technologies or to export. Norman McLennan's focus on this important area in this book is therefore timely and resonates loudly with all stakeholders. A must-read for business leaders." **Stuart R Broadley, Chief Executive Officer, EIC (Energy Industries Council), UK**

"Against the backdrop of changing working styles, the impact of data, the quest for innovation, valu and the speed of change, the importance of supply chains has never been higher. McLennan's timely publication gives private and public organizations the collateral to refresh and reframe their approach towards realizing better supply chain practice. It provides context, the why, the how, real examples and potential structures to enable positive outcomes for all parties. Now is the time to embrace change and take your business forward, and this is the guide to assist you in unleashing the power of collaboration."
William Gingles, former underwriting executive, Lloyds of London

Collaborative Principles for Better Supply Chain Practice

Collaborative Principles for Better Supply Chain Practice

Value creation up, down and across supply chains

Norman K McLennan

KoganPage

Publisher's note

Every possible effort has been made to ensure that the information contained in this book is accurate at the time of going to press, and the publisher and authors cannot accept responsibility for any errors or omissions, however caused. No responsibility for loss or damage occasioned to any person acting, or refraining from action, as a result of the material in this publication can be accepted by the editor, the publisher or any of the author.

First published in Great Britain and the United States in 2019 by Kogan Page Limited

2nd Floor, 45 Gee Street	c/o Martin P Hill Consulting	4737/23 Ansari Road
London	122 W 27th Street	Daryaganj
EC1V 3RS	New York, NY 10001	New Delhi 110002
United Kingdom	USA	India

© Norman K McLennan 2019

The right of Norman K McLennan to be identified as the author of this work has been asserted by him in accordance with the Copyright, Designs and Patents Act 1988.

ISBN   978 0 7494 8049 3
E-ISBN   978 0 7494 8050 9

British Library Cataloguing-in-Publication Data

A CIP record for this book is available from the British Library.

Library of Congress Cataloging-in-Publication Control Number

2016046148

Typeset by Integra Software Services Pvt. Ltd., Pondicherry
Print production managed by Jellyfish
Printed and bound in Great Britain by Martins the Printers, Berwick upon Tweed

*To my family – my wife Alison,
my three children Holly, Stewart and Lucy,
my late parents Kenneth C McLennan and
Audrey N McLennan and also to my sisters
Pamela and Mary for the guidance and encouragement
shown to me throughout my life.*

CONTENTS

ABOUT THE AUTHOR

Norman K McLennan is a Visiting Professor at the Robert Gordon University, Aberdeen, and a respected cross-industry leader and consultant in the areas of supply chain management, commercial practice and business improvement. He is also owner and Managing Director of Rubislaw Consulting Group (Aberdeen and London).

His professional industry experience spans over 30 years split between the energy, oil and gas engineering and traditional construction sectors. He has worked for top FTSE, NYSE and JSE-listed companies in the UK, Europe, America, Canada, Sub Saharan, South Africa, China and the Middle East and has a proven track record of strategic leadership and enhancing business performance across diverse international multi-cultural teams.

He is a Fellow of the Royal Institution of Chartered Surveyors (RICS), the Chartered Institute of Procurement and Supply (CIPS) and the International Institute of Advanced Purchasing and Supply (IIAPS) and is an enthusiastic member of the London-based Institute for Collaborative Working (ICW) and Institute of Directors (IoD).

Norman has chaired numerous pan-industry and non-executive advisory boards across energy sector industry associations. He is an accomplished thought leader, conference speaker on business and supply chain issues and is regularly invited to present at related industry and professional bodies' events.

PREFACE

Considering whether to embrace a more collaborative business model requires a comparative reflection on the way organizations currently do business versus where they could be through greater collaboration. The three questions worth asking are:

1 Where is the organization now?
2 Where does it want to be?
3 How is it going to get there (the collaborative journey)?

Relationships are important in collaboration, and recognition of this is why collaboration has grown in importance in the contemporary business world. Developing trust in business relationships is also important, alongside managing risk in that context, the challenge of leadership in a collaborative setting and positioning to strive to achieve optimum outcomes.

Businesses and the supply chains upon which they rely across most industry sectors continue to change at an alarmingly fast rate on an increasingly complex global stage for all sizes of business. The need to embrace change is apparent, however, notwithstanding that much of the current organizational thinking is still based on traditional contracting solutions having end-to-end ownership; looking forward, the author envisages that most business models will eventually change to embrace collaboration in the shape of joint ventures, partnering and alliances that will have greater emphasis on behaviours, competence, skills, integration and fit for purpose governance. The need for organizations to work together in a more integrated fashion has perhaps never been more critical than in today's global economic environment in which the impact of technological advancements is coupled with faster, slicker communications and greater transparency of business markets.

Many organizations have found it a struggle to start relationship management programmes, and there has been a lack of suitable available frameworks within which to develop ideas in this regard. The emergence of a new global standard for collaborative working in the shape of ISO 44001 and the efforts of the Institute for Collaborative Working is welcome news.

Each business or organizational relationship has its own unique considerations. Many large corporations that have been in existence for many
decades, for example, will already have well-established processes and
procedures, yet the adoption of a new collaborative framework such as
ISO 44001 still has value and will still be of benefit in terms of providing a
common language that can aid implementation and collaborative engagement. For younger or more embryonic organizations, or those starting out
on the collaborative journey, the framework creates an ideal road map for
development.

It is against this backdrop, that this book has been complied to explore
the 'art of the possible' – the collaborative principles that will unlock better
business practice and enable value creation – up, down and across supply
chains. The 'art of the possible' theme underpins the whole book, positively
exploring 'the how' in terms of transitioning toward supply chain excellence though novel collaborative commercial arrangements and behavioural
shifts, drawing on specific case study examples of collaborative working
from across a range of different industry sectors.

The book's value proposition to readers is the articulation a range of
portable 'soft' (*behavioural*) and 'hard' (*commercial*) collaborative business
principles for consideration by cross-sector stakeholders to inform them as
to how they might unlock better business practice and create value in the
context of their own organizations and the interdependent supply chains
upon which they rely.

The merits of supportive business philosophies are examined in the
context of challenging business environments – from the different perspectives of the client (looking down the supply chain), the suppliers (looking up
the supply chain) and the interdependencies of organizations horizontally
across the supply chain.

It is envisaged that the book's content will have strategic supply chain
management significance and relevance for most organizations in the public,
private and third (voluntary/humanitarian) sectors and will examine how
such organizations can harness the benefits of working with a global standard in collaborative working practice (ISO 44001) and the CRAFT 8 Stage
Life Cycle Model developed by Midas Projects Limited.

In producing this book the author has spent many hours reflecting and
drawing on his 30 years' experience of working practices in both operational
and project type environments in the energy, oil and gas, and traditional
construction engineering sectors. He has developed strong cross-industry
networks and has also dealt with many complex and internationally diverse

cultures, having worked across Europe, America, Canada, South Africa, the Middle East and China.

The book also touches on leadership and aims to have international reach and relevance for a broad audience, including but not necessarily limited to:

- business practitioners of all kinds in any sector;
- middle and senior managers in industry (both buyer and supplier organizations);
- academia – higher education establishments, universities, colleges. etc;
- professional bodies (as recommended text /learning materials);
- members of industry trade associations;
- anyone else seeking insights into collaborative supply chain/business improvement practices and principles.

In terms of leadership, the author knows only too well that it can be lonely leading organizations or functions within organizations, or at least it used to be! Traditional leadership models were built on hierarchies and managed from the top down; today we've evolved into more collaborative leadership models, with customary leadership roles moved from the one to the many. Much of the content in the book welcomes and embraces this transition. The author advocates that the fundamental driver of collaborative success, whether in business or in life, is people and organizations working together and embracing joined-up collaborative thinking.

Many famed leaders have built their success with a collaborative approach. The following quotes are personal favourites of this author:

> O wad some Power the giftie gie us, to see oursels as ithers see us!
>
> (Robert Burns (1786) 'To a Louse, On Seeing one on a Lady's Bonnet at Church')

> People must be aware of their problems in a realistic way. They must be able to analyse their problems and to work out common solutions. In other words a community is easily divided when their perception of the same thing is different.
>
> (Bantu Stephen Biko)

> I'm going to tell you the story about the geese which fly 5,000 miles from Canada to France. They fly in V-formation but the second ones don't fly. They're the subs for the first ones. And then the second ones take over – so it's teamwork.
>
> (Sir Alex Ferguson)

> When 'I' is replaced with 'We' even illness becomes wellness.
>
> (Malcolm X)

Coming together is a beginning, staying together is progress, and working together is success.

(Henry Ford)

Teamwork is the ability to work together toward a common vision. The ability to direct individual accomplishments toward organizational objectives. It is the fuel that allows common people to attain uncommon results.

(Andrew Carnegie)

It is the long history of humankind (and animal kind, too) those who learned to collaborate and improvise most effectively have prevailed.

(Charles Darwin)

A single arrow is easily broken, but not ten in a bundle.

(Japanese proverb)

Collaboration has no hierarchy. The Sun collaborates with soil to bring flowers on the earth.

(Amit Ray)

No individual can win a game by himself.

(Pelé, Brazilian footballer)

Interdependent people combine their own efforts with the efforts of others to achieve their greatest success.

(Stephen Covey)

Being in a band is always a compromise. Provided that the balance is good, what you lose in compromise, you gain by collaboration.

(Mike Rutherford, musician, Genesis)

Collaboration has been an underpinning theme throughout the author's entire career – both in terms of building relationships and also achieving the most success in projects and industry supply chain initiatives that he has been involved in.

The acronym for the discipline of supply chain management is SCM – if we reverse it to read MCS it transitions to mean 'mainly common sense' – this is the compelling case for collaboration across supply chains!

(Norman K McLennan)

This book is intended as starting point for those interested in collaboration – a trigger to create discussion, reflection and debate regarding how collaboration might make a difference in the reader's own organization in terms of creating value.

Daring to be different and having the courage to challenge organizational thinking that is still based on traditional contracting solutions offers the potential for significant value creation and gain for all parties involved, particularly if contemporary collaborative models are embraced. Remember – we don't always have to run with the pack that embraces historical methods.

It is hoped, too that this book will play its part not only in educating, but also in changing the mind-sets of current and future business, commercial and supply chain management professionals.

ACKNOWLEDGEMENTS

The author would like to acknowledge the following individuals and organizations who provided help and guidance, and permitted the use of various materials and case studies in the preparation of this manuscript:

- Professor Andrew Cox, President Emeritus IIAPS at the International Institute of Advanced Purchasing and Supply, for his insight into SCM sector modelling and for his friendship and advice.
- David Hawkins, Director of Operations and Knowledge Architect at the Institute for Collaborative Working, for his insight into the workings of the CRAFT 8 Stage Life Cycle Model developed by Midas Projects Limited and the new ISO 44001 Global Standard for Collaborative Relationship Management.
- Dr Marla Philips, Leader of Pharmaceutical and Medical Device Industry initiatives, Driving Collaborative Change, Cincinnati, Ohio.
- Mike Lakin, Chief Executive Officer of Envoi UK Limited, a highly specialist consultancy that uniquely advises the upstream oil and gas industry on the acquisition and divestment of exploration and production (E&P) projects internationally. He and I have had such fun deal making over the years.
- Darine Ndihokubwayo, Supply Chain Executive for 'Food for the Hungry', the third sector humanitarian relief organization based in the Democratic Republic of the Congo. Darine's insights into the challenges around delivering food to the one of the worlds most vulnerable populations were truly humbling.
- Malcolm Wilson, Senior Executive at Achilles Information Management Ltd, for their insight and material provided on First Point Assessment and its relationship with industry supply chain codes of practice.
- Matt Royal, Steve Bushel and Ian Nethercot, Directors at Probrand, for their fascinating insight into the future world of digital procurement in the information technology sector and also SC4 and the onset of the fourth industrial revolution.
- Steve Smith, former operations head at Texaco North Sea UK Co, for his insights into collaborative innovation and sharing lessons learned on the Captain project.

- Andrew McCallum and Luca Corradi, Senior Executives at the Oil & Gas Technology Centre for their insights into pioneer technology acceleration and the aims and objectives of the Centre.
- All my professional industry colleagues at the Institute for Collaborative Working, the Royal Institution of Chartered Surveyors, Oil & Gas UK, the Energy Industries Council, NOF Energy, East of England Energy Group, the International Institute of Advanced Purchasing and Supply, the Chartered Institute of Procurement and Supply, the Institute of Directors, the Association for Project Management and the Association of Cost Engineers.
- My academic friends and colleagues at the Robert Gordon University, Aberdeen.
- Selma Ethem, my longstanding executive personal assistant and friend who helped immensely to keep me organized and on track in terms of all the administration that goes hand-in-hand with writing and developing a book.
- Finally, all my colleagues who I have worked with across the globe in the upstream oil and gas sector over the past three decades, without whom I wouldn't have had the career and life experiences I've had.

HOW TO USE THIS BOOK

The structure of this book is designed so that the chapters, standards, blueprints, frameworks, guidelines, tools and techniques and case studies can be read either sequentially in the order they appear, or the reader can opt to 'cherry pick' and be more selective by dipping into topics of specific interest.

The content is split into three parts. Part One captures and articulates essential knowledge architecture around collaboration and why, if deployed effectively, collaboration can be the 'jewel in the crown' for organizations. Part Two exhibits exemplar case studies of historical collaborative practice that has been successful in the private sector and Part Three exhibits exemplar case studies of collaborative practice either in play or evolving, which examine the private, public and third (voluntary and humanitarian) sectors, also extending into government and academic research areas.

Throughout all the chapters in this book, the author has sought to address what he perceives as prime challenges facing businesses and their supply chains today and also the many suboptimal business practices that we continue to observe across the private, public and third sectors.

Each chapter will highlight specific issues or practical examples from industry sectors. Additionally, the author has exhibited and adapted substantive case studies to demonstrate core themes and concepts around collaboration across different industry sectors, including one major pan-industry collaborative initiative comprising multiple strands. Commercial considerations and supply chain interdependencies are also reflected on throughout.

The author has woven exemplars of joined-up collaborative thinking throughout the entire book and into the detailed case studies. These provide not just examples of what we mean by collaborative best practice, but also provide some important examples of how to get started in introducing collaborative initiatives into your own organization or how to begin the processing of partnering with an external third-party organization for mutual benefit and value creation.

The blueprints, standards, frameworks, guidelines, tools and techniques and case studies exhibited throughout all provide a window into the mind of how some organizations are working collaboratively to move things in the right direction. Businesses and the supply chains upon which they rely across most industry sectors have huge potential to harness the benefits of adopting a more collaborative working approach. Such collaboration can of course take many forms, from loose tactical approaches through to longer-term strategic alliances, partnerships or joint ventures.

The supporting material contained throughout does not enforce a single, rigid approach; rather, it has more of a focus on providing a framework that can complement existing approaches where these are already in place. This is a very sensible, pragmatic route to take because many organizations will be reluctant to 'throw the baby out with the bath water' in terms of changing existing processes and procedures simply for change sake! Indeed, this may not be possible anyway due to proven governance structures that are already embedded within the organization. Some of the theories and concepts, however, may enlighten your thinking on governance and whether more 'fit for purpose' governance is needed to enable change for the better to be implemented.

In using this book, it important that you recognize that each business or organizational relationship has its own unique considerations. Many large organizations that have been in existence for many decades will likely already have well-established processes and procedures, yet, some of the supporting material in this book still has value and will very much still be of benefit in terms of providing you with a common language that can aid implementation and collaborative engagement. For younger or more embry-onic organizations, or those starting out on the collaborative journey, the supporting material provides a road map for development.

The adoption of the CRAFT 8 Stage Life Cycle Model and the ISO 44001 standard, referred to throughout the book, should always be balanced against the value that they can deliver to the organizations that chose to utilize them, whether this is for improving internal performance or to enhance confidence in the market.

Collaboration is an ethos. It is the process of shared decision-making in which all the parties with a stake in a process constructively explore and develop a joint strategy for action. Creating an ethos of collaboration is based on the premise that the collaborative process results in a win–win situation where everyone involved can gain.

As you begin reading the book, consider what collaboration looks like to you in your environment, asking yourself three questions:

1 Where is your organization now?
2 Where does it want to be?
3 How is it going to get there (the collaborative journey)?

The journey towards collaborative success is as simple and as complex as that.

PART ONE
Knowledge architecture around collaboration (the jewel in the crown)

Introduction 01

The rationale for collaborative business practices across supply chains and why collaboration can be the jewel in the crown for organizations

In this introductory chapter we examine the rationale behind collaborative business practices from different perspectives across supply chains and explain why, if used effectively, collaboration can be the 'jewel in the crown' for organizations. We also define what is meant by 'supply chain' across different sectors.

Considering whether to embrace a more collaborative business model requires a comparative reflection on the way organizations currently do business versus where they could be through greater collaboration. The three questions that should be asked are:

1 Where is the organization now?

2 Where does it want to be?

3 How is it going to get there (the collaborative journey)?

In terms of the *why*, we look at the importance of relationships in collaboration, their main characteristics, why this has grown in importance in the business world, the importance of developing trust in business relationships and risk in that context, along with the challenge of leadership in a collaborative setting and positioning to strive to achieve optimum outcomes. The impact of organizational culture will also be considered.

The term 'supply chain' is often used glibly by many organizations and industry practitioners, across many different sectors globally. However, what does it mean? Let's start by defining what is meant by 'supply chain'.

A supply chain can be defined as the third party organizational network that supports a client's or industry's primary objective. For example, in the global upstream oil and gas sector that primary objective would be to extract hydrocarbons from licensed oil and gas reserves. The activities of such a supply chain would typically cover the front-end concept development through the reservoir, design, build, operational and decommissioning project phases. There is a vast organizational range involved – onshore and offshore contractors, suppliers and service providers, consultants and specialist advisers through to the end user clients (integrated majors and independent operators) and such complexity is the same for other industries and business. Additionally, there are significant business flows to other non-core sectors that are necessary to support the core sector. Consider the upstream oil and gas sector, for example – if the oil sector is burgeoning because of a high oil price environment then it is likely that the local and national infrastructure will also be benefiting in increasing business for hotels, shops, restaurants, transportation – taxis, rail, flights etc. So, the supply chain has a very broad reach.

We turn now to the compelling business case and rationale for collaboration and why, if used effectively, it can become the 'jewel in the crown' for organizations.

Relationships in business are important because they are a critical aspect of sustainable success and developing, performing and maintaining effective operations. This is equally true in both the public and private sectors, but ultimately it is the interaction of relationships between organizations that creates the dynamics of better business.

Inter-company relationships often have a focus on governance and compliance where the emphasis is around establishing boundaries and adherence to processes to manage risk. However, businesses would do well to acknowledge that relationships are perhaps one of the principle risks that they must assess and manage.

Over the past 20 years there has been a significant trend towards long-term business models such as joint ventures, consortia groupings, partnerships, alliances and outsourcing, to name but a few. Such models often focus on developing integrated offerings or solutions. These business models can be highly complex and encompass a high degree of interdependency where successful outcomes depend on the ability of organizations to embrace joined up collaborative thinking and work in an integrated fashion.

The risks and vulnerability of such business models are very much linked to whether effective relationship have been built.

The dictionary defines risk as 'the chance or possibility of loss or bad consequence', and typically at the outset client or customer organizations seek to remove or reduce the uncertainty and risk by contracting with others to undertake the project, operations or work, thereby transferring the risk to contractors, suppliers or other types of organization involved. Additionally, modern business practices suggest that clients or customers seek to divest themselves of non-core business activities or establish more complex business solutions through outsourcing initiatives or programmes that frequently have direct interface with end users. An integral aspect of success is third party supply chain performance, reliability and dependability. Indeed, strategy around third party organizations upon which client or customer organizations will be reliant is a critical component of building compelling business cases and value propositions to put before executive decision makers.

There are a few key corporate considerations for relationship management that will help inform the reader reflect on their own organizational focus on relationship management capability:

- Business strategy and leadership – This should be considered in the context of whether collaborative relationships are strong or weak in terms of direction and encouragement for leadership across the organizations involved in a business proposition or contractual arrangement.

- Risk assessment and management – Typical sources of high risk are visible at a strategic, operational and project level. However, the greatest probable risk for any business is a breakdown of relationships, whether that is between client and contractor/supplier or amongst partners.

- Value creation – Unlocking potential across the value chain covers many areas of benefit, not just cost, but also sharing best practice process improvements, upskilling staff and performance enhancements to become more competitive.

- Knowledge management, trust amongst people and behaviours – The phrase 'knowledge is power' is one that most business practitioners will have heard. However, embracing this concept can be a barrier to organizations interacting in a collaborative way for mutual benefit and value gain. Trust and behaviours that promote the sharing of knowledge and exploiting it for mutual benefit lie at the heart of many modern business models. Ultimately, behaviours within organizations will be linked to corporate policies and process and the need for compliance.

- Internal corporate relationships – These are important to reflect on because internal boundaries and cross-functional divisions within companies can hinder and undermine external relationships and wider objectives.

Relationship management engagement is also important to consider in project, operational, trading and business environments in general. Consider, for example, the following:

- Clients or customers engagement needs – Now go beyond just a relationship with a preferred service provider or supplier. As requirements have become more complex across all industry sectors there is a need to understand both horizontal and vertical relationships up, down and across supply chains. Because there could be a critical link cascading the chain to the overall success of a project and it would indeed be naive to not consider potential vulnerabilities around that.

- Optimization of supply chains – In the upstream oil and gas sector typically 80 per cent of client operators' spend is on third party goods and services. For operators to become more efficient and competitive they need to reduce their lifting costs (cost of lifting hydrocarbons and taking to market).

- National, regional and international relationship issues – These arise when operating in a global market across different boundaries, such as different trading cultures.

- Outsourcing – This means that organizations external to a client or customer are now moving inside operational boundaries to effectively become a crucial part of the overall delivery process, but not necessarily embracing the client's corporate ethos or culture. Across many sectors, this seems to be an acceptable trade off.

- Bundling/clusters of small to medium sized enterprises (SMEs) – These are emerging to enable them to compete with larger companies, given the modern trend across most industry sectors for economies of scale. The conventional wisdom is that competition in the future will not be company vs company but supply chain vs supply chain, hence the trend for SME clustering.

- Corporate social responsibility (CSR) and local content matters – Very few organizations seeking to do business internationally can afford to ignore these areas, which embrace:
  - sustainability;
  - corporate governance;

- human rights;
- child labour;
- ethics;
- social well-being and infrastructure development;
- supplier development;
- environmental impact;
- green issues;
- employment of local people.

There is always a natural tension between the drivers of competitiveness, shareholder value and CSR/sustainability issues.

- Alliances, partnerships, consortia groupings and joint ventures – Relationships are critical to their success. Blending or bridging different cultures, processes, performance metrics, KPIs and incentive schemes across a chain of partners can be very challenging, requiring the most skilled of transformation efforts, but nonetheless the benefits of doing so can be enormous.

- Mergers and acquisitions (M&A) – Arguably, M&A deals are the swiftest way to grow a company. However, M&A activity can be fraught with risks. Ideally, there needs to be good operational and strategic fit as a precursor. Additionally, very often an important aspect that is not given adequate consideration is the respective organizations' cultural compatibility in their approach to relationship management to drive optimal outcomes and business success. There are many examples of M&A in upstream oil and gas past and ongoing where a deal is struck, with the ensuing aftermath being that one of the merged heritage companies usually sees their employees being quickly marginalized such that they either leave or are let go. This is the harsh reality and evidence of cultural disconnect (post-merger).

- Voluntary (third) sector – This sector has linkage to CSR and organizations should be cognizant of opportunities to harness the skills and resources that may be on offer from voluntary organizations. For example, commitment to local content and social development in an embryonic emerging region may present an opportunity. Such relationships between industry partners and voluntary sectors are possible but would need to be carefully developed because the motivations and principles of each are very different.

When developing relationships (whether they be vertical or horizontal), it is important to recognize that most relationships have a finite life cycle. To optimize the benefits of such relationships it is important to reflect on the medium to longer term consequences and implications of the parties' actions towards each other in ensuring value creating potential and commitment to delivering continuous performance improvement. Clearly, there is a need in business to establish the right platform to create the collaborative relationship in the first place. Usually this would be achieved through a formal contract or memorandum of understanding (MOU) or area of mutual interest (AMI). Such formality not only protects the parties to it but also jointly sets out the appropriate governance model, clarity on roles and accountabilities, objectives etc, all of which will combine to support positive collaborative working between the parties.

Figure 1.1 provides an insight into common positive and negative attributes between collaborative relationships, which are transferrable and could apply across most industry sectors internationally.

Figure 1.1   Attributes and indicators for collaborative relationships across supply chains

Positive attributes of successful collaborative relationships across supply chains	Negative attributes that frustrate collaborative relationships across supply chains
Top down executive sponsorship	Weak communication
Leadership commitment to action	Lack of stakeholder commitment
Joined up integrated planning	Weak management behaviour
Early stakeholder engagement	Lack of clarity on goals and objectives
Clarity of objectives and risk sharing	Leadership support lacking
Transparency (open book)	Weak upfront framing, scoping and planning
Clarity on roles and accountabilities	Lack of partnering skills and know-how
Good communications	Poor decision quality and strategic direction
Stakeholder/relationship plans	Poor partner selection
Joint ownership of risk/success	Unresolvable cultural differences
Charter for behaviours	Lack of KPIs
Robust key performance Indicators	Suboptimal dispute resolution
Dispute resolution mechanism	Lack of risk sharing, success sharing
Robust transformation process	No exit strategy for either party
Integration process – early on	Suboptimal contract arrangements
Upskilling commitment	

At this point, it is probably appropriate for the reader to pause and reflect on the maturity of their own organization or business (whether that be private, public or third (voluntary/humanitarian) sectors) in terms of readiness to enter into a collaborative arrangement to stand a reasonable chance of success.

One way to do this in a structured fashion might be to consider each of the statements on business environment in Figure 1.2 in the context of your own organizations and enter a tick in the appropriate column.

Obviously, the greater number of ticks in the 'highly ready' column shows an enhanced level of readiness for a collaborative relationship that stands a reasonable chance of success. A predominance of ticks in the 'partially ready' column indicate that there is some positive trend in the right direction but that some change is needed before finalizing any collaborative deal, whilst ticks in the 'low readiness' column inform you that there are significant barriers that would seriously frustrate the success of any attempted collaborative arrangement.

Figure 1.2   Readiness checklist for collaborative relationships across supply chains

Business environment consideration	Low readiness	Partially ready	Highly ready
Business strategy and leadership			
Risk assessment and management			
Value creation			
Knowledge management, trust amongst people and in behaviours			
Internal corporate relationships			
Client engagement needs			
Optimization of supply chains			
National, regional and international relationship issues			
Outsourcing			
Bundling/clusters of small to medium-sized enterprises			
Corporate social responsibility and local content			
Alliances, partnerships, consortia groupings and joint ventures			
Mergers and acquisitions			
Voluntary sector consideration			

This relatively straightforward and quick checklist tool enables you to address the three questions posed at outset of this chapter in terms of assessing readiness to embark upon a collaborative contractual journey with other parties:

1 Where is your organization now?

2 Where does it want to be?

3 How is it going to get there (the collaborative journey)?

Those business environment consideration areas that show low readiness or are only partially ready are the areas that your organization must focus on when asking 'How is your organization going to get there?'

The terms collaboration, partnering, alliancing and join ventures also tend to be used glibly by many people and organizations without an understanding of the potential benefits, value gain and challenges of such arrangements between different organizations. Buzzwords such as the 'DNA' of an organization, the 'corporate culture' or the 'company ethos' are often used; however, it is important to recognize that the culture of a company is effectively referring to 'the way how things are done'. Such corporate culture is likely to be dictated or driven by a company's management structure or national identity, whereas the ethos (the values) of the company is more likely to be driven by those in authority through governance processes and procedures.

There are many examples of companies with distinctly different cultures that have merged or have been acquired with the immediate result being a toxic environment when precisely the opposite was needed – an environment with a more supportive philosophy. Such an outcome is usually a result of the negative attributes or indicators listed in Figure 1.1. The reality, of course, is that to fully exploit the benefits and potential of collaboration you must create an environment that fosters the right behaviours, rather than just forcing it through process changes. Figure 1.1 again informs us as to likely positive attributes that create a greater chance of success in collaboration.

The principles and concepts behind collaborative working are nothing new – alliancing, partnering and joint venture arrangements have been around for decades as well as across many different business and industry sectors with international/global reach. Many people have the perception that collaborative working and related business practices are primarily about cost cutting, and although that is clearly a business or organizational imperative, collaboration also offers organizations an enhanced capability to build an entirely new value proposition beyond the capabilities that they have as individual organizations.

I maintain the view that by 2020 there will be a growing trend towards greater reliance on collaborative networks, partnerships, alliances and joint ventures not just with big corporate entities but also with clusters of SMEs. Additionally, there is a genuine lack of skills, training and development in the collaboration arena when it comes to internal capabilities within most organizations. Typically, because of such skills shortages, it is common practice for many organizations to commission external management consultants to facilitate and manage the establishment of a new collaborative arrangement between distinctly separate organizations. This can be a costly commitment, and sometimes because of the ensuing change management issues management consultants can be difficult to 'work out of the system' because senior and middle management become reliant upon them as a form of 'crutch'. The excellent work of the Institute of Collaborative Working (ICW), and the development of a global standard framework for organizations to adopt in the form of ISO 44001 is a major step forward for organizations wishing to develop their in-house capability to implement and manage collaborative arrangements. Subsequent chapters explore this in more detail.

Anecdotal evidence suggests that many collaborations fail – again, most probably due in some part to combinations of the negative attributes in Figure 1.1. However, there are also many great examples of where collaboration has succeeded and some of these across a sample of different industry sectors are explored in subsequent case study chapters.

Another area worth reflecting upon is 'relationship risk and opportunities'. As business and organizational landscapes become more complex and challenging, the relationships between organizations take on a variety of new configurations. Often companies miss opportunities by maintaining rigid risk boundaries internally between cross functions, but as the market landscape changes so the complexity of relationships increases, which generates a wider spectrum of risks that can be addressed through proactive integration of skills, competence and ideas. There is no doubt that globalization and convergence across many business sectors have expanded the range of trading relationships up, down and across supply chains, thereby creating opportunities to create value at all stages of the process.

Maintaining competitive edge is important for organizations, and pressure in this regard encourages organizations to work in an integrated way. It is not uncommon now to see competitors working closely together in specific project ventures to help reduce or manage risk.

There are many aspects to risk in integrated arrangements, such as:

- operational considerations;
- surety of performance;
- knowledge sharing and fusion;
- business continuity planning and contingency planning;
- reputational issues;
- people issues;
- cultural issues;
- environmental impact assessment;
- technology;
- business processes and procedures;
- governance and compliance;
- efficiency and streamlining;
- effectiveness;
- innovation and creativity;
- change/transition and future-proofing (shaping long-term plans).

Analysis of risk can be focused into three main areas:

1 Those risks that can be identified by source.

2 Those risks that emanate from actual works or operations.

3 That of impact in terms of clarity around what the repercussions may be.

Essentially, the overall process of risk assessment and management for organizations covering any of the aspects and vulnerabilities across the supply chain can be summarized as:

- identify potential significant risks or vulnerabilities;
- determine the consequence of each risk and vulnerability (including who may be impacted);
- determine the likelihood of each risk or vulnerability occurring;
- assess the overall risk or vulnerability;
- remove the overall risk or vulnerability;
- manage the overall risk or vulnerability;
- re-assess the overall risk.

Figure 1.3 Probability – impact risk assessment and management tool for use across supply chains

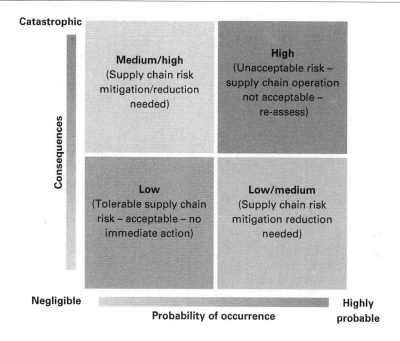

Numerous tools and mechanisms exist (such as the one in Figure 1.3) to help organizations with supply chain risk and vulnerability assessment.

The reader should reflect on the use of such tools and mechanisms because if we are to exploit the potential of more collaborative alternative business models across the supply chain then the potential impacts cannot be ignored. Moreover, in the broader sense of managing business risks the implications of relationships are not something that can be left to chance. Relationships are an integral part of business, which in turn make them a key aspect of risk management, and joint ventures can help organizations gain a competitive edge.

In the context of collaborative working it is also important to briefly consider how culture drives behaviours both corporately and at an individual personal level between different organizations. The word 'culture' is derived from the Latin *cultura* (meaning cultivation), which implies that it can be developed in some shape or form. However, in modern business parlance it generally means shared attitudes, values, goals and practices exhibited by an organization.

For collaborative working, the businesses involved need to position their partner selection and governance to support an agreed set of cultural principles that will underpin the partnership relationship. Figure 1.4 offers some

Figure 1.4   Influences on culture across the supply chain

Internal influences on culture	External influences on culture
Visions/values	Legal/regulatory
Leadership objectives	Language/education
Change and innovation	Government/political
Capability and competence	National/regional
Ethics and governance	Economy/environment
Corporate and social responsibility	Technology maturity
Diversity and quality	Social/customs
Reach to market	Ethnic

suggested high-level cultural principles that are helpful in providing a frame-work to focus organizational change. The internal and external elements listed in Figure 1.4 are examples of areas where there might be a substantial amount of influence on any business activity across supply chains and impact on behaviours. It follows, therefore, that an effective integrated partnership should have a combined culture that strives to improve performance and ultimately suppress poor behaviours by having strategic direction, goals and clear objectives, being adaptable, empowering teams, ensuring capability, adhering to core values and remaining integrated.

It is also important that we briefly discuss trust, because it is a key factor in being successful in exploiting business opportunities and managing risks at the interfaces between organizations. By building and maintaining trust we remove the time-consuming and costly controls that businesses place between themselves. Having said that, we do establish and execute formal contracts between organizations that are based on the presumption of failure or something going wrong or default between the parties! The contract will likely always be needed to protect the parties.

There are, however, three crucial factors for success with collaborative arrangements:

1 Recognize and understand the very different positions and drivers of the parties at the outset, because when two organizations enter into a collaborative arrangement there will most probably be three sets of objectives – *yours*, *mine* and *ours*!

2 Have an effective mechanism for handling disputes that may arise regarding the relationship between the two parties. This will help define

the strength of trust. For example, an 'alliance improvement governance board' could be established with senior representatives from each organization to act as the first port of call resolution group rather than arbitration or reverting to law.

3 Have rules of disengagement, an exit mechanism or strategy. In a business partnership this could simply be a 'termination for convenience' contract clause or 'termination for default of one of the parties'. In both instances there may be financial implications. However, at the time of writing, consider the UK's potential withdrawal from the EU under Brexit – essentially the exit mechanism is Article 50, and once it enters into force the collaborative EU treaties simply stop applying to the UK, unless a transitional arrangement and period is agreed. If agreeing a mutually satisfactory deal proves impossible, there is a fall-back position. The EU treaties will simply stop applying two years after the UK first notified its intention to withdraw (a period that can be extended, if needed).

The matter of trust is as much about good open communication as anything else, and as organizations move more toward alternative business models trust becomes a major consideration.

There is always the possibility of disagreement or differences in any business joint venture, partnership or alliance. So, any collaborative culture must have a mechanism to manage such situations to avoid destroying trust. Figure 1.5 advocates a win–win approach whereby the issues are out in the

Figure 1.5 Win–win versus win–lose across supply chains

Win–win	Win–lose
Flexibility	Rigidness
Joined up, collaborative thinking to arrive at a solution	Both sides seeking individual solutions in isolation
Threats avoided	Threat is power
Open and honest dialogue	Misleading information
Compromise and satisfying both sides	Power through independence
Mutual interdependence	Power owner forces solution with disregard for the other party
Conflict is a mutual problem	Conflict where one party wins and the other loses

open (in the middle ground), so that the root cause can be tackled, not just the symptoms.

Collaborative leadership has an important part to play in this. Dynamic modern leadership styles are a key facet of managing every successful joint business venture such as partnering, alliances and collaborative programmes, especially where delivery objectives and processes cross organizational boundaries. Very often, a collaborative leadership style is required to skilfully navigate through organizational structures that have been hierarchical and lacking the necessary agility and flexibility to optimize the effectiveness of interdependent organizations. In the environment of integrating relationships across such organizational and geographical boundaries, the most effective outcomes tend to come from situations where resources, knowledge, skills, competence and capabilities are pooled.

The effective collaborative leader will tend to operate not from a position of power but from his or her ability to influence, motivate and inspire, but with a good self-awareness of his or her relative power and the potential impact that they have on others. Indeed, the most effective collaborative leaders can draw and bring parties together to create practical and novel solutions that utilize the full potential of all parties to optimize performance outcomes that could not be achieved in isolation. Notwithstanding this, however, the recognition of individual contributions is essential in inspiring and fostering collective ownership and collaboration.

Collaborative working requires leadership that can take management beyond localized internal type goals to direct outcomes toward mutual return on investment for the parties involved within a culture of trust and cooperation. Additionally, collaborative working requires an emphasis on managing relationship both internally and externally.

The assessment of collaborative leadership can be examined by exploring two key aspects, *ability* and *attitude*, as shown in Figure 1.6. Essentially, ability is about business-related experience in areas that would be supportive to operating under alternative business models and ways outside the normal traditional authoritarian command–control structure. Attitude, by comparison, is about an individual's style of being able to operate effectively with others in a collaborative environment and to embrace the concept of joined up collaborative thinking to develop and implement solutions. These two key aspects, albeit distinct from each other, are also interrelated, and when combined they create the key ingredients of a collaborative leadership profile.

Figure 1.6 is essentially an adapted Kraljic matrix, which affords readers the opportunity to pause and have an honest conversation with themselves about what type of leadership profile they have in terms of suitability for collaborative programmes.

Figure 1.6 Suitability assessment for involvement in collaborative programmes – ability versus attitude across supply chains

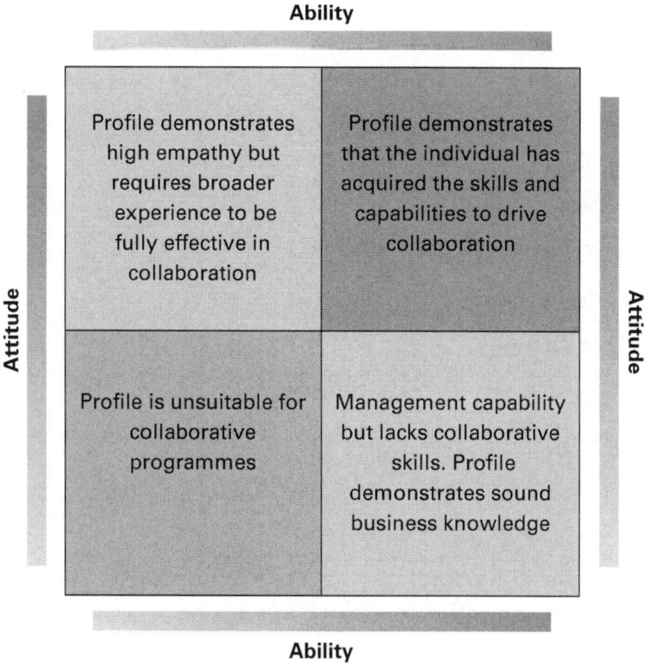

Ability

Profile demonstrates high empathy but requires broader experience to be fully effective in collaboration	Profile demonstrates that the individual has acquired the skills and capabilities to drive collaboration
Profile is unsuitable for collaborative programmes	Management capability but lacks collaborative skills. Profile demonstrates sound business knowledge

Attitude (left) — Attitude (right)

Ability

Examples of *ability* (experience, competency and skills) would include (but not necessarily be limited to):

- partnering experience;
- service delivery experience;
- product development experience;
- knowledge of international/global trade;
- market knowledge and awareness;
- project management skills;
- knowledge of supply and value chains;
- financial awareness;
- risk management skills;
- contract management skills;
- transformation and change management skills;
- performance management skills;
- benchmarking skills;

- planning experience;
- quality assurance experience;
- strategic ability;
- qualification and training.

Examples of *attitude* (personal approach) may include:

- style (Myers Briggs leadership and management style);
- communication skills;
- self-critical/aware;
- approach to business;
- varying expectations;
- the degree of importance placed on relationships;
- team working;
- sustainability awareness;
- commitment to training;
- developing, mentoring and coaching others;
- decision quality/decision making;
- personal focus toward others;
- dealing with performance failure;
- management of disputes, learning style and key success factors.

Leadership is a complex yet crucially important role in collaborative arrangements and there is an absolute need to demonstrate empathy by being actively interested in others – their challenges, their development needs, etc – and being ready to share knowledge and mentor those individuals who need to be upskilled and become confident to work in a collaborative environment.

Positioning relationships is another important aspect of collaboration in business. For certain, there will be a broad spectrum of relationships, needs and strategic requirements. The adapted generic Kraljic matrix in Figure 1.7 provides the reader with a basis for the initial positioning of a collaborative relationship and subject to movement from one sector to another as a result of changes in demand or the development of an opportunity.

Considering each quadrant in turn:

- **Lower left quadrant** – *Supply/service* contractual arrangements across supply chains would be those that would cover general products,

Figure 1.7 Relationship positioning focus matrix across supply chains

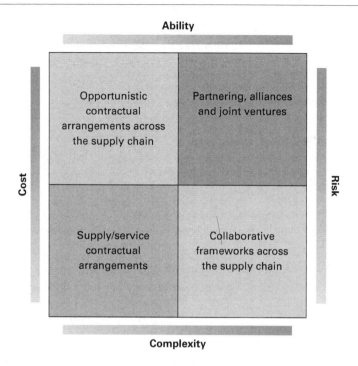

commodities or straightforward services that are relatively low in complexity, risk and value and not of strategic significance to the business. These types of arrangements tend to be frequently competitively tendered and suppliers changed out often.

- **Top left quadrant** – *Opportunistic* contractual arrangements across supply chains would be those that would generally be of a one-off nature and although not complex there is a high risk and value attached to the business. Such arrangements are usually formalized by way of a traditional arm's length type contract.

- **Lower right quadrant** – *Collaborative frameworks* across supply chains relate to those that, whilst not initially strategic in nature, are of significant cumulative value to the business, and where overall cost and performance can be enhanced through the development of a framework agreement.

- **Top right quadrant** – *Partnering, alliances and joint ventures* across supply chains relate to business-critical strategic alliances where there is long-term potential for an integrated approach that would be likely to offer significant advantages and benefit through the exchange and pooling of knowledge, competencies, skills and resource.

When considering any partnership, alliance or joint venture arrangement, it is important to consider what your potential partner or partners may look like. This is often referred to as finding your partner of choice, and in this regard there ideally needs to be a framework within which the prospective partner organizations can undertake a systematic approach to consolidating their respective internal expectations and the views of the other potential partners. It is only once this is done that you would create an appropriate development strategy. Figure 1.8 articulates at a high level the typical issues. By categorizing the key issues such as organizational, cultural, capability and commitment to action, organizations can apply their minds and focus on the fundamental issues that will drive their new partnership type relationship to a successful implementation.

The process around this is to develop the criteria that will be used to make the assessment, aimed at compiling the overall picture of the potential partner and then focusing on the areas for potential exploitation and improvement through development, or 'development areas'. There is a broad range of areas that should be probed to determine the 'suitable fit' of a prospective partner, such as those shown in Figure 1.9.

In conclusion, collaboration is essentially about exploiting the joint potential of partnering organizations in a fully transparent, open and positive manner. Exploring and probing the areas in the 'partner fit' triangle in Figure 1.9 will help to inform you as the prospective partners resolve to

Figure 1.8   Cross-partnership development areas across supply chains

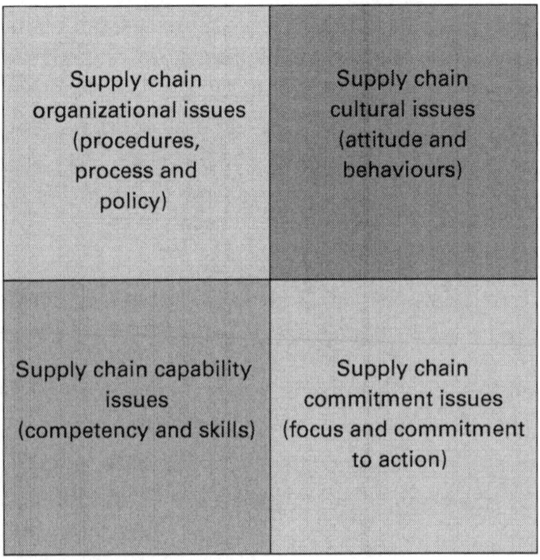

Supply chain organizational issues (procedures, process and policy)	Supply chain cultural issues (attitude and behaviours)
Supply chain capability issues (competency and skills)	Supply chain commitment issues (focus and commitment to action)

Figure 1.9 Partner fit triangle – areas to probe across supply chains

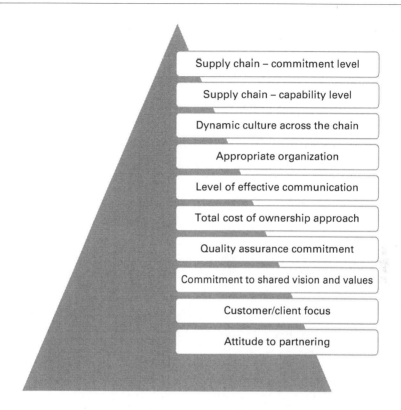

Supply chain – commitment level

Supply chain – capability level

Dynamic culture across the chain

Appropriate organization

Level of effective communication

Total cost of ownership approach

Quality assurance commitment

Commitment to shared vision and values

Customer/client focus

Attitude to partnering

participate proactively. The application of collaborative approached takes time and requires the deployment of valuable resources, so any decision to embark on a collaborative journey should not be taken lightly. It requires a serious, dedicated effort to focus on deploying an organization's assets to optimal effect.

Hopefully, this introductory chapter has provided the reader with a high-level awareness and appreciation of the rationale behind collaborative business practices from different perspectives. In terms of the importance of relationships in collaboration, its main characteristics addresses why it has grown in importance in the contemporary business world, the importance of developing trust in business relationships and risk in that context, along with the challenge of leadership in a collaborative setting and positioning to strive to achieve optimum outcomes, and the impact of organizational culture in terms of positioning for success.

Considering whether to embrace a more collaborative business model requires a serious comparative reflection on the way organizations currently do business versus where they could be through greater collaboration, addressing the three questions of:

1 Where is your organization now?

2 Where does it want to be?

3 How is it going to get there?

This is what we call the collaborative journey.

In the subsequent chapters we build on *why* collaboration can be the jewel in the crown for organizations by exploring the *how* and the *where* of development and implementation of collaborative arrangements. The *how* will provide framework guidelines on implementing collaborative practice in business and across supply chains. Such guidelines will be firmly anchored to the CRAFT 8 Stage Life Cycle Model and the business case that evolved to adopt ISO 44001, a new global standard for collaborative business working that discusses organizational knowledge, state of readiness within organizations to adopt the standard approach, and practicalities of working together. The *where* will explore the value proposition that collaborative business practices and relationships can bring in the short, medium and long term, with an emphasis on cooperation across supply chains and amongst customer or client groups.

Collaborative arrangements

02

Different supply chain perspectives, drivers and interdependencies

In this chapter we shall examine the different perspectives up, down and across supply chains. It is important for industry practitioners to have an upfront understanding of the supply chain interdependencies that make for a better business relationship and what the value drivers are to organizations, given certain variables and circumstances. A good working knowledge and understanding of this is an essential precursor to the establishment of any collaborative contractual relationship. These principles are sufficiently generic to be applied across most industry sectors where third party goods and services are being provided.

Let's start first of all by examining the perspective of a client or buyer looking down the supply chain, and what features are important. The matrix in Figure 2.1 helps us in this regard. We can see that the two key dimensions that are important to the client are whether or not the third-party goods or services that it is procuring are 'high risk or critical' and whether or not they are of significant 'procurement value or spend'. Additionally, it can be seen that nature of the business relationship can be classified into four segments, depending on the aforementioned two dimensions. These segments are critical, routine, leverage and bottleneck.

- **Critical business relationships** – In a situation where a client buyer has contracts with contractors or suppliers that are in the high risk/high procurement value category, then those contracts are critical to the client

Figure 2.1 Perspective of client looking down the supply chain

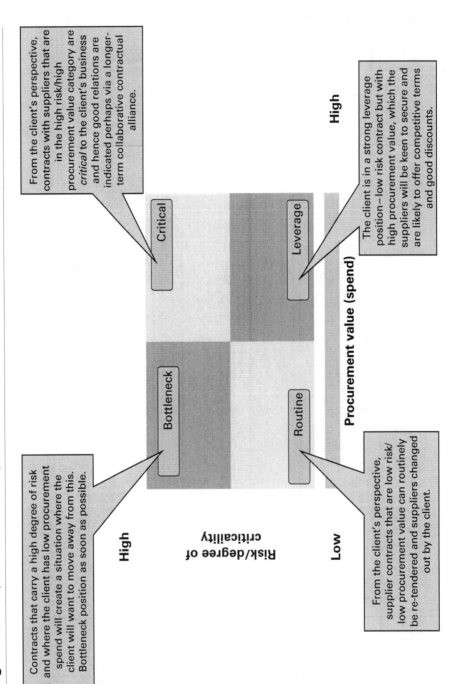

From the client's perspective, contracts with suppliers that are in the high risk/high procurement value category are *critical* to the client's business and hence good relations are indicated perhaps via a longer-term collaborative contractual alliance.

The client is in a strong leverage position – low risk contract but with high procurement value, which the suppliers will be keen to secure and are likely to offer competitive terms and good discounts.

Contracts that carry a high degree of risk and where the client has low procurement spend will create a situation where the client will want to move away from this. Bottleneck position as soon as possible.

From the client's perspective, supplier contracts that are low risk/low procurement value can routinely be re-tendered and suppliers changed out by the client.

High

Critical

Leverage

High

Procurement value (spend)

Risk/degree of criticality

Bottleneck

Routine

Low

buyer's business and hence good relations are indicated perhaps via a longer-term collaborative contractual alliance where risk and reward is shared. Under such circumstances it is likely that there will be fewer of those suppliers in that particular market segment, meaning that the client buyer does not have as much leverage as it would like. Accordingly, its tactics must be tailored to a more collaborative approach.

- **Routine business relationships** – The opposite extreme is a situation where the client buyer has contracts with contractors or suppliers that are low risk/low procurement value – they can routinely be re-tendered and suppliers changed out by the client as there is likely to be plenty of those suppliers and lots of competition in that particular market segment, meaning that the client buyer can be more bullish.

- **Bottleneck business relationships** – These reflect a situation where the client buyer is in contracts that carry a high degree of risk but where there is a relatively low amount of procurement spend. This is not a constructive relationship for the client to be in and is indeed a bottleneck scenario and one that the client should move away from as soon as possible.

- **Leverage business relationships** – As the term suggest, this is where the client is in a strong leverage position dictated by the contract being low risk (not critical to the business) but nonetheless one where there is a high procurement spend that the contractors or suppliers will be keen to secure and are likely to offer competitive terms and good discounts on. Under such circumstances it is likely that there will be many competing suppliers jockeying for position in that particular market segment. This of course means that the client buyer has significant leverage to secure more favourable commercial terms and discounts.

Flipping things completely now and turning to an entirely different perspective, we will look up the supply chain (from the perspective of the contractor or supplier looking at what it ideally wants from a client or buyer). Figure 2.2 helps us better understand this differing perspective and, as can be seen from this matrix, the features on the vertical and horizontal axis of the matrix subtly change to read 'account attractiveness' and 'value of business (revenue)'. This change reflects a shift in type of business relationships to the preferences of the contractors or supplier looking up the supply chain at its clients.

Ideally, smart contractors or suppliers can position themselves contractually such that they can prioritize their own client base to maximize revenue, with handsome profits being made and hopefully in a long-term sustainable

Figure 2.2 Perspective of contractor/supplier looking up the supply chain

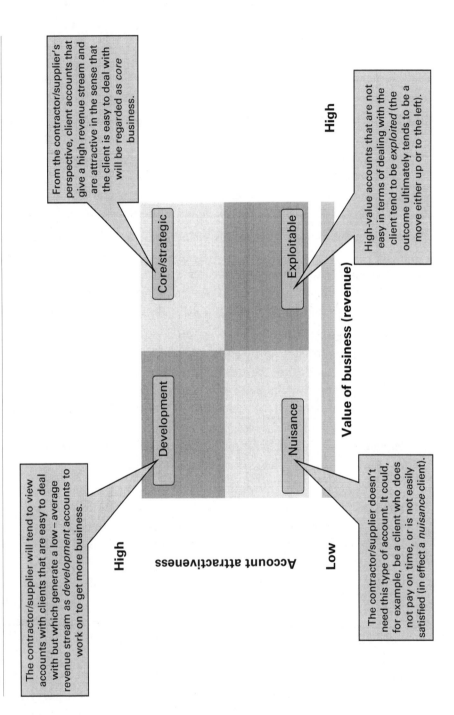

business relationship, thereby giving greater security of work. It can be seen from this adapted matrix that the nature of the business relationship from the contractor or supplier's perspective can be classified into four segments depending on the aforementioned two dimensions. These segments are core, nuisance, development and exploitable.

- **Core/strategic business relationships** – In a situation where a contractor or supplier has existing or prospective client contracts or accounts that, from the contractor or supplier's perspective, give a high revenue stream and are attractive in the sense that the client is easy to deal with, then this would be categorized as core business and would absolutely be a business relationship that one would want to work hard at retaining for as long as possible. Under such circumstances it is likely that the contractor or supplier would do everything in its power to encourage a longer-term collaborative contractual business relationship with its client. Accordingly, its tactics must be tailored with this very much in mind – deploying its best resources, not becoming complacent, etc.

- **Nuisance business relationships** – The opposite extreme is a situation where the contractor or supplier does not get much in the way of business or revenue from the client and also where the client is difficult to deal with, such as late payment of invoices, far too onerous (wants everything for nothing!), lack of repeat business, etc. In such circumstances one could refer to such a client as a nuisance client. Clearly any smart contractor/supplier would quickly establish that this type of account is not one that it needs, and as such would quickly move away from it. Unless there is a substantial improvement in client behaviour the outcome ultimately tends to be for the relationship to be terminated or run its course to expiry and not be renewed.

- **Development business relationships** – Contractors and suppliers will tend to view accounts with clients or buyers that are easy to deal with but generate a low–average revenue stream as development accounts to work on to try to get more business. Ideally the objective would be to try to shift the relationship to the right to become a new core business relationship.

- **Exploitable business relationships** – As the term suggest, exploitable accounts are those that are high value for contractors or suppliers but are not easy in terms of dealing with the client. The outcome ultimately tends to be a move either up or to the left (development) or for the relationship to be terminated or run its course to expiry and not be renewed.

Customer profiling

From the foregoing, it can be seen that customer profiling and prioritizing the client base are important activities for contractors and suppliers in determining whether or not to embark on a longer-term collaborative relationship with any client. Client prioritization in terms of the account's attractiveness to the contractor or supplier isn't just linked to the monetary size of the contract award value or order. Other factors feature – such as:

- What is the likely profit margin on the project? A large contract award value doesn't necessarily equate to one that gives the contractor a profit!

- Are there likely to be any follow-on opportunities beyond the original award? In other words, is there likely to be repeat business?

- Will the client be receptive to new ideas or innovations?

- Is it a nice market with scope for leverage, or is there too much competition?

- Does the client pay on time in accordance with contract terms or is there a tendency to stretch out payment terms?

- Is there any kudos in working with a particular client (ie public relations gains from being seen to have worked with and established a track records with a blue-chip client)? This may inform a particular strategy in commercial terms.

Figure 2.3 gives us some theoretical insight into how a contractor/supplier might go about profiling and prioritizing its client base. From the table it can be seen that there are 15 client companies that have awarded contracts to the contractor/supplier in question. Each contract has a different contract value; however, the magnitude of the contract is not the factor to consider when deciding whether or not each contract has been a worthwhile one for the contractor/supplier.

Significant effort may have been needed to secure certain contracts as opposed to others, which can be measured partially by the number of quotations and clarifications that had to be made. Additionally, if we were to allocate a score of 1 to 5 (with 5 being highest) to each of the 'attractiveness elements' (such as profitability, opportunities, receptiveness to innovation, degree of competition, payment performance and kudos) then we could arrive at an overall ranking as to which of the 15 client companies are more attractive than others and, as can be seen, contract value alone is not a reliable guide to this.

Figure 2.3 Customer/client profiling

| Company | Value (£) | Quotes | Attractiveness to contractor/supplier Receptiveness areas | | | | | | Total |
			Profitability	Opportunities	Innovation	Competition	Payment	Kudos	
Company 1	560,668	1	4	4	4	5	5	4	26
Company 2	2,733,772	8	4	3	4	4	3	3	21
Company 3	1,055,889	20	3	3	4	4	3	3	20
Company 4	496,819	1	3	4	3	5	3	2	20
Company 5	459,653	2	4	4	4	3	2	2	19
Company 6	422,836	4	3	3	3	5	3	2	19
Company 7	956,347	1	4	2	4	3	3	2	18
Company 8	469,158	1	3	3	3	4	3	2	18
Company 9	355,890	22	3	4	4	2	2	2	17
Company 10	246,484	2	3	3	4	1	3	2	16
Company 11	167,524	12	4	3	4	1	2	1	15
Company 12	4,062	6	2	4	4	2	1	1	14
Company 13	225,012	1	2	3	3	1	2	2	13
Company 14	391,454	1	3	2	2	1	2	1	11
Company 15	210,926	1	2	2	1	1	2	1	9

If we were to then ask ourselves where each of these 15 clients fit into the categorization matrix outlined in Figure 2.2 from the perspective of the contractor/supplier looking up the supply chain, we could look at the 'total client attractiveness' scores and map them onto the matrix by placing them in the categories of develop, core, nuisance or exploitable. This is an excellent supply chain management tool and technique that can be used to help position a contractor/supplier organization when focusing on more collaborative longer-term contractual relationships.

Figure 2.4 maps the total client attractiveness scores for each of the 15 companies in Figure 2.3 and groups them into these four categories. This mapping helps inform us about the salient features that must be present in an existing or potential client/customer business relationship to warrant expending time and effort in a smart fashion on the development of a longer-term collaborative alliance style contractual arrangement. Again, the matrix helps point us in the right direction.

Figure 2.5 summarizes in a very simplistic fashion the key features that lend themselves to longer-term collaborative alliance business relationships.

Figure 2.4 Client/customer attractiveness mapping

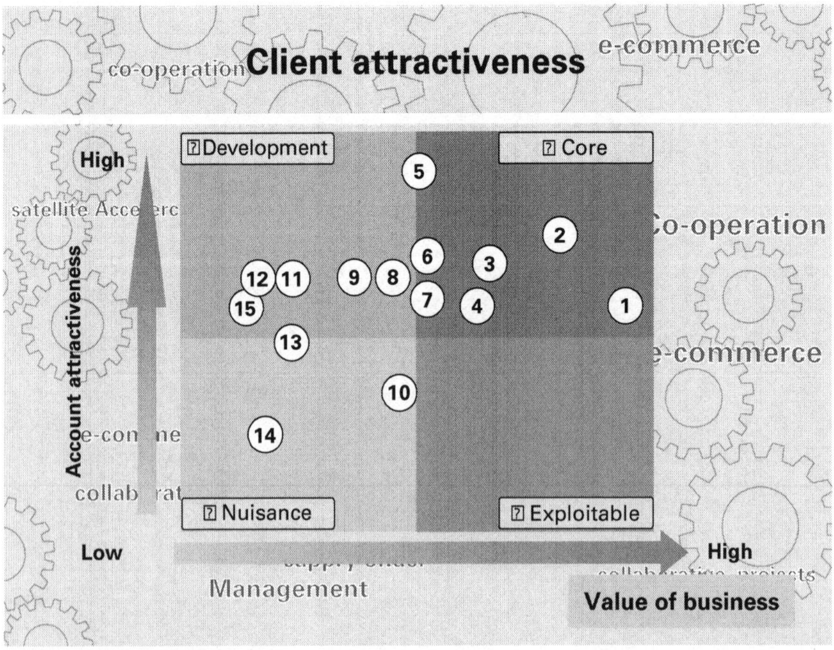

Figure 2.5 Features for longer-term collaborative alliance relationships

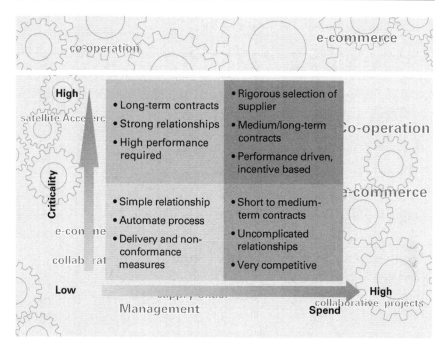

Contractor landscape analysis for awareness of interdependencies across the supply chain

The final consideration that we shall touch on in this chapter is the need for industry practitioners to be aware of the importance of understanding of the contractor landscape and interdependencies across supply chains. This is crucial in terms of positioning for realistic collaboration and supply chain cooperation. Nowadays, in almost every industry sector, it is supply chains, not organizations, that compete against each other. Moreover, the author would advocate that it is the supply chain management practitioner's role in any sector to promote joined up collaborative thinking to:

- deliver a reduction in waste and inefficiencies;
- identify value added activities;
- improve client/customer supplier relationships;
- encourage and achieve alignment of objectives along the supply chain;

- dynamically respond to market changes and understand the contractor landscape and supply chain interdependencies;
- strategically re-position as required.

A competent supply chain practitioner will always remember that *a supplier is a valuable partner resource* and will fully appreciate and respect that there are times when it is vitally important to cooperate and collaborate with suppliers.

Key questions that most customers or clients should ask key contractor or supplier organizations are:

- What can you do to reduce risk in my business?
- What competencies can you offer to me to help lower my operating or capital costs?
- How can we collaborate and cooperate to add value to our respective organizations and help us become collectively more competitive as a joined up collaborative unit?

In so doing we must think carefully about the relationships and interdependencies across supply chains. Figures 2.6 and 2.7 compare a traditional competitive tendering process amongst four bidders seeking to win a contract with a client vs the reality of what is likely to happen in practice.

Figure 2.6 shows what appears to be a relatively straightforward, simplistic competitive tendering process between four separate providers (suppliers A, B, C and D), all of whom provide both equipment and services and are seeking to win a contract with a client/prospective customer. On the face of it, supplier C is the successful tenderer; however, this view is based on a somewhat naive lack of understanding and awareness of the linkages and interdependencies that may exist between suppliers A, B C and D.

Figure 2.7 scratches beneath the surface somewhat and reveals the linkages that exist between all four providers of the equipment and services, irrespective of which supplier wins the contract with the client/customer. The successful tenderer, supplier C, is in fact reliant upon the other suppliers for components of its overall contractual obligation to the main client. It is likely that such reliance would be formalized through a subcontract or subsupply arrangement to supplier C; however, it would be a prudent client to have an awareness and understanding of such linkages and interdependencies in advance of developing its sourcing strategy. Sometimes it is smarter to be more collaborative and engaging with a supply chain upfront, rather than thinking that you hold all the ace cards!

Figure 2.6   Traditional simplistic competitive tender process

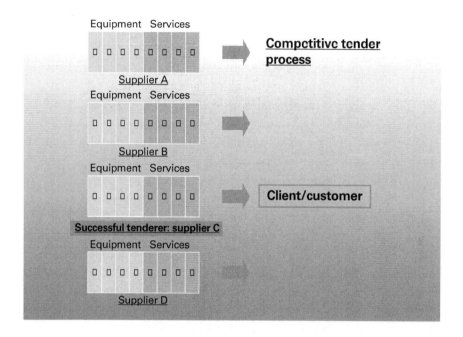

Figure 2.7   The reality of what happens in practice, acknowledging the linkages and interdependencies across the supply chain

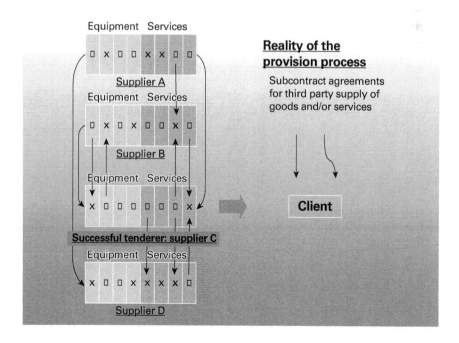

In conclusion, it is important that the reader has a reasonable grasp and awareness of different supply chain perspectives and drivers and also the myriad of complex interdependencies and linkages up, down and across supply chains when considering entering into collaborative arrangements.

One thing is certain – we cannot afford to ignore such interdependencies when crafting our supply chain management or contractual strategies or when selecting our partners of choice to collaborate with.

Businesses and the supply chains upon which they rely across the public, private and third sectors continue to change at an alarmingly fast rate on an increasingly complex global stage. It is important also to remember that the business environment has evolved such that it is supply chains that now compete, not individual companies! It follows, then, that the discipline of supply chain management (SCM) and the role of the SCM practitioner have become ever more important.

The skills of the supply chain practitioner have been in play supporting many different sectors internationally in various guises since their inception. Consider the pre- and post-contract award activity detailed in the wheel diagram in Figure 2.8. The SCM practitioner will be engaged in all three primary outer segments and all seven secondary inner sub segments in some way. A key competency for such practitioners will be an awareness of and ability to collaborate with others, both internally within the organizations and externally with partner organizations and third parties.

Figure 2.8   The role of the SCM practitioner – 'the wheel of collaborative involvement'

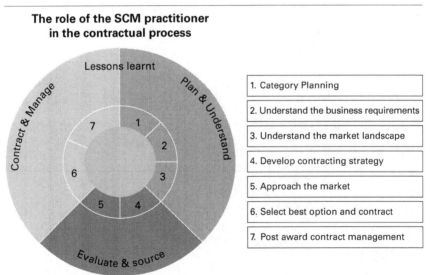

The discipline of SCM and the SCM process lie at the heart of business interface and collaboration. Moreover, there is a compelling value proposition for the use of the SCM process in companies. Consider, for example, the energy sector – it absolutely needs to use and rely on SCM process because:

- The average exploration and production company spends 80 per cent or more of its money on third party goods and services, whilst about 20 per cent goes on overheads and salaries.

- It makes sense to focus on the 80 per cent spend on third party goods and services through identifying efficiency improvements and following process.

- The role of the SCM practitioner is simply to assist in helping the company be more commercial in managing, planning and obtaining goods and services by using robust business processes.

- Performance can be significantly improved by continuous effort at safely reducing the capital employed in the business (eg Opex, Capex and G&A) in combination with other efforts (ie improving the revenues earned, good planning, execution efficiency).

- Each of the stages in the 'chain' should be one of 'adding value' (ie develop the need, scope of work/specify, contract, mobilize and deliver, operate and maintain, close-out/dispose). Non-delivery on any one of the links means that value is compromised.

- SCM practitioners tend to be great ambassadors and facilitators of collaboration and are ideally placed to do so as they sit at the heart of the business and have line of sight of most that is going on.

My acronym for the discipline of supply chain management is SCM. If we reverse it to read 'MCS' it transitions to read Mainly Common Sense – this is the compelling case for collaboration across supply chains!

Raising the game – the CRAFT 8 Stage Life Cycle Model and ISO 44001

03

The evolution and emergence of a new global standard for collaborative working

In this chapter we conduct a light-touch examination of a new global standard framework that has been developed with the aim of implementing collaborative practice in business and across supply chains. This framework will enable any organization or business, whether public, private or third (voluntary and humanitarian) sector, to exploit collaborative approaches. Organizations will almost certainly be required to 'raise their game' regarding embracing alternative collaborative thinking, which has most probably been suppressed until now.

ISO 44001 is a global collaborative business relationships standard that represents a new generation of international standards, with a focus on behaviours, organizational culture and management processes providing a common platform to underpin sustainable business relationships and harness the benefits of collaborative working. The standard is essentially a sector neutral framework that encourages best practice for collaborative and partnering programmes.

ISO 44001 was launched in early 2017; however, the journey to its creation began with the CRAFT 8 Stage Life Cycle Model developed by Midas Projects Limited in conjunction with the Institute for Collaborative Working (ICW). This model formed the basis of British standard 11000 and the international standard ISO 44001.

All CRAFT and related material from the ICW exhibited in this book have been provided courtesy of Midas Projects Limited and the ICW. Since its creation in 1990, the ICW has focused on promoting the adoption of collaborative working applications to enhance the performance and competitiveness of organizations large and small, culminating in the crafting and implementation of a new global standard. Organizations across any sector with a desire to collaborate would be wise to consider adopting this best-practice standard.

Trends in organizational thinking and the pace of change

Businesses and the supply chains upon which they rely continue to change at an alarmingly fast rate across an increasingly complex global stage. Much of the current organizational thinking, both from a customer and supplier perspective, is still very much based on traditional contracting solutions having end-to-end ownership. Looking forward, the author, along with other supply chain management thought leaders, envisages that most business models will eventually embrace collaboration in the shape of joint ventures, partnering or alliances. Such collaboration will almost certainly have greater emphasis on behaviours, competence, skills, integration and 'fit for purpose' governance. The need for organizations to work together in a more integrated fashion has perhaps never been more critical than in today's global economic environment in which the impact of technological advancements is coupled with faster, slicker communications and greater transparency of business markets.

How to collaborate

For most organizations, the hardest part of starting any relationship management programme is to find a suitable framework within which to develop ideas. A systems model based approach can be helpful in this regard.

Figure 3.1   High-level structure of management systems incorporated into ISO 44001

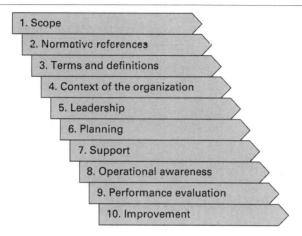

SOURCE Courtesy of Midas Projects Limited and the Institute for Collaborative Working

ISO 44001 can be regarded as a road map based on the CRAFT 8 Stage Life Cycle Model. This is shown in Figure 3.1.

ISO 44001 is precisely what it says on the tin – it is a framework approach and organizations can tailor it to suit their own specific and varied circumstances. It should also be appreciated that whilst the overriding ISO 44001 profile assumes an end-to-end application, the supply chain in any sector can of course be complex and organizations' requirements and interdependencies on other organizations will be positioned at different entry points.

Drawing on the CRAFT 8 Stage Life Cycle Model, ISO 44001 can be regarded as a process that provides a lifecycle framework for relationships that addresses the influences driving both organizational and individual behaviours, creating a cultural environment where collaboration can be fully exploited to mutual benefit.

From Chapter 1, we know that developing a collaborative approach has been shown to release potential value and innovation. We also know that integration in the supply and delivery network both locally and globally can be optimized by focusing on the boundaries between organizations to focus on what each does best in a complimentary business process. This requires organizations to 'raise their game' regarding embracing alternative thinking that is most probably currently suppressed within the confines of the existing traditional style of contracting practices that they are used to and have been applying to date. ISO 44001 offers businesses a platform from which they can begin to build new and exciting competitive propositions working, for example, as part of a consortia grouping.

We turn our attention now to the high-level ISO structure of management systems that has been also been incorporated into ISO 44001 from CRAFT and the ICW. The structure of the management systems was primarily designed as a step change in the way that organizations looked to develop more integrated relationships (Figure 3.1). The underpinning theory behind the structure was that collaborations frequently failed or had suboptimal outcomes because the concept of collaboration had only been considered at the point where a contract had been established. What was indicated, however, was appreciation that successful collaboration requires a more fundamental understanding of the benefits and potential risk long before looking to even engage partners or third parties by building a systemic approach to collaboration to ensure sustainable relationships with the right cultures and behaviours.

Figure 3.2   CRAFT 8 Stage Life Cycle Model incorporated with ISO 44001

SOURCE Courtesy of Midas Projects Ltd in conjunction with the Institute for Collaborative Working

The introduction of this structure under the umbrella of the new global standard ISO 44001 offers a very helpful approach to organizations in terms of providing a basis to enable them to integrate management systems that overlap across multiple work streams and possibly other assets that they may have globally. The value gain and benefits of this approach are apparent through progressive integration of processes and systems by harnessing existing practices rather than creating independent ones.

Figure 3.2 illustrates the eight key operational 'life-cycle' stages of the CRAFT model that have been incorporated into and lie at the heart of ISO 44001. Each of the eight stages is crucial in terms of creating a more robust foundation to build sustainable collaborative relationships. The following sections provide a brief outline of each stage, together with the important considerations at each stage.

Stage 1: Operational awareness

Typically, for the larger business corporations (both client organizations and tier 1 contractors/suppliers) the cascading of management systems across the business and the supply chain will be influenced heavily by the impact of divisional and industry sectors where client, regulatory, geography or operational factors may require certain adaptations.

Important considerations across client organizations and the supply chain companies upon which they rely are:

- **Duties of senior executive(s) responsible** – The role of the senior executive(s) responsible for championing collaborative working is usually established at a corporate level. However, for practical operational reasons some responsibilities may have to be delegated through a delegation of authority (DoA) mechanism.

- **Application and validation of a fit-for-purpose 'governance' structure** – The senior executive responsible for collaborative working shall ensure that any necessary variations to policies and processes are agreed and that an appropriate fit-for-purpose governance structure is established within the overall corporate systems.

- **Identification of operational objectives** – There will be a need to align collaborative approaches with the business objectives, ensuring that there is clear link between collaborative approaches and the organizational change that may be required.

- **Establishment of value analysis process** – Adopting a collaborative approach must clearly offer greater tangible benefits than a more traditional ownership model. It should be focused on a robust analysis of a cost-effective solution.

- **Identification and prioritization of collaborative business relationships** – Perhaps the most crucial decision is how organizations differentiate their relationships and focus their resources effectively. The spectrum of relationships and specific needs and strategic requirements will be varied.

- **Understanding different drivers and the need to verify collaborative approaches** – Understanding what drives an organization and the client, contractor or supplier are very important features of the development process. The whole spectrum of the marketplace will influence events. If these are not understood then opportunities may be missed, and the risk profile increased. Chapter 2 provides us with some helpful insights into drivers and different perspectives up, down and across the supply chain.

- **Planning for operational collaboration** – Before venturing into specific collaborative developments, it is crucial to plan how such approaches will be integrated into operations.

- **Development of competencies and compatible behaviours** – Working in a collaborative environment may not suit everyone; while they may be excellent in one domain, the competencies, capability and skills for operating in a mutually beneficial relationship may challenge some individuals. It is therefore essential to understand what skills are available and what development may be necessary.

- **Initial risk assessment and subsequent risk management approach** – Collaborative approaches can introduce alternative ways of managing risk, including a joint approach with partner(s), but can also introduce new risk elements that need to be identified and carried forward. How risk is viewed and treated contractually is discussed in detail in Chapter 2 from different perspectives looking up, down and across the supply chain.

- **Establish a relationship management or stakeholder engagement plan** – Whilst there may be a corporate relationship process in place, this needs to be reviewed to ensure that it can effectively be implemented across, for example, different organizations or geographical boundaries. Stakeholder engagement is discussed in detail in Chapter 4 along with suggested blueprints.

Stage 2: Knowledge

The success of any business venture that involves client interface with its partners and across its supply chains depends on the strategy that is behind the approach and the depth of risk evaluation that precedes action. Developing collaborative strategies should start by establishing the influences that will stimulate success. To exploit the potential, it is essential to fully appreciate the drivers, risks and pressures of the marketplace being addressed; adopting collaborative approaches requires investment from all parties and thus should be focused where it offers most benefit.

Important considerations across client organizations and the supply chain companies upon which they rely during this second stage are:

- **Strategy and compelling business case development** – The challenge is to develop an effective strategy that integrates the ideas into a practical approach to meet the business objectives and expectations of the potential partners. The four key areas for strategy development are environment, organization, people and process. These define the key parameters and focus the process of collecting and validating the new collaborative approach.

- **Specificity in identification of relationship objectives** – Understanding the objectives and drivers for collaboration are essential, since if these are not well defined it becomes difficult to communicate the rationale for seeking external partners – particularly where these relationships may affect internal functions.

- **Implementation of the value analysis for a specific opportunity** – Undertake an initial value analysis to ensure there is sufficient potential value to be obtained through a collaborative approach in relation to the investment and risks.

- **Identification of potential collaborative partner organizations** – Adopting the collaboration concept is the first step, but then organizations need to consider who is out there in the marketplace to fill the gaps as potential partners. In some cases, these partners may come from existing relationships, or partnership potential may evolve from an agreement to work together. Extensive due diligence may be needed before any final decision is made regarding selection of a medium- to long-term partner.

- **Development of an initial exit strategy** – A key aspect of developing a strategic approach is to consider the exit strategy as an essential component upfront. Understanding the issues that will arise from disengagement will highlight aspects to be addressed in development.

- **Identification of key individuals' required competences and behaviours** – It is important to also consider key individuals and the available resources to support a collaborative approach and, where appropriate, ensure development programmes and support are in place. The emphasis should be put on selecting and developing those individuals with appropriate behaviours.

- **Knowledge management** – One of the significant benefits of collaboration is the ability to share knowledge with partners. This frequently creates a challenge for many organizations to identify what can and cannot be shared to avoid clashes later. The effective exploitation of knowledge is the key to success; creating the environment necessary to ensure the sharing of knowledge should have a clear focus.

- **Supply chain and extended enterprise threats and opportunities** – Key aspects of developing the strategy are the impacts and opportunities of harnessing existing or potential partner supply chain relationships. These extended relationships may open further benefits and opportunities as well as introducing further risk to be assessed and managed.

- **Risk assessment and management** – Development of a strategy must be linked to the creation of a risk management strategy that addresses the concerns of all parties, together with identifying a profile of varying levels of acceptable risk.

- **Evaluation of the business case** – Having drawn together the knowledge surrounding a specific opportunity and the potential application of a collaborative approach, it is important to evaluate the business case before proceeding. This will ensure that the objectives, potential benefits and opportunities are balanced against risk, key resources, exit parameters and the estimated lifecycle/length of relationship.

- **Incorporation of knowledge into the relationship management plan (RMP)** – When a strategy has been established, the creation of a specific RMP will help to capture the key principles. This will provide the communications and information platform that will help to raise awareness across the organization.

Stage 3: Internal assessment

Any collaborative relationship involving client interface with its partners and across its supply chains is always a two-way process, and to achieve the desired goals it requires commitment on all sides. This is not just about processes, procedures, systems and contracts; it is a question of the leadership, skills and motivation that will govern the behaviours and approaches at the working level. It is important to understand the internal enablers that build trust between the parties based on mutual benefit and equitable reward.

Important considerations across client organizations and the supply chains companies upon which they rely during this third stage are:

- **Capability and environment for collaboration** – It is unlikely that every organization will have an abundance of skilled professionals ready to take on a collaborative role. Even those highly skilled people in a traditional environment may struggle when operating outside the command-and-control structure. In selecting a team, it is important to focus on those individuals who will best respond to the challenges of collaboration.

- **Assessment of strengths, weaknesses, opportunities and threats** – Organization should consider the extent to which current operating practices may constrain effective collaboration, then address these issues. These can vary widely but may relate to programme ownership, cross-functional barriers, incentive and performance measurement policies, together with systems and procedures.

- **Assessment of collaborative profile** – For collaboration to work effectively, potential partners must see the organization as an intelligent partner they can work openly with. The CRAFT 8 Stage Life Cycle Model incorporated into ISO 44001 is a benchmark for collaborative capability and a useful model on which to test the current position.

- **Appointment of collaborative leadership** – The key to successful collaboration comes from having the right leadership, which is a difficult role since they need to be able to engender and maintain the ethos of collaboration by supporting and mentoring those involved. Traditional management tends to focus on control through position, but in a collaborative structure it is the ability to influence that counts.

- **Definition of partner selection criteria** – As part of the internal assessment, organizations need to establish in each case what a partner should look like. This enables the organization to set its agenda and provides criteria for evaluation later in the process.

- **Implementation of the relationship management plan** – Once collaboration has been validated as the strategic way forward, the organization should develop a specific relationship management plan with the output of the internal assessment, including responsibilities to be assigned with target dates, establishing who does what, by when.

Stage 4: Partner selection

It is important to understand the differing dynamics of a collaborative approach involving client interface with prospective partners and future relationships across supply chains and also to assess the strengths and weaknesses, whatever the route to selection. Where an existing provider is perhaps a single-source option their collaborative capability is frequently ignored, as there is no other choice. It is clearly important to ensure that selection maintains the competitive edge that many see only coming from competition and to build confidence in the selection process clearly defining the endgame upfront to avoid confusion later.

Important considerations across client organizations and the supply chains companies upon which they rely during this fourth stage is again listed as follows:

- **Nomination of potential collaborative partners** – Whatever the drivers for collaboration, it is important to have a clear perspective on which potential partner(s) to approach. It is unlikely that every potential partner would meet the aspirations and it is sensible to prioritize the business objectives.

- **Partner evaluation and selection** – Assessing a collaborative partner goes beyond compliance to a contract. Organizations may have the attributes to deliver a sound proposition and an established performance record that supports their ability to meet the required performance. However, they may have not progressed in developing an appropriate performance culture that would enable them to fit into the business process of other organizations.

- **Development of engagement and negotiation strategy for collaboration** – The process of negotiation is frequently a significant weakness in the development of collaborative arrangements. The traditional engagement and negotiating models often referred to as win/lose. Negotiations will set a baseline for the relationship and need to be managed in a more structured way around the concepts of win/win. It is important to recognize that trying to force a commercial advantage at this early stage will almost certainly damage the future relationship.

- **Initial engagement with potential partners** – The end game of a sustainable relationship requires consideration as to the steps taken in engaging the market whilst this may require a staged approach each step needs to clearly support the focus for collaboration.

- **Assessment of shared objectives** – Throughout the selection process, it is advisable to work with the potential partners to understand their objectives, as well as building a dialogue around common objectives and outcomes. These may not always be the same as yours but should be evaluated for alignment and compatibility.

- **Assessment of exit strategy** – In considering the implications of a collaborative engagement the potential partners should jointly evaluate the key aspects of disengagement. Establishing potential triggers and rules of disengagement, possible transition and future development during the partner selection and contracting stage builds confidence between the parties.

- **Selection of preferred partners** – How organizations expect they will be working together will help to define the nature of the contracting relationship and the style of integration and level of interfaces. This will have a significant impact on the development of risk management approaches.

- **Initiation of Joint Relationship Management Plan** – Once a collaborative partner has been selected the organizations should incorporate all the principles that have been agreed in to a joint Relationship Management Plan and formal arrangements shall be based.

Stage 5: Working together

Effective and sustainable collaboration requires a robust approach to both organizational development and personal behaviours; these factors are inextricably linked. This starts with a focus on individual and joint partner objectives, together with agreement on roles and responsibilities. To establish a working platform on which collaboration can deliver the benefits of combining skills, resources and driving innovation, there must be clear governance that is supported by integrated business processes, measurement and people development.

Important considerations across client organizations and the supply chains companies upon which they rely during this fifth stage are:

- **Establishment of the fit-for-purpose governance structure** – Creating organizational culture or change requires a robust approach to both organizational development and personal behaviours; these factors are inextricably linked through a sound governance structure, which must be supported by integrated business processes, measurement and people development.

- **Executive sponsorship** – It is important that there is joint executive sponsorship to provide overall support. There needs to be clear and transparent executive agreement on the desired outcomes and objectives of the relationship, which reflect shared ownership of the principles that will govern in a fit for purpose way the collaborative behaviours of those involved.

- **Validation of objectives** – The blending of both common and individual organizational objectives removes many of the hidden agendas that may affect successful collaboration.

- **Operational leadership** – The appointment of the right leadership is crucial as the collaborative team has to meet the everyday demands of the business landscape and contend with the internal stresses and strains of being separated from (or out of step with) its home organization.

- **Management arrangements** – Establishing a management team, together with a clearly defined profile of roles and responsibilities, ensures that all participants fully understand their contribution. The leadership has to support the team whilst driving toward agreed objectives.

- **Shared communications strategy** – A key aspect of maintaining a sound relationship between organizations and their stakeholders is to ensure that there is a solid process of communications. Keeping people informed helps to strengthen awareness and thus maintain the support for collaboration.

- **Knowledge management process** – Effective management of knowledge and information is essential to ensure that the partners are clear on what information they need and how to share it. Information flow is a major benefit of collaboration, but frequently it is an area of conflict when working together.

- **Establishment of a risk management process** – A robust risk management programme as part of the operating process is a critical factor in being able to build sustainable and flexible operations. Evidence of a strong relationship is that the partners support each other's risks where practical.

- **Operational process and systems review** – A joint review of the delivery processes will establish the platform for effective performance and provide a basis to ensure that all key issues have been jointly addressed before formally contracting. Optimization of business processes is a key benefit of working in collaboration arrangements, but this can often create the next level of potential conflict.

- **Measurement of delivery and performance** – There needs to be a clearly defined basis of how the integrated team will deliver their objectives and how these will be measured; this is an essential aspect of establishing a sound basis for working together.

- **Improvement of organizational collaborative competence** – An assessment of the competencies and skills of the partner organizations to be engaged in delivery and, where appropriate, agree a joint development plan. Individual competencies can strongly influence behaviours and thus the success of relationships.

- **Establishment of an issue resolution process** – Managing conflict towards a constructive and mutually beneficial outcome is an essential element of effective collaboration. It is important to ensure that there is an issue resolution process that provides a mechanism and escalation procedure where appropriate.

- **Establish an exit strategy** – It is important to define the boundaries of the relationship clearly, including business risks; in any business environment there are many factors and pressures that can have an impact on the operational drivers. It also helps to avoid potential areas of conflict that reach beyond their brief.

- **Stakeholder impacts** – It is important when establishing an exit strategy to ensure that impact on stakeholders is taken into account.

- **Assets and commercial implications** – Organizations need to clearly define the individual and joint distribution of the assets they have contributed to the collaboration, in the event of controlled disengagement.

- **Management of staff** – A significant facet of behaviours stems from the future perspectives of staff working within the relationship. This should be part of any disengagement consideration.

- **Agreement or contracting arrangements** – Most business relationships need to anchor the contracting arrangements from the point of establishing what the business hopes to achieve through the relationship. In developing a contracting approach, it is essential to define the individual responsibilities and to place these obligations with the correct party.

- **Establish and implementation of joint relationship management plan** – When the decision is made for multiple organizations to work together, the RMP becomes a joint relationship management plan (JRMP) that outlines the way they intend to manage the relationship in future. There are a variety of ways this can be addressed; the principle, however, should always be that this is a mutually agreed approach between the parties.

Stage 6: Value creation

The objective of trying to harness added value across collaborative client interfaces with partners and across supply chains means challenging the traditional thinking, creating new value or alternative value propositions beyond those contracted. Innovation is a critical factor in the value creation process. A parallel benefit that comes from introducing a structured approach to value creation is that it supports organizations and teams working together. How organizations choose to encourage innovation depends on a wide variety of factors but is often managed well by establishing joint cross-functional teams that can be brought together to address specific challenges or ideas.

Important considerations across client organizations and the supply chains companies upon which they rely during this sixth stage are:

- **Establishment of the value creation process** – While there is great value in a spontaneous approach to innovation, establishing a joint process that ensures both targeted support and encourages new ideas is very powerful. A structured approach will underpin sustainable engagement. It will provide a measure of integration and continual focus on driving greater value from the relationship.

- **Identification of improvement and setting of targets** – The key to optimizing co-creation is to ensure that identified issues are regularly reviewed and, where necessary, removed if not delivering. This ensures resources are not wasted or diverted from the primary objectives. In a collaborative environment, value creation is about delivering innovative solutions or releasing value that could not be generated by one organization alone.

- **Utilization of learning from experience** – As organizations begin to work together more closely it is equally important to capture the lessons learned. This is a key aspect of creating value and setting the agenda for innovation.

- **Updating the joint relationship management plan** – The JRMP should be updated to incorporate value creation initiatives that, after evaluation and development as required, are to be incorporated into the operations.

Stage 7: Staying together

Businesses and their relationships with supply chains are constantly being impacted by an ever-changing world, with many things being completely outwith their control. It is a given, therefore, that there will be many internal and external pressures on any collaborative relationship that will lead to impacts on effectiveness. Recognize that relationships evolve as they change to reap the benefits of the agreement. Also, it is important to undertake regular validation to maintain focus and efficiency. No two relationships are the same, and the dynamics of organizational and people changes can influence performance, so it is equally important to recognize that as relationships progress they need to be monitored to ensure that appropriate focus is maintained on areas where convergence might not be happening, to maximum benefit.

Important considerations across client organizations and the supply chains companies upon which they rely during this seventh and penultimate stage are:

- **Oversight by the senior executives responsible** – The senior executives responsible should provide oversight and support to the joint management team. To ensure sustainable engagement over time, this oversight should be both via reporting processes and by maintaining a visible presence.

- **Relationship management** – The key to sustaining relationships is to ensure there is effective joint management focused on the operational level, managing the day-to-day activities of the relationship and ensuring continued focus and support. Maintaining both delivery and development focus is crucial to ensure the relationship remains proactive.

- **Implementation of monitoring of behaviours and trust indicators** – Developing trust in the relationships and ensuring the appropriate behaviours are key aspects of joint management. As trust increases, the performance of the relationship should increase the value it delivers. The wrong behaviours will quickly undermine the situation, with obvious impacts on output.

- **Continual value creation** – There should be continuous support and monitoring of innovation and continual improvement, to ensure that the partnering teams are exploiting their joint knowledge and, where appropriate, enhancing their skills.

- **Delivery of objectives** – A critical aspect of any relationship is that it delivers the performance that was initially envisaged. Any failure by a partner in a collaborative environment could lead to a breakdown in the relationship. The longer the relationship is in place, the greater the possibility for complacency to build between the various parties.

- **Analysis of results** – It is important to understand and agree how the performance of the contract and the relationship will be jointly measured and ensure appropriate reviews are undertaken. If the relationship is delivering and remains a strategic approach, then it should be periodically tested and adapted to reflect changes in the business environment.

- **Issue resolution** – Within any high-performing group it is inevitable that friction will arise and, in fact, constructive conflict can be a stimulus for innovation. The joint management team and their senior executives responsible must ensure that issues are addressed and if appropriate, defused quickly. Experience would suggest that escalation processes in many cases can be counterproductive as they will often crystallize issues rather than focus on resolution.

- **Maintenance of exit strategy** – Developing a structured joint approach to formulating an exit strategy is an important facet of collaboration. Maintaining a focus on disengagement ensures that the partners have a clear focus on the value of the collaboration. The development of a collaborative relationship will often have a defined lifespan, and during its formation the relationship take into account the process that will lead to the eventual disengagement of the partners, which needs periodic validation.

- **Maintenance of the joint relationship management plan** – The JRMP should be regularly reviewed to ensure it remains applicable, and where updates are deemed necessary the senior executives responsible should be involved to validate and approve changes.

Stage 8: Exit strategy activation

Businesses and their relationships with supply chains will always be such that there will be a finite lifespan, and this will vary between organizations and be linked to market influences. Adapting to such change is a crucial part of developing effective collaborative partnering arrangements. The development of effective integrated activities requires the building of trust between the parties, which over time will enhance the opportunities and those who expect to maximize their investment over a limited time will generally find that collaboration does not provide solutions. Many people believe that to address an exit strategy at the outset of a relationship infers an acceptance that the relationship will fail, but this is not the case. Experience suggests that being open about all possibilities allows the partners to focus on every aspect of integration.

Important considerations across client organizations and the supply chains companies upon which they rely during this eighth and final stage are:

- **Initiation of disengagement** – Where the partners mutually agree that the current activity has reached its natural conclusion, the management team should implement the exit strategy. This should take into account all commercial considerations:

  - accountabilities;
  - agreed objectives;
  - implications for the personnel involved.

- **Business continuity** – The foundation of a sound relationship is that while it continues to add value it must also recognize the implications of maintaining continuity for both the partners and their customers. The responsibilities that operating organizations accumulate may remain after the partners have agreed not to continue the relationship. In developing an exit strategy, the partners must consider the way in which current liabilities will be fulfilled. The reputations of all parties are important and support to the customer is crucial for future activities.

- **Evaluation of the relationship** – Collaborative integration offers the opportunity for organizations to extend their individual capabilities and market reach through combined operations. These may be time-limited or open-ended, but there is a need for the parties to openly address what they need to do in the event that the relationship is no longer viable. Each party must consider what they will contribute for short-term gain and what may be at risk in the longer term. How we exit from a relationship says a great deal about the integrity of the parties, the strength of their relationship and their potential to collaborate in the future.

- **Future opportunities** – If the relationship has been well managed and met its objectives then they should be open to consider future possibilities for collaboration. In future, more organizations may then look towards this approach.

- **Review and updating of the relationship management plan** – The parties should review their JRMP as part of their lessons learned for feedback to their relative management systems.

Conclusion

This chapter has been a relatively light introductory insight into the workings of ISO 44001 drawing on the CRAFT 8 Stage Life Cycle Model and related material from the ICW.

Any decision by an organization with its potential partners (and indeed also the supply chains upon which they rely) to integrate a standard (such as ISO 44001) into their own management systems is one that requires careful decision quality to be applied by the respective organizations' executive decision makers.

Arguably, many collaborative business relationships deliver a wide range of benefits that enhance competitiveness and performance whilst adding value to organizations across the supply chain and across multiple industry sectors. The ongoing determined effort of organizations such as Midas Projects Limited and the ICW and their substantive contribution into providing material that formed the basis for the subsequent publication of BS 11000 and the ISO 44001 international standard for collaborative relationships and working is a landmark for businesses and organizations globally.

The global standard seeks to address collaborative business relationships by providing a reliable consistent framework, which can be scaled and adapted to meet particular business needs. The CRAFT 8 Stage Life Cycle Model incorporated into ISO 44001 also provides an invaluable framework for organizations in the public, private and third sectors in terms of accessing a neutral platform for establishing sustainable programmes for mutual benefit, acting as a bridge between cultures to form a more robust partnership or alliance laying down a solid foundation.

Above all, the author considers the standard to be an invaluable road map for development. It will help encourage client organizations, their partners and associated supply chains to embrace collaborative thinking and significantly raise their game in how they undertake business.

The importance of stakeholder engagement in harnessing the benefits of collaborative working practices

04

In this chapter we consider how any business, public, private or third (voluntary and humanitarian) sector, can harness the benefits of working with a global standard in collaborative working practice (ISO 44001). Some of the tools and techniques that are available for use to help identify and compare where collaboration and ISO 44001 can add value will be explained, with a focus on behaviours, organizational culture and management processes that help to provide a common platform underpinning sustainable business relationships.

Additionally, this chapter offers an insight into the importance of stakeholder engagement to encourage more sustainable business relationships and working practices such that the benefits of working with ISO 44001 can be seen. Specifically, the author will discuss five guideline steps that he considers crucial to any stakeholder engagement programme: identification of stakeholders; analysis of issues and reputation; setting engagement objectives; action planning for engagement; and evaluation planning.

> Guideline tools, techniques and templates are shared with the reader on how to: map stakeholders, conduct stakeholders, conduct stakeholder relationship reviews, conduct reputation assessments, set the desired reputation, select levels of engagement, and select engagement platforms.
>
> A blueprint for the development of a stakeholder engagement programme is also featured, which is an invaluable tool for any collaborative practitioner.

Businesses and the supply chains they rely on across most industry sectors have huge potential to harness the benefits of adopting and working with a global standard in collaborative working practice. This is especially so given that most business models will eventually embrace collaboration in the shape of joint ventures, partnering and alliances, which will have greater emphasis on behaviours, competence, skills, integration and fit for purpose governance.

The benefits of the new global standard ISO 44001 on collaborative business relationships offer the potential for a wide range of benefits to organizations of all sizes in terms of enhancing competitiveness and performance and adding value. Indeed, the launch and publication of ISO 44001 can be considered a landmark for business. Why? Because, quite simply, it is the first international standard that has been created to address collaborative business relationships by providing a consistent framework that can be scaled and adapted to meet particular business needs.

As we have already noted in earlier chapters, collaboration between organizations can take many forms, from loose tactical approaches through to longer-term strategic alliances, partnerships or joint ventures.

The structure of the ISO 44001 framework is supported by a wide range of tools, techniques and guidelines. The framework does not enforce a single rigid approach; rather, it has more of a focus on providing a framework that can complement existing approaches where these are already in place. This is a very sensible, pragmatic approach because many organizations will be reluctant to 'throw the baby out with the bath water' in terms of changing existing processes and procedures simply for change's sake. Indeed, this may not be possible anyway due to proven governance structures that are already embedded within the organization.

It is important to recognize that each business or organizational relationship has its own unique considerations. Many large corporations that have been in existence for decades will already have well-established processes and procedures, yet, the framework still has value and will still be of benefit in terms of providing a common language that can aid implementation and collaborative engagement. For younger or more embryonic organizations or those starting out on the collaborative journey the framework creates a road map for development.

The adoption of the ISO 44001 standard should always be balanced against the value that it can deliver to the organizations that chose to utilize it, whether this is for improving internal performance or to enhance confidence in the market. The standard offers the collaborative practitioner a comprehensive and robust framework for the public, private and third sectors to build a neutral platform for establishing effective sustainable collaborative initiatives or programmes for the mutual benefit of all parties to the collaborative arrangement.

Commonality of language and application between delivery partners is at the heart of the standard and is essentially the core value that leads to improved or better integration between the parties involved. A further benefit is that the standard acts as a bridge between cultures, which in turn forms a more robust partnership, alliance or joint venture. This will help to minimize confusion and instil greater confidence among all participants in the collaborative arrangement, which in turn will lay a solid foundation for creativity and innovation. Figure 4.1 illustrates the primary benefits that can be harnessed by organizations through adopting ISO 44001.

Figure 4.1   Benefits to organizations that adopt ISO 44001

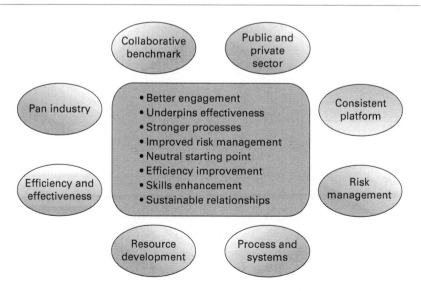

A further observation regarding the development of the ISO 44001 standard is that it was achieved because of a pan-industry effort, with input being solicited from across many different sectors. This has the advantage of offering a generic non-sector-specific standard, which carries a more flexible value proposition. It:

- enables broader adoption and engagement;
- provides a common foundation and language for relationships between the various parties;
- provides uniformity of understanding across different international cultures;
- provides a platform for developing repeatable models to enhance communication and engagement;
- builds confidence.

Additionally, the standard provides a basis for benchmarking the collaborative capability of organizations both internally and externally through its linkage to the British Standards Institute's independent assessment process. This process will help to enhance decision quality around partner, alliance or joint venture evaluation and selection, together with establishing market differentiation.

The standard also encourages the establishment of a consistent but flexible approach that provides a foundation for efficiency and repeatability across collaborative initiatives or programmes and increased opportunity to focus on developing value. It will also assist the commercial practitioner with the development of organizational capability at the working level.

Client or customer confidence is also important, and the standard helps to get a measure on this key area. Collaboration initiatives or programmes need to retain a focus on effective joint risk management in terms of challenges of specific collaboration initiatives and also those linked to relationship aspects of collaborative working. The adoption of the standard will help reduce the likelihood of misunderstandings and any disconnect of objectives, tease out and hopefully constrain any hidden agendas and most importantly minimize or reduce the probability of serious conflict.

The standard's consistent, structured, yet flexible approach helps to facilitate a focus on integration of collaborative working within operational procedures, processes and systems. This has the effect of creating a platform for more streamlined, fit for purpose governance and an optimal timeframe for development. The standard also acts as a baseline to support competency frameworks, resource development and training to increase collaborative organizational capability to enhance skills and the inter-changeability of key personnel.

The ISO 44001 framework also helps to promote better engagement and effectiveness through strengthened business processes, whilst at the same time also improving risk management, enhancing dispute resolution and providing a basis for skills development. Most importantly of all, however, is improving the potential for sustainable relationships that deliver value.

Achieving ISO 44001 certification would be the goal for an organization in terms of demonstrating collaborative capability and readiness for integrated working; however, the author also advocates that organizations can benefit from ISO 44001 without achieving full-blown certification accreditation. The benefits of collaboration will of course be company-specific, based on the business objectives, and much of this can be realized without going down the certification route.

The value of achieving certification, however, introduces a level of rigor to ensure internal processes are maintained to ensure greater sustainability in relationships and collaborative working practices. There are many different outcomes for collaborative relationships that depend on the objectives of the partners. The easy way to think about potential benefits is to consider improvements in delivery processes that could be achieved by working with external organizations with complementary skills and resources. It very much depends on the strategic objectives of the organizations involved.

Collaboration is about building trust, and this is something that you don't get from simply executing a contract. Only by all parties meeting their promises and delivering consistent performance can trust be created. That, plus a senior leadership and management focus on sustaining the relationship.

Intellectual property rights and who owns what may feature in certain collaborative arrangements. However, there is value and real benefit from working closely with a partner to create knowledge. Notwithstanding this, every agreement should clearly define ownership of any jointly created intellectual property.

A further benefit of collaboration is that it can help with the outsourcing of contracts, and in many instances this can involve such organizations sharing delivery processes and even placing outsourcing companies in direct line with clients or customers.

It is important to dispel any misperception that collaboration is about working without conflict. Collaborative relationships take effort and thus they should be focused on delivering value. In fact, once an agreement has been put in place there should be regular programmes to stretch the value proposition, as this will help to strengthen the relationship. Additionally, in any relationship there must be a degree of give and take because collaborative relationships are suboptimal if they are too one sided. Sometimes,

Figure 4.2   Comparative relationship drivers and areas of value gain

Value gained from relationships and key drivers across supply chains	Traditional contracting model		Collaborative model		
	Competitive tender	Single source/ preferred supplier	Alliance	Partnership	Joint venture
Long-term SC stability				Yes	Yes
Research and development				Yes	Yes
Reduced total cost		Maybe	Yes	Yes	Yes
Focused SC team			Yes	Yes	Yes
SC risk/reward sharing			Maybe	Yes	Yes
SC creativity and innovation				Yes	Yes
SC optimization			Maybe	Yes	Yes
Reduced quality cost		Maybe	Maybe	Yes	Yes
Reduced support cost			Maybe	Yes	Yes
Reduced technical engineering cost			Maybe	Yes	Yes
Back-to-back terms and conditions			Maybe	Yes	Yes
Realistic liquidated and ascertained damages			Maybe	Yes	Yes
Realistic guarantees			Maybe	Yes	Yes
Genuine cost reduction		Maybe	Yes	Yes	Yes
Inflation hedging			Maybe	Maybe	Yes
Lowering tender costs			Maybe	Yes	Yes
Reduced cycle time		Maybe	Yes	Yes	Yes
Winning prices			Maybe	Yes	Yes
Improved cash flow			Maybe	Yes	Yes
Finance/funding support				Maybe	Yes
Global supply	Maybe	Maybe	Maybe	Yes	Maybe
Customer support		Maybe	Maybe	Yes	Yes
Currency risk management			Maybe	Yes	Yes
Reliable delivery	Maybe	Maybe	Yes	Yes	Yes
Market pricing	Maybe	Maybe	Yes	Yes	Yes
Enhanced service support		Maybe	Maybe	Yes	Yes
Extended skills base			Maybe	Yes	Yes
Enhanced supply options			Maybe	Yes	Yes
Integrated propositions		Maybe	Maybe	Yes	Yes
Client/customer focused solutions		Maybe	Maybe	Yes	Yes

commitments can restrict one side or the other. This must be considered up front and addressed before putting any collaborative arrangement in place.

Figure 4.2 gives an insight into identifying where collaboration and the adoption of the ISO 44001 framework may be beneficial and add value to an organization, versus a more traditional contracting relationship.

When considering the implementation of the ISO 44001 standard in any organization, it would be remiss of us not to examine the importance of stakeholder engagement to encourage more sustainable business relationships and working practices such that the benefits of working with the standard can be realized. In this regard, this chapter also contains a suggested blueprint for stakeholder engagement.

Most organizations will have a wide range of stakeholders in internal, industry, market and broader socio-political environments, which can be grouped into ten broad categories. These are:

- shareholders;
- employees;
- business/joint venture partners;
- organized labour;
- customers;
- suppliers;
- organized business and industry;
- government, regulators and political role players;
- civil society;
- the media.

These categories are depicted in Figure 4.3.

Generally, in the interest of an organization's effective management of stakeholder relations, a collaborative engagement programme is developed for each stakeholder category to ensure a focused, integrated and aligned approach to the organization's engagement with stakeholders in that category. The suggested blueprint contained within this chapter provides a high-level step-by-step guideline for the development of a stakeholder engagement programme. It guides the reader on how to take into consideration stakeholder inputs (stakeholders' needs, concerns and expectations), as well as the organizational objectives or goals, when designing a stakeholder engagement programme.

Figure 4.3   Stakeholder group categories and environments

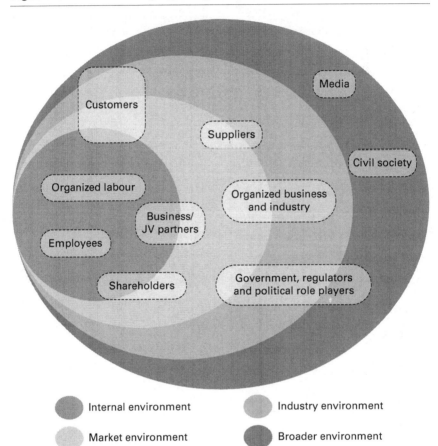

Minimum requirements for any stakeholder engagement programme are:

- The stakeholder engagement programme should align to any overarching global stakeholder management strategy and adhere to a stakeholder engagement charter.

- Priority stakeholders for the category should be identified, mapped or listed.

- A high-level analysis of issues, reputation risks or gaps between stakeholder expectations and company performance should be conducted to inform the programme.

- The stakeholder engagement programme should have specific, measurable objectives against which implementation can be tracked over time (SMART).

- The programme is more than just a high-level strategy and should include an action plan with specific responsibilities, accountabilities, etc.

- An evaluation plan should be designed to ensure measurement against the set objectives.

Stakeholder engagement charters are also a good idea. In the development of a stakeholder engagement programme, every 'what to achieve' and 'how to achieve that' should correspond with the organizational ethos (or mind-set) with which the organization engages its stakeholders. The stakeholder engagement charter is a personal commitment of every employee to display the right or desired behaviours in stakeholder engagement. However, nothing planned in a stakeholder engagement programme should violate or contradict the intent and key principles in the stakeholder engagement programme.

In addition to the minimum requirements, there are a number of quality standards that developers of any stakeholder engagement programme should consider:

- **Confidentiality** – The programme, and the processes leading up to it, could be part of an organization's strategic advantage. As such the programme is an internal organizational document and access will be limited to those who have a legitimate interest in it.

- **Alignment** – The programme should directly align with any overarching global stakeholder management strategy.

- **Integration** – The stakeholder engagement programme must integrate with all the organization's activities, which may have a bearing on engagement activities for the stakeholder category for which the programme is being developed.

- **Objectives** – Objectives set in the programme should be concrete and measurable. Objectives should state *how*: long-term positive and effective relations and goodwill will be built with key stakeholders; key business will be advanced; the organizations' reputation will be enhanced; and issues material to stakeholders will be responded to.

This blueprint includes the following tools and templates to assist with the development of the stakeholder engagement programme:

- tool 1: how to map stakeholders;
- tool 2: how to conduct a stakeholder relationship review;
- tool 3: how to conduct reputation assessment;
- tool 4: how to set the desired reputation;
- tool 5: how to select levels of engagement;

- tool 6: how to select engagement platforms;
- template 1: stakeholder relationship review;
- template 2: response plan – reputation risk;
- template 3: plan – relationship building;
- template 4: engagement road map – top and priority issues.

Figure 4.4 outlines the process for developing an engagement programme.

Alignment with any overarching global stakeholder management strategy is one of the quality standards for an engagement programme, as it directs stakeholder management irrespective of operational locale or stakeholder category.

In the same way that an organization's strategic agenda informs the strategy of a specific region or business unit, the overarching global stakeholder management strategy spells out what the organization wants to achieve in general through the management of stakeholder relations, and therefore informs the stakeholder engagement programme for a particular category or region.

Figure 4.4   The process for developing a stakeholder engagement programme

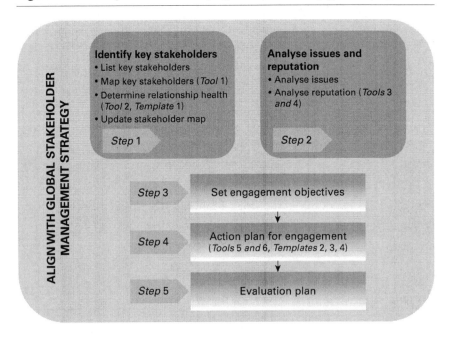

Reputation, stakeholder relations and brand are three critical intangible ingredients to many organizations. To enhance an organization's value, priorities set for stakeholder relations management and stakeholder engagement organizational-wide are to:

- enhance the organization's reputation and brand;
- build high-quality relationships with key stakeholders;
- respond adequately to issues and material concerns.

In the development of any programme there are typically five key steps that have a focus on achieving added value by addressing the priorities listed above. It is important to outline *what* each of these priorities will mean given the stakeholder and/or geographical context and, equally important, *how* these objectives will be achieved. In defining the 'what' to achieve and 'how' to achieve that, Figure 4.5 provides a generic guide on *how* to engage stakeholders and manage stakeholder relations.

Figure 4.5   Generic guide on how to engage stakeholders likely to be impacted by the collaborative arrangement

ALL stakeholder categories

- Get to know priority stakeholders affected by the collaborative arrangement.
- Ensure the organization has a direct relationship with priority stakeholders affected by the collaborative arrangement. This means having direct contact, access and in-person relationships.
- Structure engagement as an ongoing process of collaborative dialogue, engage frequently.
- Identify, acknowledge and address stakeholders' expectations, as well as the gaps existing between stakeholder expectations and the organizations' performance.
- Improve identified relationships strategic to the business.
- Deliver a stakeholder experience of the organization as responsive, committed to long-term healthy relationships, respectful of others' views, and never arrogant.
- Meaningfully involve stakeholders, deepen the level of engagement from mere information sharing to consultation, collaboration and joint problem solving.
- Engage effectively in accordance with the stakeholder engagement charter, with emphasis on planning and evaluation of engagement, and rigour in the management of data and systems established to support stakeholder engagement.
- Enable mutual understanding between the organization and its stakeholders. This means understanding each other's vision, goals, main drivers, challenges and support needed.
- Build the organization's brand: present and reinforce the positive image of the company for stakeholders in all geographical locations that it operates in.

Step 1: Identify stakeholders

This first step in developing a stakeholder engagement programme allows for the identification of stakeholders as the specific individuals or organizations that will be engaged by the organization.

Stakeholders can be defined as any group material to the organization and its operations, impacted by the organization, or with the potential to impact the organization. Identifying specifically who the organization views as the stakeholders material to the organization in a category or geographical region is very important.

Stakeholder categories can be typically unbundled into clusters at the discretion of the category owner. These clusters, referred to as level 1 stakeholders, are 'buckets' of stakeholders in a region, or country or for a particular grouping.

The actual stakeholders that the organization will engage with, thus the focus of this stakeholder engagement programme, are referred to as level 2 stakeholders. Figure 4.6 provides the positioning of both the level 1 cluster of stakeholders and level 2 stakeholders in terms of overall stakeholder architecture within a governance framework.

Identifying the level 2 stakeholders that an organization needs to engage with to achieve added value is a critical input into the engagement programme. The lenses through which key stakeholders are identified will typically include the organization's strategic intent (what is important to the organization) and the stakeholder agendas (issues, expectations, needs important to stakeholders). Criteria to be used to identify key stakeholders include:

- their ability to either enable or hinder the organization in achieving its objectives;
- their relevance to the priorities and strategic goals set in any overarching global stakeholder management strategy;
- their relevance to top/priority issues.

Usually, a stakeholder identification exercise can be used to list lots of potential stakeholders. However, mindful of the fact that organizations will typically be constrained in terms of available resource to engage stakeholders and manage stakeholder relations, part of developing a stakeholder engagement programme is to prioritize stakeholders and focus on those most material to the organization.

Figure 4.6 Stakeholder architecture within an overarching governance framework

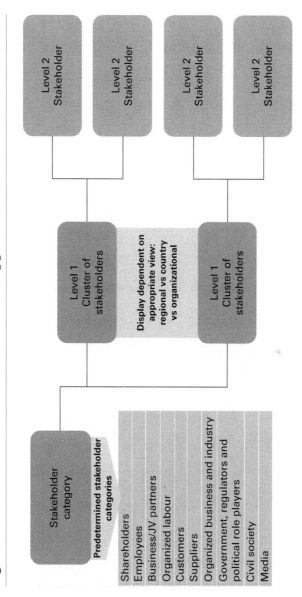

The prioritized key stakeholders can be mapped on a stakeholder map as illustrated in tool 1 in Figure 4.7. The tool assists with plotting key stakeholders on a stakeholder map. The X and Y axes can both be read as a 10-point scale. The Y axis represents the stake of the stakeholder in the organization (mutual importance/interdependency) on a scale from 0 to 10 where 0 is very low and 10 extremely high. The X axis expresses the level of the stakeholder's influence over other stakeholders, where 0 is no influence and 10 is very high influence. The two ratings out of 10 form the coordinates on the X and Y axes, and are used to plot each key stakeholder on the map in the form of a dot. The four quadrants are used as a further consideration to determine the most appropriate positioning of a stakeholder on the map.

Once this initial position on the map has been determined, the positions of stakeholders relative to each other are considered, and through a process of benchmarking influence and importance the dots are moved around until the stakeholder landscape offers a valid representation of the priority stakeholders.

Figure 4.7   Tool 1: Example of a populated stakeholder map

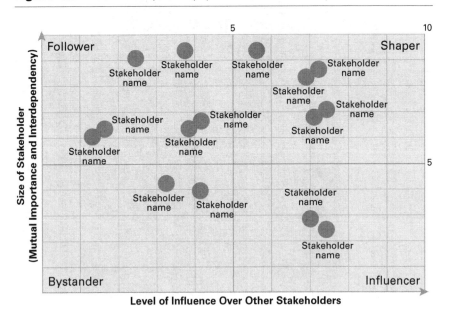

A further consideration to determine the most appropriate placement of a stakeholder is the four quadrants on the map:

- **Bystanders** have a low stake in the organization, and low influence over other stakeholders. The level of engagement is usually either monitoring of the stakeholder in view of any change or a deliberate attempt to move the stakeholder to become an influencer, shaper or follower (if such a move would equate to business value).

- **Followers** have a high stake, but a low influence. The level of engagement with these stakeholders is usually information-sharing, ensuring high levels of mutual awareness and understanding.

- **Influencers** have a low stake, but high influence. The most appropriate level of engagement is consultation to obtain endorsement, influence opinion or get advice.

- **Shapers** have a high stake and a high influence. The level of engagement required is co-creation, problem solving, robust, ongoing and open dialogue.

A stakeholder map is a living document that should be adapted as the stakeholder landscape changes. New stakeholders can be added, or stakeholders can be removed or repositioned, as required.

As a further optional step, the current relationship health between the organization and each of the identified key stakeholders can be assessed using tool 2: how to conduct a stakeholder relationship review (Figure 4.8). Understanding the current relationship health is a good departure point in determining the issues impacting on the relationship and the need for relationship building. The outcome of the relationship review is capturing the results on the stakeholder relation review template (template 1), which may result in a relationship building plan in step 4 of the blueprint.

Once the relationship health has been rated (see tool 2 and template 1), it can be interpreted and mapped on the stakeholder map. Relationship health is indicated by the colour of the dot on the stakeholder map. The current relationship health between the organization and each of the level 2 stakeholders can be coloured to indicate whether a relationship is poor (red), average (amber) or good (green). Figure 4.8 will help to determine the interpretation.

Where sufficient information is not available for specific stakeholders, no rating should be done. These stakeholders can be colour-coded on the stakeholder map. Stakeholders with whom a relationship has not yet been established, and no engagement has taken place, are also colour coded blue.

Figure 4.8   Tool 2: Stakeholder relationship/health review

Mean	Nature of relationship	Descriptor on map	Colour
1–3	Any of the following:	Poor	Red
	Strong opposing views in a generally antagonistic/adversarial relationship		
	Frequent unsolved or destructive conflict that weakens the relationship		
4–6	Any of the following:	Average	Amber
	Impartial relationship: not too close, but not antagonistic (ie with a regulator)		
	Stakeholder will sometimes criticise, and sometimes offer mild support		
	Supportive on some issues, but contesting/opposition on other issues		
7–10	Generally mature, supportive and robust relationship	Good	Green
	Constructive disagreement and conflict resolution, that strengthens the relationship		
No rating	Insufficient information available	None	Blue
	No relationship established		
	No engagement taken place		

Step 2: Analyse issues and reputation

Identification of issues that may impact on an organization's reputation, relationship with key stakeholders or the organization's achievement of its objectives is an important step in the development of a stakeholder engagement programme. Understanding the issue from the stakeholder's perspective and the inherent risk to the organization should the issue not be resolved are key considerations in determining how to address or manage these issues through stakeholder engagement. The insight gained though issue analysis should inform stakeholder engagement planning. It is important to consult issue owners or subject matter experts as they often have more detailed information on the issue and better understand the response.

Analyse issues

Issues can be viewed from the perspective of the stakeholder as well as from that of the organization. Stakeholder issues generally arise when there is a gap between stakeholder expectations and the organization's actual performance. If material stakeholder issues are not actively managed or addressed, these issues may develop into reputation risks, which in turn will affect trust levels and ultimately the achievement of engagement objectives. The inclusion of reputation risks as issues is important, as measures to mitigate these risks should be factored into engagement planning.

Analyse reputation

An organization's reputation is based on how well it performs compared with the interests and expectations of stakeholders. The organization's actual reputation and desired reputation need to be considered to identify the gap between stakeholder perceptions and expectations on the one hand, and actual performance on the other.

In considering how this gap can be bridged, specific items need to be identified that can be used to drive the organization's reputation, items that are material to the stakeholder and can be delivered upon by the organization. These drivers or levers are the content on which to engage key stakeholders. Reputation drivers can be applicable to any aspect of an organization's bottom line performance.

The following tools will assist in the determination of organizational reputation reality and bridge the gaps between perceptions, expectations and actual performance:

- tool 3: how to conduct a reputation assessment;
- tool 4: how to set the desired reputation (and determine leverage to drive reputation).

During the process of analysing issues and reputation, additional stakeholders to engage may be identified for inclusion in the list of key stakeholders.

Step 3: Set engagement objectives

Having analysed stakeholders, issues and reputation drivers, the engagement objectives need to be set. Setting engagement objectives is the most important step in the development of a stakeholder engagement programme. Engagement objectives articulate *what should be achieved through stakeholder engagement* over an exacting forward timeframe. Measuring performance against these objectives enables evaluation of the success of stakeholder engagement.

The overall intent of engagement should be clear, covering areas such as:

- enhance the organization's reputation and brand;
- build high-quality relationships with key stakeholders;
- respond adequately to issues and material concerns.

But what exactly the above will mean in the context of this stakeholder engagement programme – given the identified stakeholders and analysed issues – is what needs to be pinned down in specific, measurable objectives.

In setting the 'what to achieve' objectives, differentiation is often needed between (1) impact and (2) process or output objectives. Impact objectives describe the impact on the stakeholder in terms of new perceptions, enhanced relationships, higher awareness and understanding or changed behaviour. It states what impact the programme will have on the prioritized stakeholders. Process or output objectives are the incremental steps to be taken to achieve the desired impact. Often these process or output objectives clearly describe 'what we have to do' to achieve the desired impact. The heart of the stakeholder engagement programme is the set of impact and process/output objectives.

Step 4: Action plan for engagement

Having set the engagement objectives for the stakeholder engagement programme, you will then be in a better position to begin planning the 'how to' engagement activities, techniques and tactics that will make up the programme for the upcoming year. We arrive at the action plan by completing Figure 4.9.

The following should be taken into consideration when developing the action plan:

- Engagement activities with stakeholders should only be undertaken if they directly contribute toward the achievement of the objectives set. Therefore, a direct link between the engagement activity and the objectives is the first step in completing the template.
- In identifying stakeholders involved in engagement, it is good practice from a planning perspective to also list the specific representative of the stakeholder. It is possible that more than one stakeholder and several representatives will be involved the activity.
- Responsibility for the engagement activity should be assigned to specific organizational interfaces.

Figure 4.9 Action plan for engagement

Objectives									
Engagement activity (name and description)	Relevant objectives (referenced by number)	Level 2 Stakeholders involved	Stakeholder rep	Organizational interfaces involved	Engagement platform	Timing			Organization funds? Y/N
						Q./year	Month	Start date	

- When only one stakeholder is involved this is straightforward and self-explanatory. However, when multiple stakeholders are involved, one clearly identified role player in the organization should be accountable for engagement.

- As a backdrop for engagement planning, it is also essential to revisit and consider the existing stakeholder engagement platforms (ie multi-stakeholder forums, steering committees, working groups, advisory panels and others) that have been used to good effect to engage stakeholders to date, as well as their purpose and effectiveness. Based on the effectiveness of these platforms, decisions can be taken on continued organization involvement (if stakeholder owned), changes to engagement platforms (if organization owned), or the creation of new engagement platforms. Tool 5 (select levels of engagement) and tool 6 (select engagement platforms) are helpful to guide the selection of appropriate engagement methods for inclusion in the action plan.

A stakeholder engagement programme may comprise a number of plans to be implemented in achieving the set objectives. The following templates may be useful in developing these plans:

- template 4: response plan – reputation risk;
- template 5: plan – relationship building;
- template 6: engagement road map – priority issues.

Step 5: Evaluation plan

The evaluation plan should indicate how you will measure the impact and output against the set objectives. General guidelines for the development of your evaluation plan are discussed below.

The plan can be structured according to the key performance areas (KPAs) that you will focus on, differentiating between impact KPAs and output/process KPAs.

- Outputs/process – What are the products, process steps or services that should be delivered?
- Impact – What are the stakeholder changes or benefits resulting from engagement?

KPAs will correlate with set objectives, and within each KPA the following could be included:

- The key performance indicators (KPIs) – What do we need to measure to determine if the objective has been achieved?

- Performance target – To what extent or degree do we need to perform on the KPIs to be successful (usually indicated by numbers or percentages)?

- Measurement methods – How will we measure whether we have achieved the required performance target or not (this can refer to formal measurement, or research, or own evaluation in the form of document analysis, structured feedback, or physical verification, amongst others)?

- Timing – When the measurement needs to be done, indicating when we should have achieved our objectives.

The tools and templates

This section reviews the remaining tools and templates already referred to in this chapter.

Tool 2: How to conduct a stakeholder relationship review

Stakeholder relations reviews are conducted to determine the relationship health. This informs the objectives that are set for the stakeholder engagement and the action plan in the stakeholder engagement programme. The relationship health should be reviewed on a regular basis. The review consists of three basic steps:

1 Obtain inputs from organizational interfaces that have regular contact with the stakeholder.
2 Rate the relationship health.
3 Record the results of the relationship review.

Obtain inputs from relevant internal stakeholders

Relationship reviews should be conducted with all the identified interfaces of a particular stakeholder, to obtain a balanced and informed input into the review. During a stakeholder relationship review, changes to and influences on relationship health with the relevant stakeholder are discussed. Template 1 has been developed to review the effectiveness of engagement with stakeholders according to the objectives set in the stakeholder relationship building plan and should guide the review. Practical matters are also reviewed, with a view to future improvement.

Considerations to focus discussions in the meeting include:

- the nature of engagement with a stakeholder over the recent period;
- any new intelligence obtained about a stakeholder:
  - from engagement;
  - from other sources, such as newspaper reports or internal/external research reports;
  - new profiling information, new issues that are emerging or insights about a stakeholder's linkage/s with other stakeholders;
- consider the implications of new intelligence gained, on engagement with the stakeholder, going forward;
- any possible changes in relationship health during the past quarter. Did the relationship improve, deteriorate or stay the same? Engagement partners to debate their experience;
- reasons for changes in relationship health, if any;
- how to address changes in relationship health, especially if the relationship has deteriorated, with a clear plan of action and responsibilities (see template 5: relationship building plan).

Rate the relationship health

During a stakeholder relationship review, participants can rate the relationship health using the constructs in Figure 4.10, on a 10-point scale, where 1 = very low and 10 = very high. Once each of these constructs has been rated, a mean score out of 10 is calculated.

Figure 4.10 Relationship constructs

Relationship constructs	Description
Trust	The degree to which the partners in the relationship believe the other: <ul><li>is acting in good faith;</li><li>demonstrates general sincere and honest conduct;</li><li>is able to do what they say they will do.</li></ul>
Long-term commitment	Willingness to invest time and effort in the relationship over an extended time period.
Satisfaction	Degree of satisfaction with the level, nature and outcomes of engagement in the relationship.
Control mutuality	The ability of both partners to influence and direct engagement.

Record the results of the relationship review

The results of the stakeholder relationship review are recorded using template 1: stakeholder relationship review.

Figure 4.11 Tool 3: How to conduct a reputation assessment

Consider and agree on the 'what' to be measured
- Levers/drivers of reputation.
- Existing perceptions that need to be changed.
- Unmet expectations of stakeholders.

Consider and agree on the 'how' to be measured
- Decide on a self-assessment or a formal research survey.

Self-assessment   Survey

Review existing indicators/information	**Decide on a self-executed or outsourced survey**
Consider:	Consider the following criteria to determine outsourcing:
• all anecdotal/formal reports on stakeholder perceptions of the organization;	• significance, magnitude or consequence of measurement;
• previous objectives set for reputation management.	• available skills and experience;
	• conceptualization required;
	• level of complexity;
	• need for third party neutrality;
	• availability of infrastructure and resources.

Identify additional information needed and ways to obtain it | **Determine the research methodology and select respondents/draw a sample**

Source information | **Design the measuring instrument**

Design template/criteria | **Perform data collection**

Perform an evaluation using the template/criteria and sourced information | **Conduct data analysis**

Tool 3: How to conduct a reputation assessment

This tool (Figure 4.11) provides a step-by-step process to determine reputation reality.

Tool 4: How to set the desired reputation

Tool 4 (Figure 4.12) guides the process to set the desired reputation for the organization.

Tool 5: How to select levels of engagement

This tool (Figure 4.13) will assist with the selection of the appropriate levels of engagement, which in turn will assist with the selection of appropriate engagement platforms. Engagement can be categorized into different levels, on a continuum of low/no interaction, to high interactivity and involvement. The different levels of engagement are helpful to ensure that engagement is planned appropriately for the objectives to be achieved, as well as the nature of the relationship with stakeholders.

In terms of the general application of engagement levels, for a more significant scope of collaborative change through engagement, higher levels of engagement will be required.

Figure 4.12   Tool 4: How to set the desired reputation

Consider all anecdotal/formal reports on stakeholder perceptions of Sasol

Consult the previous year's objective set for reputation management

Perform a gap analysis to identify areas for improvement where big differences exist between stakeholder perceptions and actual performance

Articulate how to bridge the gap
(including key drivers, perceptions to be changed, expectations to be better met)
Drive reputation through specific levers

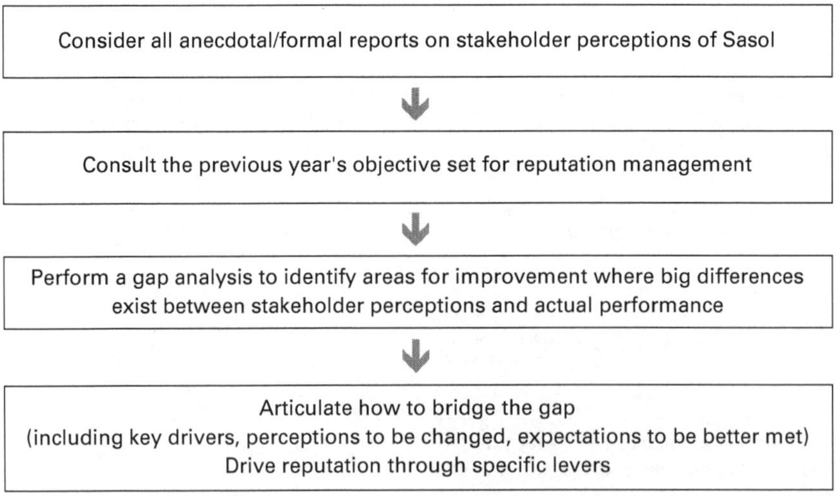

Figure 4.13   Tool 5: How to select levels of engagement

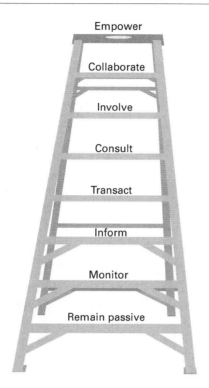

- Change can refer to either a change in the relationship with a stakeholder, or a joint project to achieve change, such as local economic development.
- Higher levels of engagement imply more resources to be pooled between the organization and the relevant stakeholders, while lower levels do not require as many resources.
- Resources refer to one or more of the following: knowledge, people, capacity, finances or influence.
- Higher levels of engagement also imply a higher level of control mutuality in the relationship (control mutuality is the ability to influence the content/direction or outcomes of engagement).
- Engagement with a stakeholder will consist of a combination of engagement levels, with some levels more applicable at times, than others. For example, sometimes it will be sufficient to merely inform a community leader of progress on a project, while consultation on how to proceed with a project may be needed at another time.

- All relationships include a degree of informing, while some relationships will require higher levels of engagement, over and above informing – for example collaboration with provincial government on local economic development.

- Strictly speaking, the first three levels of engagement (remain passive, monitor, inform) are not regarded as 'true' engagement, as they are not interactive. However, they are often the first steps in forming a relationship, or, in the case of inform, supporting an existing relationship.

- To summarize, the appropriate level of engagement will generally be determined by:
  - the organization's objectives for engagement;
  - the scope of relationship changes or of the project at hand;
  - the maturity of the issue that engagement focuses on (more mature issues require higher levels of engagement to manage risk or avert a crisis).

Tool 6: How to select engagement platforms

This tool summarizes some of the most commonly used engagement platforms. The decision about which engagement platform to use should be guided by key considerations regarding:

- the organization objectives and needs;
- stakeholder preferences, perceptions and needs;
- the nature of the relationship with the stakeholders involved;
- the context of issues relevant for the engagement;
- the advantages and disadvantages of the various engagement platforms.

Key considerations to guide the decision of which platform to use are shown in Figure 4.15. Figures 4.16 to 4.19 show the remaining templates.

Figure 4.14   Tool 6: How to select engagement platforms

Description	Most appropriate application	Main advantages and disadvantages
One-on-one meetings		
Personal interviews		
Workshops and presentations		
Focus groups		
Small group/committee meetings		
Round table discussions		
Think tanks		
Public or town hall meetings or road shows		
Open days/open house meetings		
Comments/response/feedback sheets/slips/boxes		
Surveys		
Advisory committees/stakeholder panels		
Online engagement mechanisms		
Multi-stakeholder forums		
Multi-stakeholder alliances, partnerships, voluntary initiatives, joint projects		
Hotlines		

Figure 4.15   Key considerations to guide the decision of which platform to use

Organization's objectives and needs	**1** Does it help to establish the kind of relationship wanted? **2** Will it contribute to the organization's reputation? **3** Can it generate the short- and/or long-term outcomes needed to reach strategic goals? **4** Will it generate the outcome that the organization needs? **5** Are there sufficient resources and time for applying this method/mix of methods?
Stakeholder context	**1** Would this platform appeal to the stakeholders that are to be engaged with? **2** Considering the stakeholders' mobility, is it suitable for their current location? **3** Does it suit the stakeholders' current level of awareness and understanding? **4** What practical matters need to be considered and addressed in order to make the engagement accessible/attractive to them? **5** Do the stakeholders have previous experience of participation in this kind of platform? **6** Are there signs of stakeholder fatigue or cynicism with a specific type of platform? **7** Is the platform culturally appropriate?
Relationship context	**1** Is there a current relationship with these stakeholders, making this approach applicable? **2** How willing are the relevant stakeholders to engage in a group with other stakeholders present? **3** What benefits/risks will there be in bringing different stakeholders together? **4** Are the stakeholders known long enough for the platform selected? **5** Is it suitable for the number of people needed to deal with? **6** What expectations will be created through using a particular engagement platform?
Issue context	**1** Is the platform appropriate for the level of maturity of the issue? **2** Is the issue maybe too sensitive for this approach? **3** Does it match with existing policy or legislative requirements that apply to the stakeholders or issue? **4** If the issue requires multi-stakeholder involvement, does this approach work for it?

Figure 4.16   Template 1: Stakeholder relationship review

Overview			
Review period quarter		Date	
Stakeholder category		Stakeholder	
Stakeholder relationship owner - name		Position	
L1 Stakeholder relationship owner - name		Position	
Review of delivery against relationship building plan			
Achievement of engagement and relationship building objectives	●		
Review of issues			
Issues impacting on this relationship	●		
Relationship health rating			
Trust: The degree to which the partners in the relationship believe the other: ● Is acting in good faith ● Demonstrates general sincere and honest conduct	1___2___3___4___5___6___7___8___9___10 Very low Very high **Motivation for rating:**		
Long-term commitment: Willingness to invest time and effort in the relationship over an extended time period	1___2___3___4___5___6___7___8___9___10 Very low Very high **Motivation for rating:**		
Satisfaction: Degree of satisfaction with the level, nature and outcomes of engagement in the relationship	1___2___3___4___5___6___7___8___9___10 Very low Very high **Motivation for rating:**		
Control mutuality: The ability of both partners to influence and direct engagement.	1___2___3___4___5___6___7___8___9___10 Very low Very high **Motivation for rating:**		
Overall relationship health rating [Mean score of previous four components]		**Comments on current rating**	
Comparisons with previous relationship health rating			
Overall relationship health rating from previous relationship review		**Comments on movement in relationship health**	

Figure 4.17   Template 4: Response plan – reputation risk

Risk title					
Stakeholder concern	*Briefly summarize stakeholder concern*				
Associated risk	*Unpack risk associated with not addressing stakeholder concern*				
Affected stakeholders	Stakeholder		Relationship owner		
	L2 stakeholder name		*This stakeholder's relationship owner who can be consulted on other interfaces*		
Mitigation owner	*Assign responsibility for oversight and guidance on mitigating the reputation risk*				
Planning timeline	From		To		
Engagement history	Date	Engagement activity and outcome			
Organization position					
Mandate	*Regarding this stakeholder concern: What are the margins of movement? What can the organization promise? What can it not promise?*				
Risk mitigation objectives	*Specific, measurable, attainable, results for business oriented, time conscious (SMART) objectives are set for mitigation of the reputation risk*				
Action plan	Action				
	List action steps that will enable the achievement of the objectives set				
Senior management participation	Required participant	Engagement activity	Stakeholders involved	Date	
		Name and explanation of engagement activity to provide indication of the role to be played		*Provide date as specifically as possible*	
Attachments	Background document				
	Frequently asked questions				

Figure 4.18 Template 5: Plan – relationship building

Stakeholder relationship to improve	List the L2 stakeholder name						
Relationship owner	Individual responsible for reporting on the health of this relationship						
Planning timeline	From			To			
Relationship health – current stakeholder perceptions/ opinion/concern	Concise description of current relationship by describing what the stakeholder thinks of the organization, their perceptions and opinions. Traffic light metaphor may be used to further quantify the health of the relationship						
Relationship building objectives	Specific, measurable, attainable, results for business oriented, time conscious (SMART) objectives are set for the improvement of the relationship.						
Action plan	Action		Due	R	A	S	C	I
	List action steps that will enable the achievement of the objectives set			Initials				
Senior management participation	Required participant	Engagement activity	Stakeholders involved			Date	
Attachments	Last relationship review						
	Research findings						
	Stakeholder profiles						

Figure 4.19   Template 6: Engagement road map – priority issues

Issue name	Issue engagement is being planned for									
Issue owner	Assign responsibility for oversight and guidance of the engagement road map									
Planning timeline	From			To						
Impacted stakeholders	Stakeholder			Relationship Owner						
	L2 stakeholder name			This stakeholder's relationship owner who can be consulted on other interfaces						
Organization position										
Mandate										
Engagement objectives	Specific, measurable, attainable, results for business oriented, time conscious (SMART) objectives are set for the management of this issue									
Action plan	Action									
	List action steps that will enable the achievement of the objectives set									
Senior management participation	Required participant		Engagement activity		Stakeholders involved				Date	
Attachments	Issue brief									
	Issue map and motivations for stakeholder positions on it									

Conclusion

Any business or organization, whether from the public, private or third sector, has the potential to harness the benefits of working with a global standard in collaborative working practice (ISO 44001). This potential also extends to include the supply chains upon which the organizations rely. Hopefully this chapter will have provided a useful insight into some of the tools and techniques that are available for use to help identify and compare where collaboration and ISO 44001 can add value.

Stakeholder engagement is also crucial in order to encourage more sustainable business relationships and working practices such that the benefits of working with ISO 44001 can be realized. Hopefully the guidelines and blueprint for the development of a stakeholder engagement programme will likewise prove to be an invaluable tool for any collaborative practitioner.

Pan-industry supply chain collaboration

05

An exemplar of solutions developed by and for the industry

In this chapter we examine a substantive industry case study of the United Kingdom Continental Shelf (UKCS) upstream oil and gas sector, which, because of its dynamics and historical challenges, has evolved to develop a better, more collaborative way to manage the business relationships across the supply chain. This is achieved through joined up collaborative thinking to drive cost waste and inefficiency out of the supply chain for the benefit of both clients and contractors.

Industry context

Let us start first by defining what the UKCS oil and gas supply chain is. Essentially it is the organizational network supporting the industry's primary objective to extract hydrocarbons from the UKCS licensed oil and gas reserves. The activities of those organizations cover front end seismic and processing, reservoir discovery, exploration and appraisal drilling and subsequent well delivery, and then design and build of offshore facilities, and then into operational, production and decommissioning project phases. The third-party supply chain covers a vast organizational range, such as onshore and offshore contractors, suppliers and service providers, consultants and specialist advisers all the way through to the end user clients

Figure 5.1 The client and contractor landscape

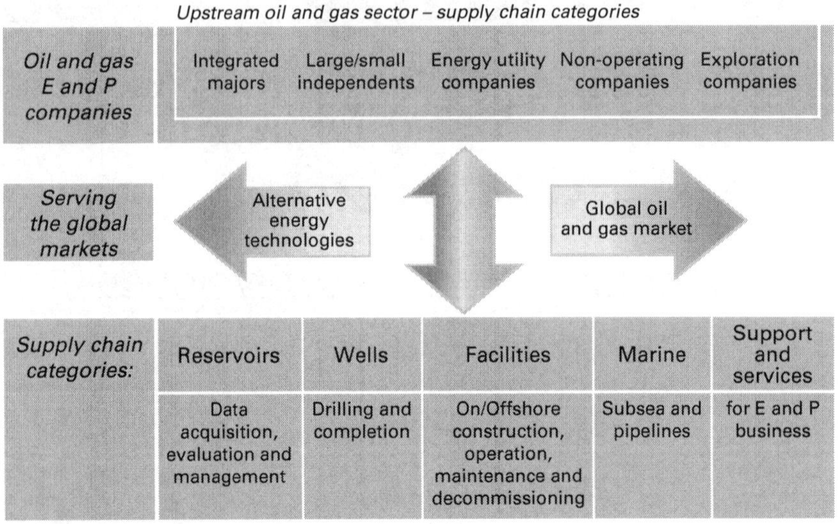

Upstream oil and gas sector – supply chain categories

Oil and gas E and P companies	Integrated majors	Large/small independents	Energy utility companies	Non-operating companies	Exploration companies

| Serving the global markets | Alternative energy technologies | | Global oil and gas market | |

Supply chain categories:	Reservoirs	Wells	Facilities	Marine	Support and services
	Data acquisition, evaluation and management	Drilling and completion	On/Offshore construction, operation, maintenance and decommissioning	Subsea and pipelines	for E and P business

(integrated multi-national client majors and independent client operators). Additionally, there are significant business flows to other non-core sectors that are necessary to support the sector.

Understanding the client and contractor landscape is an important precursor to the case study. As can be seen from Figure 5.1, there are different types of oil and gas exploration and production (E&P) client companies and different contractor tiers. There are integrated multinational majors like BP, Chevron Total, ExxonMobil, Equinor, Sasol and Shell; and there are also small, medium and large independent oil companies like Premier Oil, Nexen, Apache, TAQA Britani, INEOS, Hess and utilities companies like Centrica. Additionally, there are companies that are non-operated and simply form part of a partnership group of three or four oil companies to spread risk, with one of the other companies acting as operator on behalf of the consortium. Finally, there are pure client exploration companies who focus more on acquiring an embryonic exploration licence to prove up reserves by further technical study of the geology. They enhance the value of the licence this way and trade equity on the licence to realize value.

The supply chain categories cover many tiers, with some offering bundled integrated product service lines to the clients, and there are many specialist logistics and transportation providers, such as helicopter companies. Most serve global oil and gas markets now, having used the UKCS as a platform for growth internationally, and many also support alternative energy technologies through diversification.

We also need to understand the sector dynamics – and the link between oil price volatility and cyclical behaviour shift towards the disciplines of supply chain management and value management.

Generally, two primary dimensions dictate the influence and importance that the discipline of supply chain management can have in a sector – these being the size of profit margins being made (or not, as the case may be) and also the percentage of spend on outsourced third-party goods and services. Professor Andrew Cox's model shown in Figure 5.2 helps us to understand this.

It is also possible to broadly categorize different industry sectors into the undernoted four categories dependent on the typical percentage spend on third party goods and services and the typical profit margins seen in those sectors. From Figure 5.2 there is:

- **Category A: transactional** – Where profit margins tend to be positive and high, coupled with a relatively low percentage of outsourced third party spend. Here supply chain management and value management have very low strategic significance. Typically, professional services, wholesale financial services and software services sectors sit in this space.

Figure 5.2 Sector dynamics: comparison of the oil and gas sector with other industries

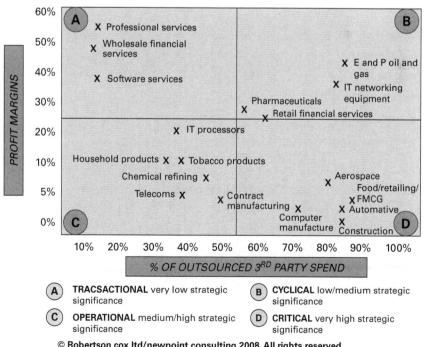

SOURCE Courtesy of Professor Andrew Cox, Newpoint Consulting Group – (2008, World class or best in class, CPO Agenda (Summer))

- **Category B: cyclical** – Where profit margins fluctuate between high and low, coupled with a high percentage of outsourced third party spend. Here supply chain management and value management have fluctuating strategic significance. The E&P oil and gas sector sits firmly in this cyclical category because when the oil price falls then profit margins are squeezed, and in a sector where there is a high percentage reliance on third party goods and services the significance of supply chain management becomes greater. Conversely, when the oil price rises, and the industry burgeons again, organizations tend to 'take their foot off the pedal' and place less strategic significance on supply chain management and value management. It is under those circumstances that we see low/medium strategic significance. Typically, pharmaceuticals, IT networking equipment and retail financial services sectors also sit in this space.

- **Category C: operational** – Where profit margins tend to be low or sometimes negative, coupled with a relatively low percentage of outsourced third party spend. Here supply chain management and value management have medium to high significance. Typically, telecommunications, tobacco products, chemical refining, household products and IT processors sit in this space.

- **Category D: critical** – Where profit margins tend to be low or sometimes negative coupled with a high percentage of outsourced third party spend. Here supply chain management and value management have medium to high strategic significance. Typically, aerospace, food retailing, fast-moving consumer goods, automotive, construction and computer manufacture sectors sit in this space.

Oil price fluctuations and consequences

The cyclical nature of the oil and gas sector is evidenced by the chart in Figure 5.3, which shows how the oil price has fluctuated between 1985 and 2017. Prices have ranged from as low as $10 per barrel of oil equivalent (boe) in 1986, rising to a high of $147 per boe in 2008 with influencing events.

The consequence of this cyclical behavioural shift for the disciplines of supply chain management and value management in the oil and gas sector due to fluctuating oil prices is that there is:

Figure 5.3 Twenty-year snapshot of oil price volatility

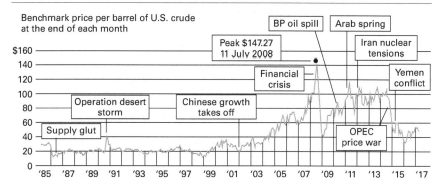

- greater focus on outsourced third party resource/spend when oil and gas prices fall, and cost reduction becomes paramount;

- greater focus on short-term cost reduction targets rather than long-term value for money considerations when oil and gas prices fall and again cost reduction becomes paramount. This plays out in practice by behaviour such as 'slash and burn' of existing contracts, early termination of commercial arrangements for convenience of the client, stretching out or delaying payment terms, etc;

- continuous crisis management with limited collaborative planning of innovation and adaptation within the supply chain;

- a lack of continuous supply chain management/value management competence development within the business.

Wild West vs sustainable commercial practice

All these behaviours are reminiscent of the days of the Wild West, where those who tended to prevail were the more aggressive on the draw in a shoot-out, with little regard for the carnage they left behind and the direct and indirect consequences of their actions!

There is a compelling case for better, more collaborative, sustainable commercial practices to be applied and also that the disciplines of supply chain management and value management should have equal strategic significance within organizations, irrespective of whether it is a high, medium or low oil and gas price environment.

The starting point and compelling case for greater cross-industry collaboration

Clearly the economic circumstances of $10 per boe in 1987 (in money of the day) was not sustainable, and this, coupled with the fact that the oil price continued to remain low throughout the early to mid-1990s, was the catalyst for change, forcing the industry to think differently and essentially embrace the capability dimensions now being advocated by the new global ISO 44001 standard for collaborative working and relationships, as seen in Figure 5.4, under the auspices of a collaborative industry initiative.

Key industry stakeholders involved in driving this forward at the time were the then United Kingdom Offshore Operators Association (UKOOA) now superseded by Oil & Gas UK (the primary industry association on behalf of operators and contractors), the Government body the Department of Trade and Industry (DTI) now superseded by the Oil and Gas Authority (the regulator), the Government PILOT initiative and LOGIC (leading oil

Figure 5.4   CRAFT 8 Stage Life Cycle Model incorporated with ISO 44001

SOURCE Courtesy of Midas Projects Ltd in conjunction with the Institute for Collaborative Working

and gas industry competitiveness), along with representative members of the operator and contractor communities in the sector.

In 1993 it was identified that the oil and gas industry was facing fundamental challenges to its future prosperity (at this time real oil prices were expected to continue to remain at low levels). With this, capital and operating costs continued to escalate, and it was acknowledged that urgent action was required to reverse this trend. So Cost Reduction Initiative for the New Era (CRINE) was established to address these issues, with the ultimate objective of achieving a substantial reduction in the cost base of the UKCS development and production activities. The CRINE initiative comprised a mixture of operators, contractors and suppliers to ensure a balanced fair and representative view. Key outputs from the CRINE report in 1994 highlighted the following:

- a need to cut UKCS costs (Capex and Opex) by 30 per cent;
- a need for standardization (technical and commercial);
- a need to eradicate duplication of effort (especially around contractor pre-qualification for operator business);
- the formation of a new standard contracts committee to develop a suite of standard contracts for the industry, to minimize legal cost and effort.

New development costs at the time were rising rapidly and it is the technical costs that drive the economics of new developments. As can be seen from Figure 5.5, over a more recent snapshot seven-year period, unit technical costs ($/boe) have risen significantly, which illustrates the difficulties when oil and gas prices decline. Additionally, as can be seen from Figure 5.6, the Northern North Sea, where the majority of activity was taking place, was the most expensive area when comparing the various unit operating costs by region (assuming sustained investment case).

Cost remains a major concern for UKCS today, linked to oil price volatility, global competition, rising labour and material costs. Additionally, there are still ongoing challenges around:

- boosting investment in small and challenged UKCS reserves and also in new technology development solutions;
- unlocking the full potential of emerging and existing plays;
- attracting and retaining skilled people and promoting business and technical training courses;
- contracting models to encourage long-term basin sustainability;
- controlling costs;
- maintaining the availability of crucial contractors.

Figure 5.5   Technical lifting costs and operating costs by UKCS region

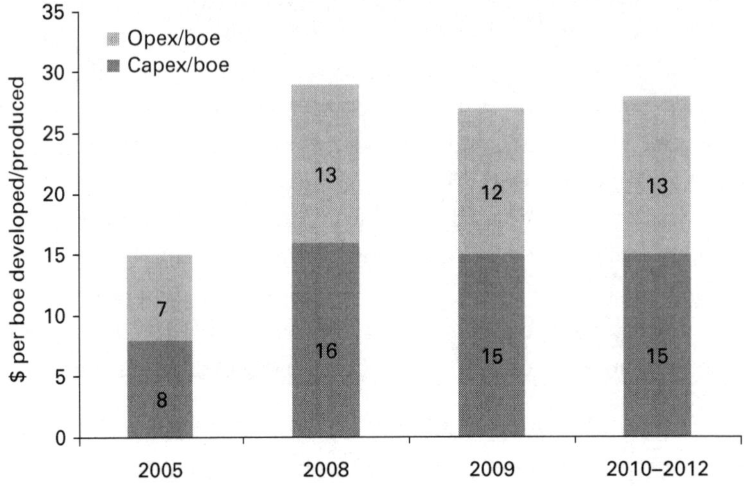

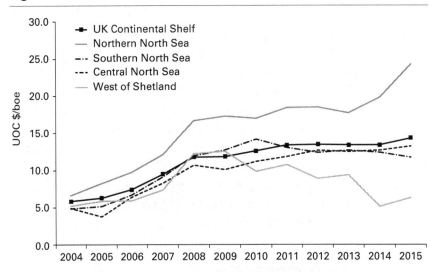

SOURCE Courtesy of Midas Projects Ltd in conjunction with the Institute for Collaborative Working

Figure 5.6   Unit Technical costs 2004–15

SOURCE Unit Technical costs 2004–15

These behaviours are damaging to the sector, when what is needed is a more supportive philosophy to towards the supply chain across the sector to ensure greater sustainability.

So, the key message back then was that time will not wait and that the industry collectively, collaboratively needed to seize the 'window of

Figure 5.7 Example of a typical offshore oil and gas – UK hub life extension

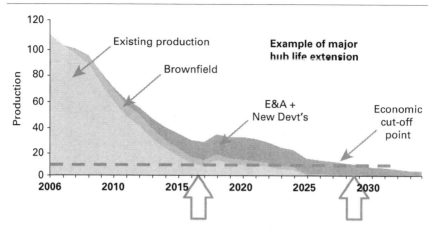

SOURCE Based on information from Oil & Gas UK

opportunity' – as a significant percentage of UKCS oil and gas infrastructure could be decommissioned by 2025 unless current activity is sustained. Moreover, if investors' confidence is maintained, decommissioning could be delayed by 10–15 years in many of the existing production systems. Figure 5.7 illustrates this point in terms how a major offshore oil and gas hub life could be extended.

What had transpired therefore was a 'tale of two futures' for the UKCS upstream oil and gas industry. If nothing were to be done in terms of addressing the challenges of the sector, then the path of decline in overall industry production against a backdrop of burgeoning demand would be steeper, with an earlier end date. However, with meaningful sustained collaborative intervention then the extent of production decline would be gentler, resulting in a better, longer future for the UKCS – as can be seen in Figure 5.8.

Even with the emerging new energy mix, the reality about fossil fuels and dependence on oil is that for the foreseeable future to 2030 it will continue to provide most of the world's energy vs renewables, hydro, and nuclear.

As if the economic and behavioural challenges of the industry weren't enough, to further compound matters the bureaucracy of emerging European Utilities legislation threw a 'curve-ball' at the UKCS oil and gas industry. The EC Utilities Directive 2004/17/EC applied to oil and gas exploration companies in the European Union for contracts over the threshold value (£279,785 (€412,000) for supply & service contracts and £3,497,313 (€5,150,000) in the case of works contracts). The impact was that it required all commitments above these thresholds to be advertised in the Official Journal of the

Figure 5.8   Production decline versus demand – the tale of two futures

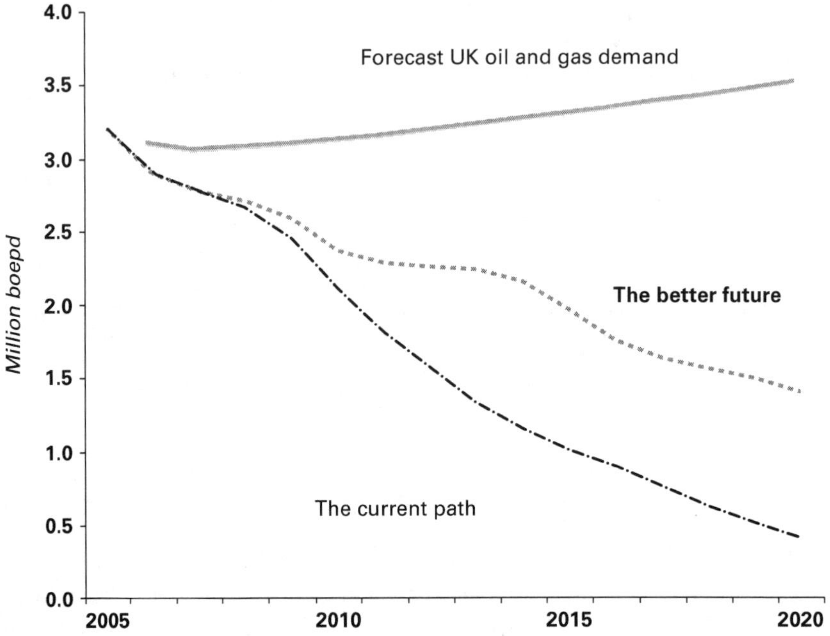

SOURCE Based on information from Oil & Gas UK

European Communities (OJEC), leading to a bureaucratic and unworkable process.

The OJEC (which became the Official Journal of the European Union in 2003) was published weekly and any company expressing an interest in bidding in response to one of these journal publications would be entitled to, on the grounds of transparency, objectivity, competition and non-discrimination in the way that EU oil and gas exploration and production companies select their suppliers. In reality, what this meant in practice was that if several hundred companies responded to a single enquiry with one client operator then that operator would have to evaluate all bids, and that just for one enquiry. The need for pragmatism is indicated here.

There was, of course, also the Piper Alpha North Sea oil platform disaster in 1988, which resulted in 167 men losing their lives. Piper Alpha, at the time, was operated by Occidental Petroleum (Caledonia) Ltd. It accounted for around 10 per cent of the oil and gas production in the North Sea. Flames from the disaster could be seen 100 miles away. To date, it is still the world's worst offshore oil disaster in terms of loss of human life.

The Lord Cullen Inquiry that followed made far-reaching recommendations for offshore operations, all of which were accepted by the industry without question, culminating in revised and new legislation. As one might imagine, a plethora of legal court cases followed, surrounding alleged negligence and compensation. Additionally, there was a lack of clarity between countless third parties as to who was responsible for indemnifying who, in terms of injury and damage to personnel and equipment, resulting in protracted legal cases at huge cost to those organizations involved. It was fair to say that the industry was in turmoil at this time.

The application of good principles to address stormy waters

So, it is against this backdrop and myriad of challenges that combined to create stormy waters for the sector that we can now examine the remarkable set of collaborative principles and solutions that were developed by the industry for the industry to manage the risks associated with those challenges.

Although not all the solutions were developed at the same time, the component parts combined to be embraced under an umbrella industry-wide supply chain code of practice that effectively relates to an aspiring set of good principles to be applied in a sustainable way, not just during stormy waters! The Supply Chain Code of Practice (SCCoP) is essentially a set of best practice guidelines that the UK oil and gas industry is now encouraged to follow in order to help businesses:

- improve overall performance;
- eliminate unnecessary costs;
- add value and boost competitiveness.

As can be seen from Figure 5.9, there are three commercial stages that apply to the SCCoP:

- plan;
- contract;
- perform and pay.

Signatories to the SCCoP are senior officers from within organizations that should aim to comply with the code during each of these three stages. This will help companies achieve the highest standards of business ethics and comply with all relevant legislative requirements. It is acknowledged that full compliance with the code will not be achievable by all signatories. However, they should all aim to comply as fully as possible.

Figure 5.9   Three key stages of the SCoP regarding commercial process

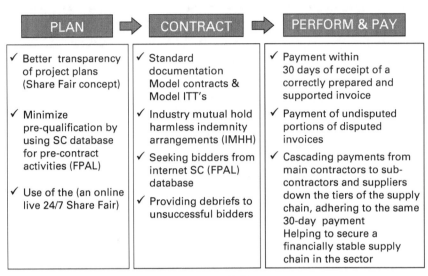

SOURCE   FPAL/Achilles Information Management Ltd/Oil & Gas UK

It should also be noted that purchasers could be both client operator purchasers who purchase from main tier 1 contractors but also contractor purchasers who buy or contract with sub-contractors and other third parties.

Purchasers have the opportunity to achieve an industry award of bronze, silver, gold or excellence (three consecutive years of gold), depending on their level of compliance with the SCCoP.

The industry association Oil & Gas UK's Industry Behaviours Charter was also launched. The Charter, signed by members of Oil & Gas UK and supported by the Oil and Gas Authority (the regulator), is a collective commitment to work effectively, efficiently and cooperatively. Many of the signatories to the Charter are also signed up to the SCCoP, thereby embracing the collaborative values advocated by the author.

Sitting at the heart of the SCCoP is First Point Assessment (FPAL), a database developed by the industry for the industry, which is now run and empowered by the Achilles Group. The database focuses on supplier sourcing, evaluating, auditing and monitoring of suppliers while ensuring commercial requirements are met, as well as the selection of suitable suppliers for purchasers of goods and services in the upstream oil and gas industry. Figure 5.10 illustrates at a high level the type of information available

Figure 5.10 High-level information on suppliers in FPAL

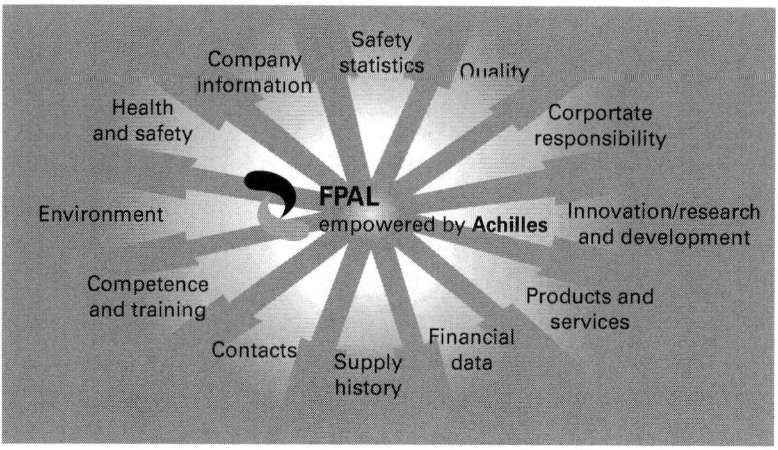

SOURCE Courtesy of Oil & Gas UK

on suppliers. However, there are other aspects of the system that will be explored in more detail shortly.

We will turn now to the component parts of the SCCoP itself.

Stage 1: Planning

Planning is all about the transparent planning of forward contracting activity by major purchasers to improve supply chain capability and keep the supply chain anchored in the business region. There are several component parts to this:

- **Transparency of forward work plans from major purchasers** – The online FPAL forward work plan facility allows purchasers to reveal their forward work plans, which enables suppliers to identify potential business opportunities within the industry. This offers huge benefits to the supply chain to access online information on projects very efficiently and at low cost to pre-qualify or bid for. Traditionally, to establish this type of information would have involved much time, effort and cost on the part of suppliers. Purchasers can improve their use of the FPAL forward work plan facility to engage with a wide range of suppliers and promote competition within the supply chain. Suppliers can make use of this tool to uncover potential business opportunities and ultimately add value to their organizations.

- Up-to-date contact lists – In a dynamic, ever-changing environment with people moving all the time, maintaining up-to-date company contact information on FPAL is vital to facilitate discussions within the industry. Under the code obligations purchasers are encouraged to maintain this performance, as it helps to establish clear lines of communication throughout the pre-qualification and tendering process.

- Share fair events – The annual Oil & Gas UK Share Fair provides an opportunity for all firms active on the UKCS to network and discover new business prospects. The vast majority of purchasers who are signatories to the SCCoP attend this annual event, as do companies in the supply chain serving the sector. Presenting companies are encouraged to identify and share current efficiency challenges facing their businesses, allowing attendees to identify and raise awareness of any potential solutions or mechanisms that could help unlock the full potential of the UKCS. Purchasers also present their forward work plans and offer one-to-one meetings with suppliers in compliance with the code.

The aforementioned commitment by the industry to ensure that the supply chain has 'line of sight' as to what is coming up in terms of future work to try and win is a lighthouse example of joined up collaborative thinking at play and one that many other industry sectors would do well to embrace.

Stage 2: Contracting

In the main, the impact on contracting is on standardization, alongside decent business behaviours, as opposed to the Wild West of the past.

Again, there are component parts to this, which we will now review.

The development of LOGIC model forms

LOGIC supports a suite of 10 standard contracts (LOGIC model forms, as they are referred to in the sector) that are available for use throughout the oil and gas industry for the main onshore and offshore activities, as indicted in Figure 5.11. They were developed by a standard contracts committee made up of representatives from both the client operator and contractor communities, the objective being to arrive at a standard framework of common pre-agreed contract terms and conditions that could be applied without the need for protracted and repetitive negotiation between contracts and legal representatives of companies seeking to enter into an

Figure 5.11 Suite of LOGIC Model forms of contract for upstream oil and gas activities

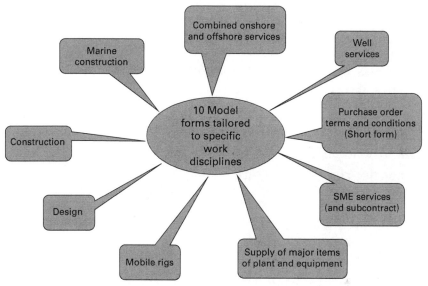

❖ Suite of 10 models covering most of high-value, high-risk activities associated with offshore oil and gas

Model forms
❖ Available at www.logic-oil.com

❖ Originally published in late 1990s, updated in 2000s

SOURCE Courtesy of LOGIC and Oil & Gas UK

agreement with each other. The cost and inefficiency associated with doing so had become unreasonable.

The suite of standard contracts that were established follow a generic structure, the main elements being:

- form of agreement;
- general conditions of contract;
- special conditions of contract;
- remuneration;
- scope of work;
- administration instructions;
- health, safety and environmental issues;
- quality management;
- training;

- documents and drawings;
- materials and facilities to be provided by company (client);
- contractors' plans.

Notwithstanding that the general conditions tend to be accepted by most parties in advance, there are always new or special things that come along that need to be bolted on to form part of the contract. This is achieved by means of a special conditions section that forms part of the contract. An example of this would be provisions to ensure awareness of the need to comply with the 2010 Bribery Act and the more recent Modern Slavery Act. At period points the standard is updated by LOGIC, who govern this standard solution, to incorporate such additions.

Again, this is another lighthouse example of joined up collaborative thinking at play to reap the benefits of standardization.

The development of model/standard invitation to tender documentation

The use of LOGIC model invitation to tender documents is a further means to drive efficiency and good practice within the industry and streamline pre-qualification, tendering and negotiating processes to reduce bidding costs for the supply chain seeking to win work. Again, this is another great example of an initiative to eliminate waste, add value and increase competitiveness. Historically, many client operators solicited tenders or proposals from the supply chain using very different formats but essentially seeking the same thing. This was not consistent with collaborative values as it was more labour intensive for those bidding.

Industry mutual hold harmless agreements and model parent company guarantees

The case law emanating out of Piper Alpha was the catalyst to establish an industry mutual hold harmless deed (IMHH) to address the contractual gap that traditionally exists between contractors working on the UKCS regarding the allocation of liability. On an offshore installation an operator will award contracts to a contractor who may sub-contract to its sub-contractors. This provides a vertical relationship between some of the parties but no relationship across contractors and sub-contractors. The IMHH is designed to sit as a background agreement where there is no direct contract between the contractors.

The use of mutual hold harmless provisions within the industry's contracts is common practice. In fact, some operators have their own version of the IMHH. These are, however, limited to specific contracts or companies, and as a result an industry scheme was developed.

The IMHH applies to the UK's territory of the North Sea and the Irish Sea. It is intended to underpin all offshore activity (with a few exceptions) in the oil and gas industry and participants should be able to enter into it for the long term (although there are limited rights of withdrawal and termination). Parties who are not members initially will be able to join at any time. The IMHH scheme has been created to manage the risks inherent in the industry in a much more comprehensive and effective manner. It operates on the premise that a company is in a much better position to protect and insure their own people and equipment. In doing so, companies can be more certain of the risks they need to insure and this, in turn, reduces multiple policies insuring the same risk.

Post Piper Alpha disaster, IMHH began operating in mid 2002, with over 400 participants having knock-for-knock indemnities between fellow contractors working offshore, covering their own people, property and consequential/indirect losses. Pollution was excluded.

Additionally, model parent company guarantees, and performance bonds were developed, and recommended model formats can also be found on www.logic-oil.com.

Of course, there are other benefits in that it reduces the need to negotiate or litigate such matters, as companies should understand their liabilities. In any event, the IMHH has proved to be a success within the industry.

Meaningful debriefing and feedback for unsuccessful contractors

A further obligation placed on purchaser signatories to the SCCoP is to provide meaningful constructive feedback to suppliers who have been unsuccessful in bidding for work with them. Many suppliers expend considerable time and effort in bidding for work and indeed can incur tendering related costs running into hundreds of thousands of pounds sterling. It is fair and reasonable practice to receive constructive feedback on where they might improve in readiness for future tenders. To receive a brief letter simply advising 'with regret' that they have been unsuccessful 'on this occasion' doesn't do it!

Ideally, for large projects or operational tenders feedback should be given on things such as:

- financial aspects (not precise amounts – but were they significantly off the pace?);
- technical proposals/contractor plans/methodology – any gaps;
- health, safety and environmental proposals – any gaps;
- quality assurance – any gaps;
- compliance with terms and conditions – exceptions – any gaps.

From an industry collaboration angle, there are only benefits all round to taking the time to provide constructive feedback as it enhances the quality and commercial and technical attractiveness of future bids and is good, courteous business practice.

Other industry initiatives to eradicate unnecessary duplication

Flightshare

This provides a mechanism for companies to share excess seat capacity on North Sea helicopter flights. Sharing companies are required to have at least one contract in place with the service providers currently subscribed to Flightshare (Babcock Mission Critical Services Offshore Limited; Bristow Helicopters Limited; CHC Scotia Limited; CHC Holding (UK) Limited; and NHV Helicopters Ltd) and, once signed up, may share flights with companies holding contracts with the respective service provider.

Flightshare provides the legal mechanism for such shares by establishing the legal matrix between sharers and providing provisions for appropriate payment and indemnities in the unfortunate event that there is some form of incident.

Master Deed

The Master Deed is a well-established part of the legal framework of the oil and gas industry relating to asset transfers in the UKCS. The arrangements cover two areas: (i) pre-emption (the right of co-ventures in the field (or pipeline) to purchase the percentage interest that is for sale); and (ii) the process for transferring interests, including the standard documents to be used.

Developed by the Progressing Partnership Working Group, a subset of the Pilot Taskforce, the Master Deed was a result of industry and Government's examination of commercial and behavioural barriers to UKCS development. The review noted specific concerns relating to protracted negotiations and the ability of a co-venture to purchase an interest ahead of a proposed purchaser; therefore it was agreed that the system ought to be amended. The Master Deed aims to:

- standardize existing pre-emption provisions;
- create pro forma transfer arrangements;
- reduce complexities around signature;
- allow greater certainty around the timing of completions.

Offshore personnel on board (POB) dynamic monitoring system

Another exemplar of collaborative pan-industry working was the development of a dynamic POB monitoring system for all people working offshore in the UK upstream oil and gas sector. This system became known as Vantage POB, which is essentially a shared service of oil and gas operators for personnel and certification tracking at onshore and offshore installations. Each operator previously had independent systems in place. In 2000 the UK oil and gas industry initiated a project to establish a shared solution. Founded in Aberdeen and based on the findings of the Piper Alpha Cullen Report, Vantage POB was designed by logistics personnel in the industry, embodying industry best practice in aviation logistics, and has been available to the industry since 2003. It is available for use within the EU by any user; however, funding member companies have a licence for use globally.

A single Vantage POB instance can support collaborative sharing on a large scale, for example:

- oil and gas operators share the service;
- thousands of personnel movements tracked per annum;
- hundreds of locations managed;
- thousands of users supported.

The safety benefits of the system covered such things as emergency response cooperation and security. Vantage tracks days spent offshore and ensures that passenger data is up to date and accurate. Other benefits of this collaborative service include:

- accurate information on personnel trips and a picture of who has been where;
- accurate information on certification;

- personnel training details for every passenger;
- verified offshore industry training details;
- passenger eligibility checked automatically at booking and check-in;
- check-in staff can handle multiple flights at the same time, without switching systems;
- handles cross-border flights and multiple time zones and can view several countries' flights on the same screen.

Helimet

Helimet is a shared weather information tool used by the helicopter industry that supports the offshore oil and gas industry in the UK. The system was developed under the leadership of Oil &Gas UK as a cross-industry collaborative aviation safety tool, where each company's regional weather information is validated and then shared with the helicopter operators and oil and gas companies. The success of this collaborative tool has been such that the Civil Aviation Authority has mandated its use by the offshore industry in the CAP 437 (standards for offshore helicopter landing areas).

Streamlining and making the pre-qualification process more efficient for both operators and contractors

The bureaucracy associated with the EU Utilities Directive 2004/17/EC, which called for transparency, objectivity, competition and non-discrimination in the way that EU oil and gas exploration and production companies select their suppliers has already been touched on in this chapter. The impact was that it required all commitments above these small procurement thresholds to be advertised in the Official Journal of the EC (OJEC), leading to an unworkable process.

However, what is important is the smart way in which the UK upstream oil and gas sector overcame this, by means of utilizing the FPAL supply chain database, which itself was advertised annually in the OJEC as a pre-qualification system. This database has around 3,000 contractors/suppliers on it, capturing most of the companies that oil companies do business with annually. Since 1997 oil and gas companies in the UK have had the benefit of derogation under the relevant EU procurement directive, allowing them not to adhere to the full spectrum of obligations under that directive. Instead, the obligation has been for companies, when putting contracts out to tender, to hold a non-discriminatory competition (of their own design) unless there is objective justification not to do so. In practice, though, most companies still elected to utilize the FPAL supply chain database as it was considered to be best practice supply chain methodology.

FFPAL was established by the UK oil and gas industry as a way of streamlining the tender process. This streamlining is achieved in two ways. First, FPAL has a number of features such as supplier registration, performance feedback, capability profiling and verifying, which serve as a central hub of supplier information and remove the need for duplicate requests for information. Second, as a response to the EU Utilities Directive 2004/17/EC, FPAL is regarded as a qualification system under EU procurement rules. Since the inception of FPAL as a qualification system, most European oil and gas exploration companies and their main contractors are now using it as a convenient method of compliance with the EU Utilities Directive. The benefits of the FPAL system are that it provides any company in the EU with:

- an efficient method of supplier selection from a comprehensive list of around 3,000 'qualified' suppliers without the need to publish a separate notice for each contract;

- a way of awarding contracts quickly without risk of challenge under the Utilities Directive and its companion Remedies Directive.

Protection therefore exists for the supply chain (should any companies feel they have been treated unfairly) because:

1 UK oil and gas companies will continue to use FPAL for the same reasons that they have used it since 1997, despite there being no formal legal requirement to comply with the full range of EU procurement obligations. That is driven by a need to demonstrate internally (eg to internal audit functions) and externally to shareholders that value for money has been secured in awarding contracts and to support a healthily and competitive supply chain.

2 The industry's supply chain code of practice continues to exist and Oil & Gas UK (the industry's representative association) will continue to promote its use by all member companies and other signatories. The code itself encourages adherence to a set of best practice guidelines and the use of FPAL. One of the key objectives underpinning the code is to ensure transparency in respect of supply chain requirements. Recent work to award tier compliance levels to major purchasers is an example of energizing good practice across the supply chain.

3 Competition law (primarily under the UK's Enterprise Act 2002 and Articles 81 and 82 of the EU Treaty) will continue to prevent restrictive

practices, cartels or abuses of dominant market positions in respect of, for example, pricing and terms and conditions. Common law restraint of trade rules also acts as a check on anti-competitive practices.

4 The Unfair Contract Terms Act offers protection in respect of certain provisions in business-to-business contracts, for example in respect of unreasonable attempts to deny liability.

Collaborative purpose of FPAL

In summary, the purpose of FPAL is:

- to provide purchasers with a structured way of identifying and selecting potential suppliers and contractors;
- to provide suppliers with an easy mechanism of advising their interest in supplying products or services;
- to understand and record actual performance in order to facilitate continuous improvement;
- to eliminate duplication and unnecessary repetitive activities within the bid process.

Figure 5.12   Pre-qualification data available from FPAL

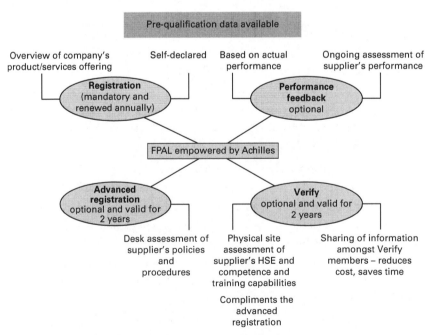

SOURCE Courtesy of FPAL/Achilles Information Management Ltd

As can be seen from Figure 5.12 there are four main parts to the FPAL database:

- basic high-level registration data which enables crucial information on a company to be shared rapidly via the FPAL internet;

- advanced registration capability profile showcasing what product/service lines the supplier can offer prospective customers;

- performance feedback/track record information on what existing or past clients or customers think of that supplier;

- verification of the robustness of the supplier's health, safety, environmental and quality assurance working practices through audit.

These four areas combine to provide a prospective client or customer with a very comprehensive assessment of a supplier's suitability and capability to undertake work on their behalf or to include that supplier on a shortlist of preferred tenderers to bid for work. This funnelling concept is shown in Figure 5.13 where information from the FPAL database can be used to reduce a large potential tender list down to a more manageable shortlisted number.

Figure 5.13 Funnel concept – using information to shortlist tenderers

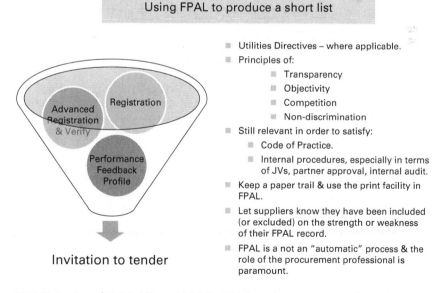

SOURCE Courtesy of FPAL/Achilles and Oil & Gas UK Information Management Ltd

Effectively, such information is invaluable due diligence to better inform the client regarding decision quality as to the selection of suppliers. The database is also an excellent means by which contractors and suppliers can raise awareness of their capabilities to prospective clients or customers in an extremely efficient and cost-effective fashion online via the internet. The majority of clients in the sector participate in the database so by being registered on the system suppliers will have exposure to and coverage of most of the buyers in the sector. This represents a huge shift from inefficient working practices many decades ago where suppliers had go round knocking on doors and hope that they were granted access to raise awareness of their product/service lines to clients, expending considerable time, effort, resource and cost.

The concept also provides client/purchaser organizations with a robust and objective reporting mechanism to demonstrate why they have de-selected certain potential suppliers from bidding for work as part of a shortlist of tenderers. This may be needed to ward off a legal challenge from a disgruntled supplier who has been excluded from bidding.

Figure 5.14 exhibits an example of the basic supplier capability Gantt chart that can be accessed on a supplier via the FPAL database. The information is extremely easy for the reader to encode – for example of the vertical axis essentially imparts a set of high-level yet very relevant KPIs – product quality, service quality, project management capability, documentation management capability, planning and delivery capability, supplier/sub-contractor management experience, installation and commissioning experience, health, safety and environmental capability, policies and capability around skills, competencies, and training. The horizontal axis is a basic score line running from 0 to 10, with 0–2 poor, 3–4 mediocre, 5 average, 6–7 good, 7–8 very good and 9–10 excellent.

The bars on the chart depict the pre-assessed capability score against each of the 11 high-level KPIs with the three ticked areas being verified through quality engineer on site assessments.

The conclusion, looking at this capability profile, would be that this supplier has a very good profile, averaging scores of above seven. It is this type of information that enables clients to differentiate between suppliers and decide which ones to select or deselect.

Not only does this concept enable supplier capability to be assessed and reviewed, but it also provides an excellent structure and basis for performance management.

The very same KPIs can be applied in a collaborative fashion to facilitate and measure performance feedback at appropriate stages during any contract to improve mutual performance, minimize waste, learn from

Figure 5.14 Capability Ghantt chart enabling clients to consider including this supplier on a tender shortlist

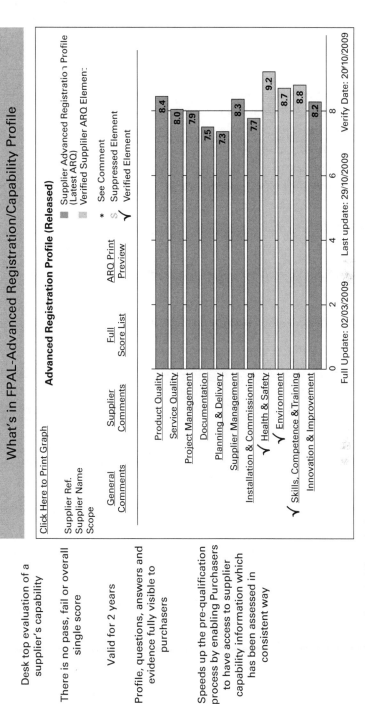

SOURCE Courtesy of FPAL/Achilles and Oil & Gas UK

mistakes and best practice, and report on the extent of compliance with the supply chain code of practice (referred to earlier in this chapter) achieved by both parties. Such information can also be captured on the database to help inform interested parties as to the historical performance track record of a supplier.

Figure 5.15 is an example of a completed performance feedback profile for a supplier, showing a range of feedback from different clients who have used the services of that supplier over a period. The bars show the range of feedback specific to each of the KPIs previously discussed. What is important is to look at the average score (as shown by the slider), which is indicative of the general consensus view of clients about that particular supplier. The system also allows for feedback to uploaded onto the system, which is either agreed (as depicted by the 'A' column in the far left) or not

Figure 5.15   Example of a performance feedback profile on a supplier

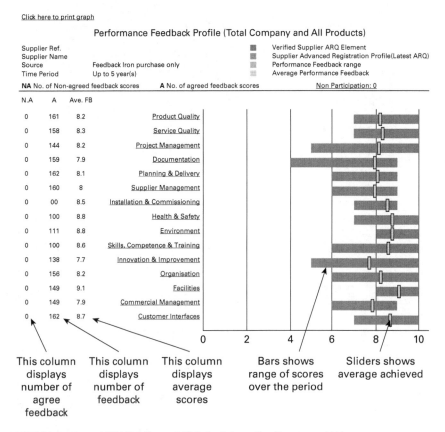

SOURCE Courtesy of FPAL/Achilles and Oil & Gas Information Management Ltd

Figure 5.16 Example of benchmarked supplier performance feedback profile

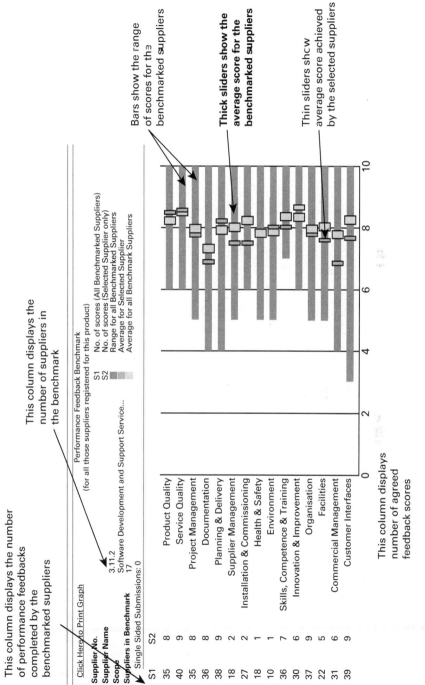

SOURCE Courtesy of FPAL/Achilles and Oil & Gas Information Management Ltd

agreed (as depicted by the 'N-A' column in the far left). Ideally, what you want to observe is a good representative sample number of feedbacks mutually agreed by the two parties rather than a small number of agreed or large number of not agreed feedback. In the case of the latter, this would send a subtle message (ie that the supplier was not receptive to agreeing feedback).

The very same concept can also be used in an enhanced fashion to conduct performance benchmarking to compare the performance of a supplier with that of its competing peers across the sector. This is shown in Figure 5.16 where the horizontal bars show the range of scores for the benchmarked supplier, the wide sliders show the average scores for the benchmarked suppliers and the narrow sliders show the average scores for the selected supplier. This type of profile is very powerful and can be used by the:

- client/customer to have a robust informed discussion based on objective data as why there are gaps or lags between the level of service it is has been receiving versus the average level of service that has been given by that supplier to rest of the industry (perhaps the supplier has allocated its 'C' team to that client rather than the its 'A' team);

- supplier to compare its level of service offering with its competitor peers (at a high anonymous level as perceived by customers across the sector). This represents a very mature way of reflective thinking in terms of receptiveness to critical feedback, which in turn creates the potential for improvement.

The collaborative nature of the Achilles FPAL database is such that it also embraces two-way performance feedback. This is an important consideration if client organizations are to adopt the global ISO 44001 standard for collaborative relationships.

In examining the effectiveness of any contractual relationship it is equally as important for clients to be receptive to receiving constructive feedback on how they have performed or are performing in terms of the working practices, interactions and behaviours that they exhibit to the supply chain upon which they rely. Indeed, sometimes it can be the poor behaviour of a client that can lead to a suboptimal outcome in terms of contract success for both parties.

The KPIs that we have discussed thus far in this chapter have focused on the perspective of the client purchaser looking down the supply chain in terms of performance expectations on the supplier. However, what if we turn the whole thing on its head and look at what is important to the suppliers looking up the supply chain at their client purchaser base? The FPAL Achilles database also facilitates feedback in this area.

If we look at Figure 5.17 we see a similar performance feedback profile to that already discussed, except that the KPIs have subtly changed to reflect things that are important to the supplier in terms of client attractiveness and what it wants out of the relationship. For example, all the following have value to the supplier:

- Specification – How well does the client specify the requirement and work scope?

- Tender process – How well does the client manage the tender process?

- Bid clarification – Does the client conduct bid clarifications properly?

- Purchase order/contract documents – Are they comprehensively managed by the client?

- Communications – Are there regular and effective flows of communication from the client?

- Manufacturing/service support – Is this present within the client organization?

- Quality control – Is this present within the client organization?

- Change control – Does the client have good contract administration around variations and contract amendments?

- Documentation – Does the client have good contract control systems in place?

- Delivery – Does the client have delivery receipt arrangements in place?

- Commercial management – Does the client have sound commercial management processes and procedures in place?

- Interfaces with client systems – What is this like?

- Post-delivery experience/feedback – Is there any feedback/ongoing dialogue?

- Cooperation and relationships – What has this been like?

Additionally, the three component parts of the industry supply chain code of practice – namely plan, contract, perform and pay – have value and meaning to the supplier community in terms of a client purchaser's compliance with the objectives and aims of the code.

Figure 5.17 reveals a range of feedback on a hypothetical client (The AAA Company) from suppliers who have dealt with it. Some record good experiences whilst others have had mediocre experiences in certain areas of the clients working practices and behaviours. Overall, however, we are

Figure 5.17 Example of a performance feedback profile on a client/purchaser

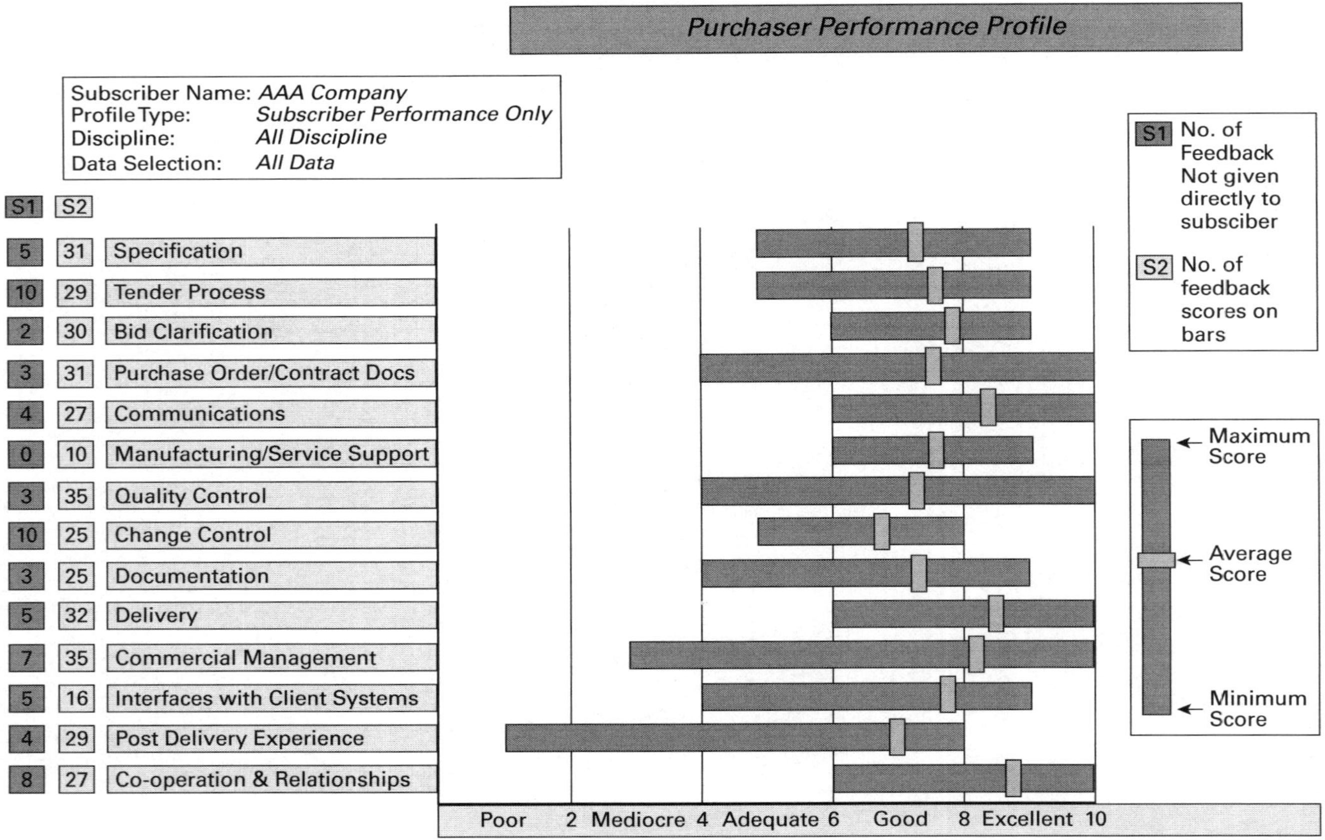

Purchaser Performance Profile

Subscriber Name: AAA Company
Profile Type: Subscriber Performance Only
Discipline: All Discipline
Data Selection: All Data

S1 No. of Feedback Not given directly to subsciber
S2 No. of feedback scores on bars

← Maximum Score
← Average Score
← Minimum Score

S1	S2		
5	31	Specification	
10	29	Tender Process	
2	30	Bid Clarification	
3	31	Purchase Order/Contract Docs	
4	27	Communications	
0	10	Manufacturing/Service Support	
3	35	Quality Control	
10	25	Change Control	
3	25	Documentation	
5	32	Delivery	
7	35	Commercial Management	
5	16	Interfaces with Client Systems	
4	29	Post Delivery Experience	
8	27	Co-operation & Relationships	

Poor 2 Mediocre 4 Adequate 6 Good 8 Excellent 10

again interested in the slider average feedback to gather a balanced view on what this client is like to work for (from a supplier perspective). Overall, on balance this client has a favourable average score.

Similarly, the very same concept can also be used to benchmark the performance feedback on that client purchaser with those of its competing client peer group across the sector. This is shown in Figure 5.18 where the horizontal bars show the range of scores for the benchmarked client purchaser (The AAA company), the white bars show the average scores for the benchmarked client purchasers within the same peer group and the black bar shows the position of that purchaser compared with its peer group. Again, this type of profile is very powerful and can be used both by the:

- client/purchaser to ascertain what its industry supply chain thinks about its working practices and behaviours compared with its competitor peer group. This may very well be important if the client purchaser organization wants to position itself as partner or customer of choice for crucial members of the supply chain upon which it may rely. Under such circumstances the organization would do well to begin embracing some of the principles of ISO 44001;

- supplier to prioritize its client base and decide which are the more attractive client/purchaser organizations to work with. This is especially true in niche product/service line market areas where the suppliers have greater leverage in terms of contractual negotiations with clients.

A very clever feature of the system is that feedback on client purchasers can be solicited with anonymity to dispel any concerns from the supply chain who might be reluctant to record negative feedback on a client for fear of retribution in terms of not being awarded any future work from that client. Such feedback would of course be recorded as N-A (not agreed by both parties) so ideally, we would want to see a mature adult discussion taking place between the two parties and for a mutual agreement on the performance feedback ranking for each of the KPI elements.

Again, receptiveness to critical feedback and joined up collaborative thinking on how things can be improved going forward are underpinning themes of ISO 44001, thereby creating the potential for mutual value creation.

Performance feedback under the auspices of FPAL Achilles is a collaborative method of assessing performance of both suppliers and buyers and maintaining an objective record of performance. It can also be used

Figure 5.18 Example of a benchmarked performance feedback profile on a purchaser

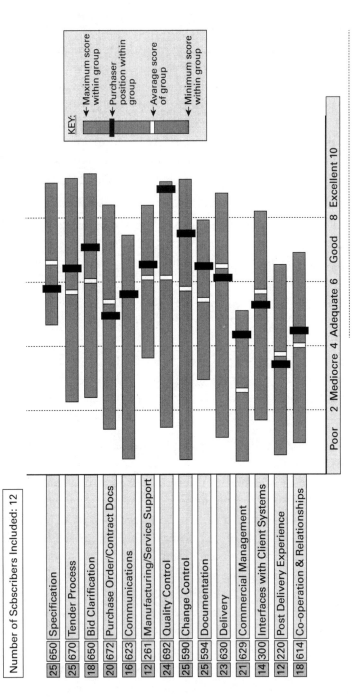

Purchaser Benchmarked Performance Profile

Number of Scbscribers Included: 12

25 650	Specification
25 670	Tender Process
18 650	Bid Clarification
20 672	Purchase Order/Contract Docs
16 623	Communications
12 261	Manufacturing/Service Support
24 692	Quality Control
25 590	Change Control
25 594	Documentation
23 630	Delivery
21 629	Commercial Management
14 300	Interfaces with Client Systems
12 220	Post Delivery Experience
18 614	Co-operation & Relationships

Poor   2   Mediocre   4   Adequate   6   Good   8   Excellent 10

KEY:
← Maximum score within group
← Purchaser position within group
← Avarage score of group
← Minimum score within group

SOURCE Courtesy of FPAL/Achilles and Oil & Gas Information Management Ltd externally as a marketing tool, internally as a business improvement tool and to develop business relationships and future opportunities. A further positive aspect is that it meets the requirements of ISO 9001 with regard to customer feedback. Additionally, buyers can use it as a filtering tool to differentiate and select suppliers for tendering or contract award and it can be presented in database records as a validated profile.

Blueprint for capturing the performance feedback in practice

Capturing and agreeing performance feedback need not be complicated, in fact the following blueprint offered by Achilles FPAL provides a very simple yet robust mechanism for doing this. By means of an outline as to how this works:

- Both parties (buyer and supplier) agree when to complete the performance – during ongoing operations or at end of work.
- Both parties agree a level of performance against relevant product/ service line codes and complete the forms (see the simple self-explanatory diagrams in Figures 5.19 onwards).
- Online submissions, once agreed by both parties, are automatically uploaded and made available on the database.
- For paper, the signed and agreed (or agreement to disagree) reports are returned to Achilles FPAL for input onto the database.
- Report details are only seen by the buyer and supplier involved.
- Performance Feedback data is aggregated and displayed as a Performance Feedback profile on the database for five years.
- There is no pass, fail or overall company score. Essentially there are eight very simple steps involved:
  - Step 1: Basic preparation – meeting request, who to attend, where, when etc.
  - Step 2: Access the form(s) via download from the internet.
  - Step 3: Assign product/service line codes.
  - Step 4: Complete work details.
  - Step 5: Add the scores (preferably by agreement).
  - Step 6: Gain agreement and sign off the forms (both parties).
  - Step 7: Report on your respective contractual party (buyer/supplier).
  - Step 8: Get it on the database.

Figure 5.19 Template for capturing supplier performance feedback information and scoring – initial product/service line coding entry

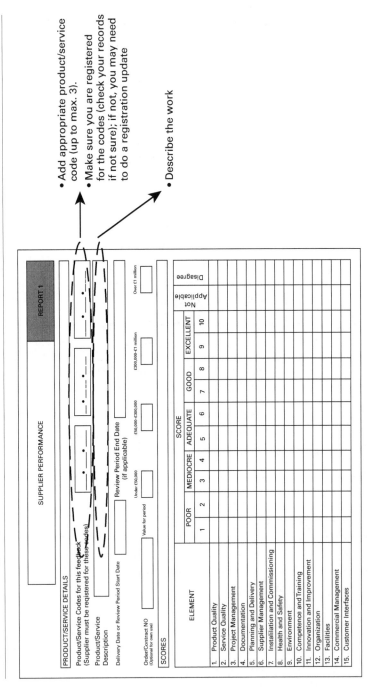

- Add appropriate product/service code (up to max. 3).
- Make sure you are registered for the codes (check your records if not sure; if not, you may need to do a registration update
- Describe the work

SUPPLIER PERFORMANCE

REPORT 1

PRODUCT/SERVICE DETAILS

Product/Service Codes for this feedback
(Supplier must be registered for these codes)

Product/Service Description

Delivery Date or Review Period Start Date

Review Period End Date (if applicable)

Order/Contract NO
(Optional for own use)

Value for period

Under £50,000   £50,000–£300,000   £300,000–£1 million   Over £1 million

SCORES

ELEMENT	SCORE											
	POOR		MEDIOCRE		ADEQUATE		GOOD		EXCELLENT		Not Applicable	Disagree
	1	2	3	4	5	6	7	8	9	10		
1. Product Quality												
2. Service Quality												
3. Project Management												
4. Documentation												
5. Planning and Delivery												
6. Supplier Management												
7. Installation and Commissioning												
8. Health and Safety												
9. Environment												
10. Competence and Training												
11. Innovation and Improvement												
12. Organization												
13. Facilities												
14. Commercial Management												
15. Customer Interfaces												

SOURCE Courtesy of FPAL/Achilles Information Management

Figure 5.20 FTemplate for capturing supplier performance feedback information and scoring – review period entry and high-level contract details

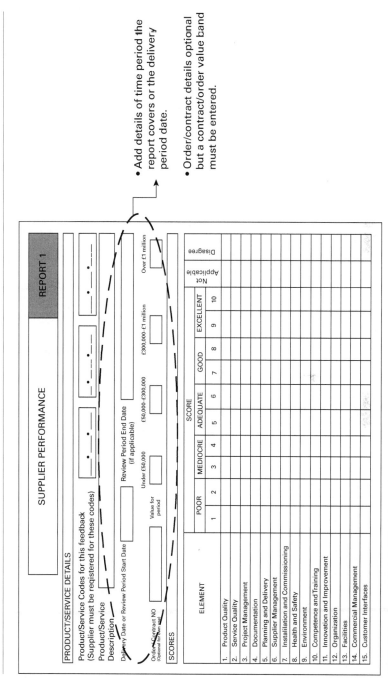

SOURCE Courtesy of FPAL/Achilles Information Management

Figure 5.21 Template for capturing supplier performance feedback information and scoring – insertion of feedback scores

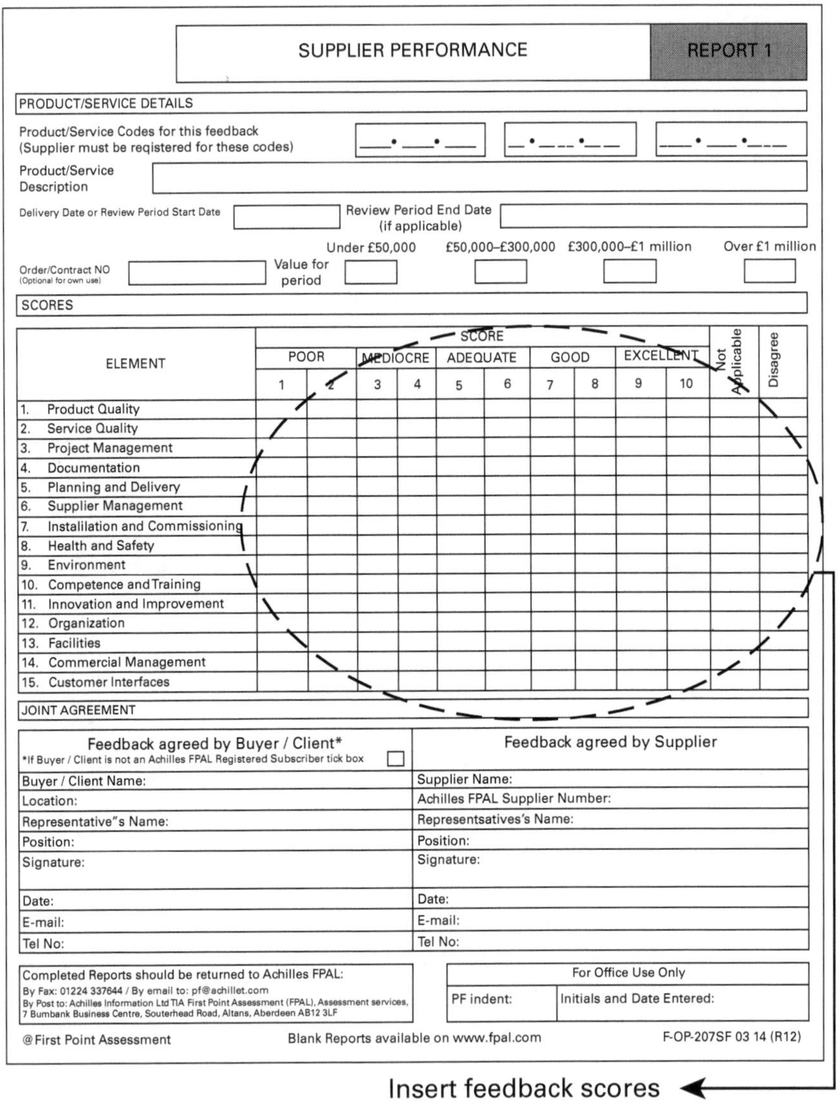

SUPPLIER PERFORMANCE | REPORT 1

PRODUCT/SERVICE DETAILS

Product/Service Codes for this feedback (Supplier must be reqistered for these codes) ___•___•___ | ___•___•___ | ___•___•___

Product/Service Description

Delivery Date or Review Period Start Date | Review Period End Date (if applicable)

Order/Contract NO (Optional for own use) | Value for period: Under £50,000 | £50,000–£300,000 | £300,000–£1 million | Over £1 million

SCORES

ELEMENT	SCORE											
	POOR		MEDIOCRE		ADEQUATE		GOOD		EXCELLENT		Not Applicable	Disagree
	1	2	3	4	5	6	7	8	9	10		
1. Product Quality												
2. Service Quality												
3. Project Management												
4. Documentation												
5. Planning and Delivery												
6. Supplier Management												
7. Installilation and Commissioning												
8. Health and Safety												
9. Environment												
10. Competence and Training												
11. Innovation and Improvement												
12. Organization												
13. Facilities												
14. Commercial Management												
15. Customer Interfaces												

JOINT AGREEMENT

Feedback agreed by Buyer / Client* *If Buyer / Client is not an Achilles FPAL Registered Subscriber tick box ☐	Feedback agreed by Supplier
Buyer / Client Name:	Supplier Name:
Location:	Achilles FPAL Supplier Number:
Representative"s Name:	Representsatives's Name:
Position:	Position:
Signature:	Signature:
Date:	Date:
E-mail:	E-mail:
Tel No:	Tel No:

Completed Reports should be returned to Achilles FPAL:
By Fax: 01224 337644 / By email to: pf@achillet.com
By Post to: Achilles Information Ltd TIA First Point Assessment (FPAL), Assessment services, 7 Bumbank Business Centre, Souterhead Road, Altans, Aberdeen AB12 3LF

For Office Use Only	
PF indent:	Initials and Date Entered:

@First Point Assessment | Blank Reports available on www.fpal.com | F-OP-207SF 03 14 (R12)

Insert feedback scores

SOURCE Courtesy of FPAL/Achilles Information Management

- Jointly agree the scores – preferably in a face-to-face meeting but can be by phone/email.

- Scoring should be done by those best positioned to make judgements; do not assess an element outside your own detailed knowledge – ask for input from others.

- Not all elements may be applicable.

Suppliers are encouraged to complete a performance feedback on a client at the same time as the client provides a supplier performance report on them. It should include:

- details of the buyer/customer along with details of the work provided;

- scores the buyer's performance – suppliers are encouraged to openly discuss the feedback.

It should be noted that not all elements may be applicable.

In order to introduce a degree of objectivity in what can sometime be accused of being a subjective process FPAL Achilles developed a blueprint set of guideline templates that could be used to help buyer and purchaser representatives reach agreement on what constituted scores such as poor, mediocre, good, very good, excellent against each of the buyer and purchaser KPIs. Figures 5.22 to 5.26 show examples of this.

Figure 5.22 Definitions for feedback banding scores

Score	Band	Description
1–2	Poor	Supplier standard of performance below that needed for repeat business; severe deficiencies in service performance.
3–4	Mediocre	Supplier performance did not satisfactorily meet all the specified requirements; buyer incurred additional support costs to achieve required performance.
5–6	Adequate	Supplier performance generally satisfied expectations and met requirements but needed some support to ensure required performance was achieved; improved opportunities identified.
7–8	Good	Supplier performance fully satisfied all expectations; met requirements without support; no identifiable improvements.
9–10	Excellent	Supplier performance exceeded all expectations and fulfilled all specified.

SOURCE Courtesy of FPAL/Achilles Information Management

Figure 5.23 Template for capturing client/purchaser performance feedback information and scoring – insertion of data and feedback scores

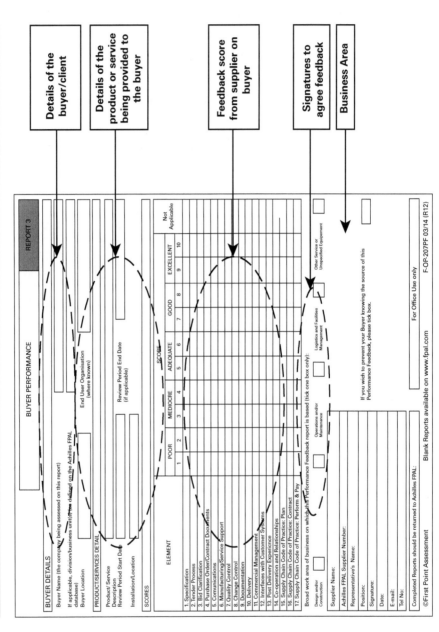

SOURCE Courtesy of FPAL/Achilles Information Management

Figure 5.24 Template examples showing area for mutual sign off and agreement to feedback by both client purchaser and contractor/supplier

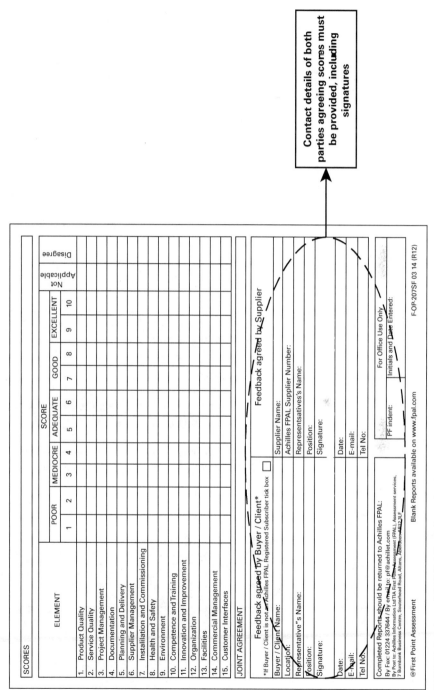

SOURCE Courtesy of FPAL/Achilles Information Management

Figure 5.25 Guidance template for feedback scoring – planning and delivery

Report 1 - Guidance Template				

5. PLANNING & DELIVERY

Poor	Mediocre	Adequate	Good	Excellent
PRE-ORDER INITIATIVE				
PLANNING				
SCHEDULING Work schedules not always available to identify potential deviations	Detailed schedules could be improved in order to identify potential deviations	Maintained adequate detailed schedule to identify potential deviations in a timely manner	Good detailed schedules allowing anticipation of potential deviations	Excellent and detailed schedules which assisted in the identification of pre-emptive improvements
PROGRESS MONITORING				
DELIVERY PERFORMANCE				
1	2	3	4	5	6	7	8	9	10

SOURCE Courtesy of FPAL/Achilles Information Management

Figure 5.26 Guidance template for feedback scoring – specification writing

Report 3 - Guidance Template				

1. SPECIFICATION

Poor	Mediocre	Adequate	Good	Excellent
STANDARD OF SPECIFICATION				
CLARITY AND COMPLETION Specification was vague and/or ambiguous resulting in major clarification exercise	Specification was partially incomplete and/or imprecise	Specification was reasonably clear and comprehensive but needed some work prior to proceeding	Specification comprehensive requiring minimum clarification	Fully comprehensive, well structured and very clear
ACCEPTANCE CRITERIA				
PLANNING ACCURACY				
INDUSTRY SPECIFICATIONS				
1	2	3	4	5	6	7	8	9	10

SOURCE Courtesy of FPAL/Achilles Information Management Ltd

Stage 3: Perform and pay

The final key stage of the commercial process under the SCCoP is that in exchange for a contractor or supplier performing its obligations under the contract then all invoices should be settled within a period of 30 days. This encourages prompt payment, reduces the potential for any disputes to arise, ensures good working relationships between firms and improves overall business performance. The code also encourages payment of any non-disputed portion of an invoice to ensure cash flow is cascaded down the supply chain

Conclusion

There are benefits up, down and across the supply chain for an entire industry sector. The benefits of cutting edge best practice technology and collaborative industry solutions are also two-way – both to client organizations (or purchasers) and to contractor organizations (or suppliers).

Consider the benefits to client organizations:

- more sustainable supply chain anchored to the sector with greater surety of supply;
- drives waste, cost and inefficiency out of the supply chain;
- introduces standardization across the sector and model contractual solutions;
- eliminates the need for non-job specific pre-qualification;
- modern internet-based technology, ease of use, easy internal and global access, contractor website linkage;
- easy and cost-effective compliance with EU procurement and competition laws;
- eliminates the need for internal company databases (up to date and industry wide);
- provides an objective, structured basis for performance monitoring against a pre-agreed capability profile;
- user-friendly capability Gantt chart – easy to understand;
- more aligned with longer-term partnership style working.

Consider also the benefits to contractor organizations:

- gives greater transparency of client's forward projects and work plans through an industry focus on forward planning;
- introduces standardization across the sector and model contractual solutions;
- reasonable payment terms cascade across the supply chain;
- it is a key marketing tool, exhibiting products and services to the prospective client base;
- provides extensive coverage of the prospective client market;
- avoids repetitive effort and related costs in pre-qualifying for prospective client work (established profile is online and available for prospective clients to access);
- creates an objective structure to receive and agree/record client feedback against capability;
- independently assessed and agreed profile of own organization (eliminates repetitive pre-qualifications);
- provides a structured basis for benchmarking analysis with competitors;
- more aligned with longer-term partnership style working.

There are more winners than losers in this type of holistic industry approach, which it is hoped will avoid a tendency to drift back towards the bad, old Wild West ways during times of challenge.

Commercial risk and pricing considerations associated with collaborative versus traditional contracting arrangements

06

In this chapter we compare commercial risk and different pricing and remuneration mechanisms in the context of collaborative arrangements versus traditional contracting arrangements across supply chains.

Limitation of risk associated with different remuneration regimes is an important consideration when deciding whether to enter into a more collaborative partnership type agreement as opposed to a more traditional contracting solution.

Whilst contractual or judicial areas of responsibility are important in offering protection and managing risk for the parties to an agreement, it is also important to understand the concept that guarding against risk and financial loss can also be achieved by establishing key drivers and defining scope early on, and having a good working knowledge and understanding of the very distinct advantages to clients (buyers) and contractors (suppliers) of adopting specific:

- remuneration and pricing regimes;
- contracting strategies and procurement approach.

Fundamentally, there are four factors that influence successful contract management between two or more parties. They are:

- cost – completion of a specified scope within budget;
- time – completion of a specified scope on time;
- quality – completion of a specified scope to the appropriate level of quality;
- health, safety and environment – completion of a specified scope in compliance with all mandatory legislation around health and safety of all those involved and with minimal impact on the related environment.

We know that complexity in any project or operation can lead to increased uncertainty over completion of the work or project and in final out turn cost and risk for the customer, client or purchaser. We also know from our definition in Chapter 1 that risk is the chance or possibility of loss or bad consequence, and that typically at outset under traditional contracting models the client or customer organization seek to remove or reduce uncertainty and risk. Additionally, modern business practice suggests that clients or customers seek to divest themselves of non-core business activities or establish more complex business solutions through outsourcing initiatives or programmes that frequently have direct interface with end users.

So, what then would be examples of possible loss and transference of risk? The possibility of loss could be the prospect of cost exceeding the original estimate upon which the viability of project or work commitment was based at outset. To guard against this potential pitfall at the outset, the client or customer organizations may seek to contract with other third parties to undertake the project, operations or work, thereby transferring the risk to contractors or suppliers or other types of organizations involved. This transfer can be achieved by traditional contracting means or by sharing and placing risk (and reward) where it best lies. This latter mind set starts to stray into the natural territory of collaborative partnership arrangements.

There is a myriad of considerations at outset before the choice of traditional versus collaborative contracting models can be made, including which procurement, contract and pricing or remuneration strategy is best suited. Figure 6.1 gives us some insight into the pieces of the 'jigsaw puzzle' that come into play in terms of decision quality around this area. The pieces

Figure 6.1 Considerations at outset before choice of procurement, contract and pricing / remuneration strategy can be made

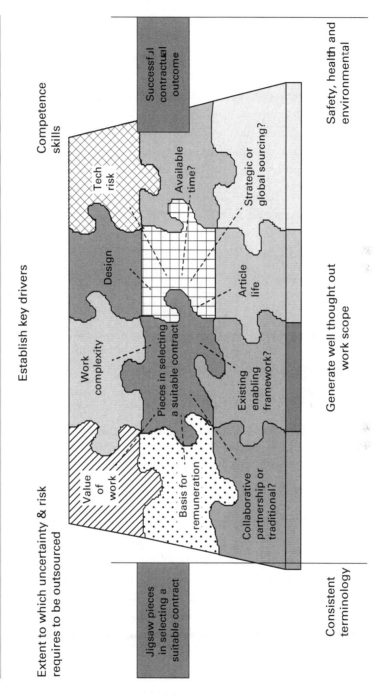

are indicative only and are by no means exhaustive. All of the pieces of the jigsaw in Figure 6.1 come into play in selecting which is the more suitable contract approach, and if key pieces of the jigsaw are missing then there is more likelihood of a suboptimal contractual outcome.

There will need to be significant dialogue internally within client or customer organizations, necessitating cross-discipline function collaboration to determine answers to each piece of the jigsaw, which in turn will help inform better decision quality as to which procurement, contract and pricing strategy is best suited to the project or requirement at hand.

The following approaches are amongst the more common options considered by the initiating party (usually the customer or client):

- Competitive tendering – Where tender enquiry documentation is issued to a pre-agreed list of tendering contractors seeking formal competitive offers to contract with the client or customer.

- Single sourcing – Where the client or customer chooses to contract with a contractor or supplier even though there are alternative providers of that particular service available. Caution and sound rationale for this approach is needed, taking cognizance of the risk of a challenge from a disgruntled supplier that has been excluded from the shortlist of bidders. This is particularly so with public sector contracts, to which EU Procurement Directives and pertinent aspects of competition law apply.

- Sole sourcing – This approach is used where realistically there is only one possible contractor or supplier for the client or customer to utilize to undertake an operational work requirement. This may, for example, be due to proprietary equipment rights for after-market support services for a major item of purchased equipment (for warranty reasons) or it could be for intellectual property reasons.

There are two distinct types of negotiation:

- Direct negotiation – Where negotiation is between client or customer and contractor or supplier to formulate a contractual and commercial relationship that offers a suitable commercial arrangement (preferably a market competitive deal). Benchmarking information is often needed here for reassurance.

- Indirect negotiation – Where negotiation is between a third party acting on behalf of the client or customer and contractor or supplier to formulate/broker a contractual and commercial relationship offering a suitable commercial arrangement (preferably a market competitive deal). Benchmarking information is often needed here for reassurance.

Partnership arrangements can ultimately be achieved by any one of the aforementioned routes; however, some areas are more traditional and better suited than others. It is nonetheless important to have a high-level awareness of these types of routes when reflecting on collaborative arrangements versus more traditional ones.

Limitation of risk associated with different contract pricing or remuneration regimes

Collaborative partnerships or traditional contractual arrangements and project or operations type work scopes can be conducted under the auspices of several different remuneration regimes. These are:

- Lump sum – This is where a client or customer requires the contractor or supplier to perform a defined work scope for an all-inclusive fixed price.
- Reimbursable – This is where a client or customer reimburses the full net cost incurred by contractor or supplier plus an agreed amount to cover overhead and profit (ie net cost plus fixed fee, net cost plus per cent, net cost plus hourly rate).
- Schedule of composite rates (unit rates) – This is a measured rate form of remuneration where pre-agreed composite rates apply for specific personnel and/or equipment.
- Day rates – This is where a client or customer requires the contractor or supplier to offer daily rates for various categories of labour and/or specialist equipment.

Hybrid regimes include:

- Management fee – This is where a client or customer requires the contractor or supplier to offer a fixed management fee (either lump sum or monthly) for managing agreed aspects of the work, including all interfaces with personnel, sub-contractors and other nominated contractors of the client, plus performance monitoring and reporting.
- Incentivized/risk reward schemes/guaranteed maximum price scheme – This is where a client or customer requires the contractor or supplier to enter into a mechanism that involves a degree of risk-sharing in terms of the costs that are incurred/absorbed by both parties and the level of remuneration to be paid to contractor. Typically, such schemes are linked to achieving pre-agreed performance levels within exacting timescales. A variation on this scheme is where a guaranteed maximum price (GMP)

is offered by the contractor or supplier. Cost in excess of the GMP will be to the contractor or suppliers account. If the final out turn cost is less than the GMP agreed, then the contractor or supplier may be entitled to a gain-share type bonus.

Figures 6.2 to 6.6 provide a simple bullet point comparison of each of the aforementioned contract pricing/remuneration regimes, highlighting the advantages and disadvantages of each regime to the client or customer.

Figure 6.2 is the traditional method preferred by clients or customers provided sufficient upfront planning has taken place and also the project requirement or work scope has been developed to a comprehensive stage such that it can be relied upon for pricing.

Figure 6.3 is the extreme opposite to 6.2 and is the contractor or supplier's preferred method to undertake a project or work scope.

Figure 6.2 Lump sum contracting

Advantages to client or customer	Risks to client or customer
• Highest level of risk assumed by contractor. • Greater incentive on contractor to perform. • As uncertainties are reduced this tends to lead to a lower cost. • Higher risk assumed by the contractor means that he is more likely to employ best resources. • Evaluation of tenders is generally easiest (client can compare 'like with like'). • Generally easier to administer, especially for large, complex projects or works contracts. • Greater certainty over final out turn cost for the client. • Greater ability to forecast cash flow.	• Low opportunity to influence contractor performance. • Cost may be more important than programme to contractor? • Possibility of contractor 'cutting corners' on quality. • Complex design requires longer contract durations and higher indirect costs. • Failure to control change by client may result in claims. • Not suited for multiple work scopes. • Requires significant effort upfront to agree a specification. • Scope must be well defined to be effective.

Figure 6.3 Reimbursable contracting

Advantages to client or customer	Risks to client or customer
• Allows the client to make early selection of contractor if time is of the essence. • Reduces the need for claims as client pays for costs to contractor automatically. • Client can influence contractor performance.	• Client retains majority of risk. • Greater uncertainty over final out turn cost. • Client pays for inefficiency of contractor. • Less incentive on contractor to offer best resources. • Difficult to assess tenders (may not be 'like with like').

Figure 6.4   Schedule of composite/unit rate contracting

Advantages to client or customer	Risks to client or customer
• Contractor risk is same as for lump sum. • Work may be conducted without a well-defined scope. • The quantity of work, within limits, may vary without changes in pricing or administration. • Composite/unit rate estimate of final cost offers more certainty and accuracy than reimbursable. • Higher risk assumed means that contractor is more likely to employ best resources. • Greater certainty in comparing tender proposals. • Provides a good basis for estimating costs of alternatives and variations.	• Low opportunity to influence contractor performance (ie little incentive for contractor to keep costs to a minimum as profit is increased by simply expending more hours). • Cost may be more important than programme to contractor. • Possibility of contractor 'cutting corners' on quality. • Failure to control change by client may result in claims. • Final out turn cost is dependant on measured quantities (may still exceed estimate). Hence close monitoring required. • The level of profit being earned is usually unknown and can't be adjusted to improve performance. • Requires higher client administration.

Figure 6.4 is the basis for a measured form of contract such as a bill of quantities developed by a chartered quantity Surveyor (QS) appointed by the client. A schedule of composite items of work is prepared by the QS and this is priced by the contractor or supplier. This then provides a structured basis or guideline framework that is used to arrive at a final contract value based on measured quantities of work or services completed.

Figure 6.5 is self-explanatory and is simply a slight variation of Figure 6.3.

Figure 6.5   Day rate contracting

> The advantages and risks to the client of the day rate regime are similar to the reimbursable regime, albeit that the day rate element and related working parameters will probably have been quantified and agreed in advance.

Figure 6.6 outlines a regime that starts to stray into the territory of pricing and remuneration mechanisms used in longer-term, more collaborative alliance partnerships between clients or customers and contractors and suppliers. This type of mechanism embodies a degree of trust and risk/reward sharing between the parties, engendering a sense of shared accountability and responsibility for the project or contract outcome. Openness and

Figure 6.6 Incentivised/risk reward schemes/GMP mechanisms

Advantages to client or customer	Risks to client or customer
• Contractor cost and profit levels are known in advance (ie not buried in a single overall cost factor).	• Considerable effort may be required for adequate contract-wide financial management.
• Contractor has clear incentives to reduce the cost of work if the contract is incentivized properly.	• The scope of work must be well defined when setting benchmarks.
• Client and contractor can have more joint influence on the level of performance due to the setting of benchmarks.	• Complex arrangements can be difficult and time-consuming to administer.
• Incentivization is a flexible arrangement that lends itself to contractor self-motivation and innovation.	• Can require a certain element of judgement in measuring performance against benchmarks, which can lead to client/contractor friction.
• More responsibility can be passed to the contractor.	• Relating contractor goals (especially financial) to client's asset specific goals.
	• Difficult to track costs in real time.
	• Inappropriate benchmarks selected can lead to significant challenges.

transparency are indicated here also. Both parties to such an alliance effectively have a vested interest in solving problems and working together with joined up collaborative thinking. These are precisely the types of values that are encouraged by the global standard for collaborative working under ISO 44001.

Understanding contractor or supplier risk

When reflecting on and considering risk in the context of either collaborative or traditional contracting arrangements, it is important for prospective clients or customers to have an appreciation and understanding of contractor or supplier risk. This is because if losses do occur due to the contractor or supplier failing or defaulting then there will most certainly be direct or indirect consequences for the client or customer.

Figure 6.7 highlights some of the common risks that contractors or suppliers can be exposed to sometimes through no fault of their own or completely out of their control. Notwithstanding this, they may still be contractually obligated to perform and deliver in a hard business world.

Figure 6.7 Understanding contractor or supplier risk

Understanding risk assumed by the contractor is important because if losses do occur then there will be direct or indirect consequences for the client. Consider these examples:

- errors in pricing;
- escalation of labour rates;
- escalation of insurance costs;
- sub-contractor failing to perform;
- unable to meet performance targets;
- underestimate of compliance with quality assurance, quality control and health, safety and environmental parameters;
- material supply and price differences;
- plant and equipment breakdown/maintenance/renewal;
- misunderstanding of contract responsibility;
- fluctuations in interest rates/currency exchange, etc;
- changes in employment legislation;
- TUPE legislation;
- weather conditions;
- wastage and theft;
- ability to retain the necessary level and quality of resource during periods of competition;
- lack of cash flow due to poor payment record from other customers.

The joint alliance steering group concept versus more adversarial contractual provisions to safeguard against failure or default

Despite the best intentions of all parties to a collaborative alliance, it is still prudent practice to consider how or what remedies are available to safeguard the client or customer against potential contractor default or to safeguard the contractor or supplier should the client or customer have challenges or difficulties.

Longer-term collaborative partnership type arrangements such as alliances or joint ventures usually have joint leadership or alliance steering groups in full force and effect, the composition of which will include senior management representatives from the respective parties to the alliance. Such groups tend to intervene early on should it become apparent that either party is at risk of defaulting under the alliance arrangement. Such interventions tend to take the form of a more supportive business philosophy where assistance is provided either by shared resource or financial support, because the cost to both parties in terms of what has already been invested in time, effort and resource is too great to simply give up.

The more traditional safeguarding remedies that fall into the traditional or adversarial camp are as follows:

- Liquidated damages – 'Liquidated damages' is a term used in the law of contracts to describe a contractual provision that establishes a predetermined amount to be paid by one party to another should the contract be breached. For example, if the contract had a mutually agreed completion date and that date is exceeded then there may be a predetermined sum in the contract to be paid for each week that the contract goes beyond its original completion date.

- Performance bonds – A client or customer can call on a bond put in place by the contractor/supplier for a pre-agreed amount if the contractor/supplier defaults. Usually these bonds take the form of security from a bank.

- Parent company guarantee – The parent company of the contractor/supplier essentially acts a guarantor in the event of its subsidiary company defaulting.

- Retention monies – The client withholds monies from interim payments due to the contractor/supplier as the contract proceeds (usually up to around 10 per cent of the contract value). The retention is held as a form of security by the client and is released upon satisfactory completion of the work or contract.

- Termination – Termination is the ultimate remedy for non-performance of a contractor/supplier. Any number of compensatory rights and provisions can be incorporated into a contract, should termination occur due to a contractor/supplier defaulting. Termination can, however, be for convenience or at fault. In the case of the former, compensation would usually have to paid.

Consider also the practicalities of what each provision is trying to achieve, clearly spelling out the protection it is giving. For example, liquidated damages clauses are not to be regarded as penalty clauses; rather, they are there to put the party back into the position they would have been in had the contract completion had not been delayed. Essentially, liquidated damages are a mechanism to secure performance under a contract.

Whilst contractual or judicial areas of responsibility are important in offering protection and managing risk for the parties to an agreement, it is also important to convey to the reader the concept that guarding against risk and financial loss can also be achieved by establishing key drivers and defining scope early on, and also having a good working knowledge and understanding of the very distinct advantages to clients (buyers) and contractors (suppliers) of adopting specific remuneration and pricing regimes, and contracting strategies and procurement approaches.

As we draw this chapter to a conclusion it is important to reinforce that longer-term collaborative partnership type arrangements such as alliances or joint ventures normally tend to adopt and embrace a more supportive business philosophy where assistance is provided either by shared resource or financial support.

Finally, to close out this chapter in an interactive fashion we shall now pose a chess game challenge to the reader to self-test knowledge and understanding of the fundamental points around limitation of risk associated with different commercial remuneration regimes.

Figure 6.8 Challenges

Challenge
Consider each risk statement in Figure 6.7 against the three pricing/remuneration regimes (lump sum, unit rate and reimbursable). Decide whether you consider the risk to be: ● high (H) ● medium (M) ● low (L)

Figure 6.9 Comparison of contract remuneration types

Risk statement	Lump sum	Unit rate	Reimbursable / day-rate
Transfer risk from owner/client to contractor			
Incentive for contractor to assign his best resources			
Ability to accurately define final cost at contract award			
Confidence in commercial evaluation of tenders			
Opportunity for owner/client to influence contractor performance			
Effort by owner/client to administer the contract			
Avoidance of claims			
Incentive for contractor to work efficiently and complete on programme			

PART TWO
Case studies of exemplar historical collaborative practice

Case study 1 07

The Team Marine story – putting logic back into logistics

Exemplar of collaborative practice in the marine/shipping service sector involving multiple partner organizations

In Chapter 5 we analysed a collaborative pan-industry initiative referred to as Cost Reduction in the New Era (CRINE) in the United Kingdom Continental Shelf (UKCS) upstream oil and gas sector. The Team Marine story was one that was spawned out of the underpinning principles being advocated and encouraged at the time by CRINE. Indeed, the author of this book was personally engaged in spearheading the Team Marine effort, which at that juncture was widely regarded across the sector as a lighthouse example of meaningful collaboration in play across the industry.

This case study seeks to give the reader a high-level insight into the history behind the Team Marine story and the rationale at the time for 'daring to be different' and changing. It explores the facts around how the various participants arrived at a multi-operator alliance partnership to maximize logistics performance offshore. The case study also gives a fascinating insight into why the Team Marine initiative succeeded in conjunction with the core shared belief system and principles that were needed to overcome the many obstacles encountered along the way.

The benefits and size of the shared prize for all the participants are also discussed, alongside the cost allocation and organizational mechanisms that were jointly developed to ensure equitable sharing of risk and financial exposure. Landmark milestones and the practical timeline needed to progress and manage such an initiative from concept inception though to conclusion are also examined.

The operator companies involved at the time either no longer exist as corporate entities, as they have either been acquired through corporate mergers and acquisitions activity or no longer operate in the UKCS sector. For reasons of confidentiality they are referred to in the case study as companies T, E, A and M.

Background history

By means of some background to the Team Marine story, in the early 1990s a small group of four companies – T, E, A and M – were significant offshore oil and gas operators in the UKCS with large, equal sized volumes of production and exploration activity. Like many businesses, they relied upon physical supply chains that ran in parallel which each other and were competitors.

The Team Marine story is one of how this small group of oil companies cooperated and collaborated for mutual benefit and risk sharing. As we touched on in Chapter 1, 'What's new about that?' the reader might ask. Oil and gas client operators share joint ventures for exactly those reasons in the field of exploration and production all the time all over the world.

The general wisdom around this was that those involved would gain a competitive edge from their respective areas of operation. At that time, the industry had an attitude that it wasn't simply enough to succeed – others had to fail at the same time! This was the crux of the matter in terms a group of like-minded operators daring to be different and move away from that attitude toward a different type of approach with more joined up collaborative thinking, especially in relation to supply chain management matters, because the opportunities of synergy are boundless.

Why change?

In terms of the rationale for these four companies changing, quite simply, as has already been stated, the acronym for the discipline of supply chain management is SCM. If we reverse it to read MCS it translates to read mainly common sense. This, then, is the compelling case for collaboration across the supply chains of the four companies.

Figure 7.1 gives the reader some insight into why the organizations felt compelled to change their marine logistics approach. In Chapter 5 the reader

Figure 7.1   Oil price graph informing the case for change: Crude oil price trends 1972–94

Figure 7.2   Bar chart showing the decline in size of average field size

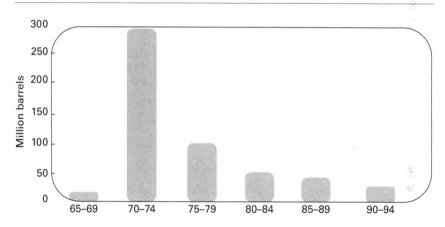

was afforded an insight into the cyclical nature of the oil and gas sector and how fluctuations in oil price caused behaviour shift. Figure 7.1 shows that the oil price had dramatically dropped and levelled out to between $10 and $20 per barrel of oil equivalent (boe) over an eight-year period. This informed the need to reduce operating costs and modify existing supply chain arrangements and practices.

A further consideration at the time was that the size of the average offshore oil and gas field being found by companies was dramatically smaller than in the past. This point is illustrated by Figure 7.2. Clearly, such a shift also contributed to informing a different way of managing the third party suppliers and contractors that supported the sector.

In times of high oil price (the 'peak' shown on the graph in Figure 7.1), the supply chain cost base including logistics had increased to levels that were not sustainable when the oil price plummeted to between $10 to $20 per boe. Clearly there was an urgent need to 'put the logic back into logistics'.

To reflect on one famous statement that is quite apt in the context of the prevailing situation at the time:

> It's not necessary to change. Survival is not compulsory.
>
> W Edwards Deming

The facts

Why did the parties involved arrive at an operator alliance partnership to maximize logistics performance?

In the spirit of the CRINE initiative to drive waste and inefficiency out of the supply chain and to look at more collaborative ways of working and sharing risk (and benefits), the four companies were aware that the close geographical proximity of their respective offshore installations (as can been from Figure 7.3) were such that it merited a feasibility study.

The logistics department of each company was tasked to ascertain the feasibility of an alliance partnership to maximize logistics performance. Members from each company were chosen to undertake a benchmark study to review marine, aviation, and shore-base performance and examine three areas:

- cost saving potential through sharing;
- contractual restrictions;
- how a joint venture could be run.

During the first few weeks of the study, it became apparent that 'big-win' sharing savings were available in the marine support category due mainly to geographical location synergies. Accordingly, this was the priority area to focus on going forward, and a revised study team was formed that had a specific remit to:

- identify cost savings;
- address issues to facilitate combining marine logistics operations;
- establish a joint operating agreement between all four companies with a view to implementing the Team Marine concept.

Figure 7.3 Map showing geographical synergy opportunity

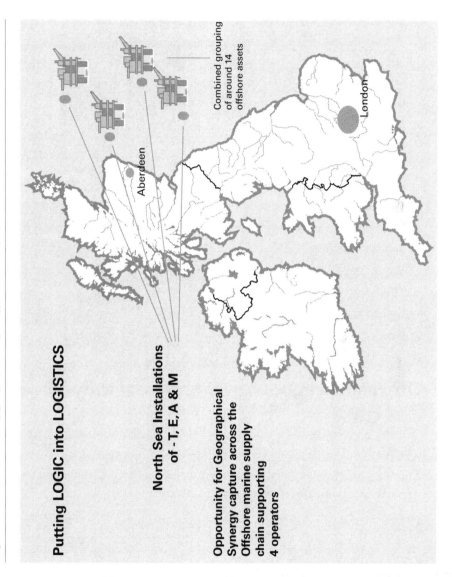

Putting LOGIC into LOGISTICS

North Sea Installations of - T, E, A & M

Opportunity for Geographical Synergy capture across the Offshore marine supply chain supporting 4 operators

Combined grouping of around 14 offshore assets

Aberdeen

London

The 'marine support service' category to platforms in the region covered activities such as offshore platform support vessels for general logistical delivery, supply vessels, diving support vessels for routine subsea inspection repair and maintenance, and anchor handling and towing supply/services (AHTS) vessels.

Salient features stemming out of this included:

- The Team Marine alliance partnership was officially formed to create optimum marine logistics mode of operation, fleet composition, schedule of support and cost allocation methodology, whilst ensuring equitable spreading of risk and savings to the participants.

- A management, steering committee and Team Marine operations structure was established.

- A combined team with representatives from all four organizations were co-located in a dedicated area in the lead procurement partner's office. This helped cement a sense of new shared identity.

- Insurance, procurement, and financial issues were worked out, and solutions put in place.

- The implementation phase established customer buy-in and created the Team Marine identity.

- Benchmarking and measurement aspects were identified and reported.

- Results were analysed.

Obstacles encountered and how they were overcome

As with any aspirational initiative of this kind, there were of course obstacles along the way. Examples of some of these, including the actions that were taken to mitigate and resolve them, are:

- Four companies with differing logistical strategies – This was addressed by identifying and then cherry-picking the best parts of each of the participating organizations.

- Existing contractual obligations across the prospective participants – This was resolved by the participant with the strongest procurement function taking the lead and acting on behalf of Team Marine.

- Onshore and offshore personnel would need to be re-educated in the new alliance concept – This was addressed via a concerted communication campaign cascaded across all key stakeholders.

- Insurance and indemnity arrangements would need to be reviewed and revised – This was resolved by putting in place a new vessel sharing agreement.

- Novel creative procurement methodology would need to be created – This was achieved via the partnership's lead procurement function and involving the use of a dedicated shipbroker.

- Cost allocation – how would this be done? This required an equitable system to be created and administered by one of the participants on behalf of the alliance partnership. This extended to include a mechanism for equitable sharing of risk and reward.

Cost allocation and management mechanisms jointly developed, and the benefits of Team Marine

As one might imagine, bringing together four separate companies into an arrangement whereby cost, risk and benefits are to be shared carries the propensity for challenge and disagreement. Notwithstanding this, however, joined up collaborative thinking was applied with many innovative and pragmatic arrangements being put in place. For example:

- Costs for term and spot hired platform support vessels were pooled and allocated by geographical location monthly based on boat usage. This afforded the partnership protection from market vessel price fluctuations, plus vessels were only taken when needed and released when not (ie treated as spot hires).

- Costs for AHTS vessels were pooled and allocated monthly by location, based on boat usage. This also afforded the partnership protection from market vessel price fluctuations, plus vessels are only taken when needed and released when not (ie treated as spot hires).

- Pay-as-you-use cost allocation delivers very small fixed costs.

- Larger combined group activity meant more term vessels could be attained, and there were associated benefits of longer-term contracts, safety, quality, operations and economies of scale.

- Joint procurement leverage raised Team Marine to become the third largest combined UKCS vessel charterer (17 per cent of North Sea market at that time).
- A joint rig move programme could be 'sold' to the lowest bidder, controlling cost and improving availability.
- Vessel productive time was high due to geographic synergy, and this encouraged sharing as vessels pass directly from job to job.
- Vessels were released back to the pool after each job, and this gave alliance participants access to term vessel rates without the utilization risk.
- The pooled fleet of vessels gave access to a larger number of vessels, increasing availability and exposure to the market.
- The pooled fleet of vessels gave access to a more diverse range of vessel type and ability.
- The opportunity of shared voyages contributed to lowering overall cost, improving utilization and increasing service level.
- Logistics learning was shared, service was improved and overheads were shared.
- Procurement effectiveness and resource sharing were developed for waste management, warehousing, shore-base, marine services, helicopters, diving support vessels, etc.
- There was also joint procurement of tank cleaning, fuel provision and quayside services, including waste disposal.

Scale of combined activity, and the benefits and results achieved under Team Marine

By way of an indication of the scale of combined activity/volumes under Team Marine, the following statistics are quite revealing:

- circa 14 offshore assets/installations serviced each year;
- up to 55 rig moves completed annually;
- 500,000 tonnes cargo delivered annually (average cost/tonne $50);
- eight vessels on charter each day (four long-term vessels plus a varying four from spot market);

- 50,000 tonnes of fuel purchased annually (some from members of the alliance);

- 230,000 nautical miles steamed each year;

- 200 plus charters completed each year;

- $10.5mm saving from AHTS call-off contract;

- 28 per cent reduction in marine costs (normalized) in year one, likewise quayside costs.

These are just some of the results achieved, and indeed the alliance partnership truly embraced the concept of collaboration by constantly striving for continual improvement year on year.

Why the Team Marine initiative succeeded: Core shared belief system and principles

Given all the complexities associated with this transformation initiative, coupled with all obstacles and things that could go wrong, why then did Team Marine succeed? What were the core belief systems and principles that made it work?

It was widely believed that Team Marine was an exemplar of collaborative working practice for the following reasons:

- The mantra for all those involved was the fundamental logical belief that benefits existed. This was the focus. A resource shared is a cost saved. That core proven belief must remain, while all barriers can be changed in its pursuit.

- The initiative was supported at the most senior level. It had top-down backing.

- It embraced an open-book benchmarking and fully transparent review process

- All those involved adhered to a simple mantra of being fair and reasonable.

- Trust between the parties was core, demonstrated and returned.

- It had an equal risk, equal reward arrangement – equitably shared with aligned goals and drivers.

- There were equal participant member rights.

- There was an active cross-operator management, steering committee, and Team Marine structure.
- The Team Marine identity was created, branded and activated, which helped with people issues and change management.
- Systems were built around the designed optimum performance, not optimizing a system.
- Key performance indicators were identified and actively managed.

If you can measure something, then you can manage performance. Examples of some of the robust KPIs that were developed and implemented under Team Marine were areas such as (years 1994–2003):

- cost/tonne normalized (retain vessel costs at £5k per day for year on year benchmarking);
- cost/tonne actual;
- deck utilization;
- port standby time;
- offshore standby time;
- dead time;
- tonnage shipped;
- boat days;
- tonnes/boat day.

These KPIs were by no means an exhaustive list, with new areas for improvement always being found through stretch targets and challenge.

Concluding reflections

By way of some concluding reflections on this case study, it is evident from the success that was achieved through Team Marine that there was joined up commitment to embracing collaboration, which had the positive effect of the perceived barriers being overcome. In this case, key observations on the exemplar behaviours and working practises of those involved were as follows:

- The operators quickly realized that they could do it themselves.
- Logic was king, and it could prevail.

- There was robust focus on rational optimized solutions.
- Key principles were identified and upheld.
- Shared team responsibilities were created.
- There was robust comprehensive measurement against KPIs.
- The combined team spirit was to think collectively and strive for the greater good.
- Trust was generated through fairness, openness and transparency.
- All team members were encouraged to retain a long-term view striving for constant, continuous improvements.
- Similarly, all team members were encouraged to have fun, acknowledging that cross-company initiatives of this kind just take time, effort and more time!

Once final thought is that that alliance partnerships in one single area, if successful, can lead to other similar initiatives in other areas. So, for companies like those engaged with Team Marine, there is obviously significant scope beyond the initial initiative to improve in other areas, or to afford the benefits of the existing collaboration to other incoming companies.

Case study 2   08

Captain – the impossible dream

The story of a record-breaking novel contractual solution to develop a challenged discovered reserve opportunity

In this chapter we give the reader a brief insight into the story of the Captain project. The project was unique in the history of the UK North Sea oil discoveries at the time. Everything about it was different, from the scale of the challenges that had to be overcome to the collaborative way that people and organizations worked together and the solutions they came up with.

Although the multinational operator involved at the time (Texaco North Sea) no longer exists as a distinct corporate entity as a result of being acquired through merger, the author considers that the historical story around this field's development to be shining example of relentless collaborative determination to succeed, despite the challenges.

Furthermore, it is also considered to be an exemplar of a multidiscipline project team engaging and working with external partners and 'daring to be different' by having the courage to pursue unconventional and unorthodox routes to achieve success.

For many, at the outset the project was considered an 'impossible dream'.

Background history

When the first dinosaurs were just starting to crawl from the sea into a young, hostile world Captain's oils were beginning to form. Gradually the ancient forests became seams of coal and the debris of over a million years filtering to the bottom of the sea helped to create hydrocarbon deposits. In the case of Captain, the oil became very viscous, lying in a shallow but extensive reservoir of loose or unconsolidated sand, and there it stayed waiting for a use. Like a riddle waiting to be solved!

Our story then jumps forward millions of years to a time when man found a myriad of uses for oil and gas under the UK North Sea. Texaco's connection to the Captain field began in 1971 when it was successful in being awarded a licence in UKCS License block 13/22 area under the UK Government's fourth licensing round. The code name of 'Captain' was given to the promising block 82 miles north of Aberdeen, which lay in 350 feet of icy North Sea water in the Moray Firth.

The evaluation that prompted Texaco's bid for the licence block was based on slim evidence; only five seismic lines of less than 50 miles in length had been used to support the geologists' view that this was a most promising structure, and despite the intense competition Texaco was awarded the Captain block.

As with any licence award, this places obligations on the successful operator to progress further technical evaluation and exploration appraisal well drilling within an exacting timeframe, as specified in the licence. Failure to do so would result in the operator having to relinquish the licence back to the Government, who would then offer it up to other interested parties under a future licence round. The UK Government wants to see demonstrable activity on the licences granted to companies because it has a vested interest in petroleum and the supplementary tax revenue take from producing fields.

The post-licence award challenge

In the hectic years that followed, competition within Texaco for corporate funds for further technical evaluation globally across the company's portfolio of exploration opportunities was fierce, and Captain was pushed back in the queue by more immediately promising projects such as Tartan, Highlander and Petronella. But, even then, Captain had its believers. Documents at the time showed a concerted battle for funds for further exploration, and in April 1977 exploration started in the block. By May the operator had struck oil.

However, very shortly after the extracted early oil from the field had been analysed it was revealed that the company was dealing with a very heavy, viscous oil and at that time the company just didn't have the technology to proceed further. It was calculated that the technology that existed at that time would require up to 300 wells from 10 different locations just to drain the reservoir. By conventional thinking, it was a financial impossibility. Even the oil itself posed problems, its viscosity making it difficult to produce and its acidity posing problems for refineries, which at that time had not equipped themselves to handle such liquids.

All of these obstacles were high in the minds of Texaco personnel who had to decide whether the Captain block should be relinquished back to the Government or retained as a long-shot prospect. The decision by Texaco senior management was that Captain should be retained for its future potential.

Resilience and the development of new technology

As the years rolled on, it became clear that the development of new horizontal drilling technology would be one of the keys to unlock the Captain puzzle. Funds for further exploration drilling were secured and two new wells were drilled with a 1,000ft horizontal well section to prove it could be done. This was completed, and an electric pump was installed which flowed that well, producing test oil at a flow rate of 6,600 boe per day. This created real excitement, showing a fabulous flare out in the North Sea and demonstrating that Texaco had an oil field of real substance.

Notwithstanding this positive news, the field economics still didn't add up – a 1,000ft horizontal well wasn't enough. What was needed was a 6,000ft horizontal well in order to reduce the number of wells required to develop the field because it had covered such a large area – to make the economics right. Furthermore, it was subsequently realized that these wells would need to produce at greater than 10,000 boe per day, not 6,000 as previously thought. The higher rates would in turn create problems of sand control and water coning; what water was produced would need to be separated from the oil – and larger, more powerful pumps would need to be designed to lift the heavier, more viscous oil.

Until the project could demonstrate that these technological hurdles could be overcome, it would fail to prise loose the vast sums of money needed to develop the field from a still sceptical executive board. Once again, Captain was still firmly stuck in the pipeline.

Then the company underwent a major shake-up and restructuring of its European upstream operations, which was to have a radical effect on the fortunes of Texaco's most reluctant project.

Unconventional and unorthodox project route achieved through collaboration

Because it was seen that there was a lot of oil in place, a dedicated Captain focus team was formed with the support of senior management and tasked to come up with a development plan that would reduce the cost through some innovative thinking, because the conventional ways just wouldn't succeed. The team had to be unorthodox and unconventional in order to get the field on stream.

One of the first steps was to secure funding for an extended well test. The team devised a simple step-by-step appraisal development plan to help persuade Texaco's reluctant executive that the perceived risks could be overcome. The team was successful in securing a $50 million fund to carry out the extended well test and appraisal activity.

The drilling rig *John Shaw* was contracted to work on this part of the project and nine exploratory wells were drilled to prove up the prospect. A tenth well with a 6,000ft horizontal section pumped oil at the rate of 12,000 boe per day during an extended well test lasting three months. This had the positive effect of proving up the volumetrics, revealing where the field boundaries were, and enabling the geologists to home in on their models. The 10th 6,000ft horizontal proved that a 6,000ft horizontal section could be drilled, but more importantly it proved the well contributed along the whole of the well bore, and demonstrated that they were able to improve the well cost. By improving the well cost they were able to improve the economics of the project. So, this was a very critical point in making the project viable.

However, although the economic viability of the project had once and for all been undeniably proven, it still wasn't enough. Before the company would approve full project funding the team would have to present a complete development plan not only to get the oil out of the ground/sea but also to provide the surface facilities to process and transport the extracted hydrocarbons to their final market destination. Once again, the project team took an unconventional and unorthodox route.

In an innovative approach, three consortia each with their own development plan were contracted to advance their ideas competitively to arrive at the fastest and most cost-effective way of developing the Captain field. At the same time, the Texaco project team proposed a novel style of collaborative alliance in which Texaco would work alongside the specialist companies involved in the winning consortium. This would have the positive effect of removing a whole tier of design and supervisory management and save the company over £100 million. This would also help to ensure that the goals of the successful contractor consortium and Texaco would become aligned, helping to achieve a faster schedule and also a lower cost of development.

Formation of a new collaborative contractor consortium

The successful consortium was made up of project engineering specialist ABB Lummas Global, along with offshore installation experts Coflexip Stena, Spanish shipyard Astano, and Clydeside fabrication yard UIE. Together they formed the first joint venture management alliance with Texaco. Their plan was very different to the usual traditional platform approach used in the North Sea. When the produced liquids from the Captain field reached the surface, they would go straight to a ship-like floating production, storage and offloading vessel (FPSO) for processing before being transferred directly to a shuttle tanker and brought onshore. The proposal was submitted to the Texaco board of directors, and after a short wait for decision quality discussions to take place the corporation approved £500 million to go ahead the development of the Captain Area 'A'.

A novel fast track project approach

A conventional project approach, even without the difficulties of Captain's oil and reservoir, would normally take up to four years to go from *concept* stage to *production*. But economics and corporate strategy at the time demanded that the project be brought on stream as soon as possible. Accordingly, the project team set themselves the seemingly impossible objective of producing oil in just two years. Discounted cash flow techniques such as net present value showed that the faster the project was brought on stream the more value it would have to the corporation and its shareholders.

So the two-year countdown to production began:

- ABB led the design and procurement phase.
- Coflexip Stena concentrated on the offshore preparations for installation.
- The FPSO and shuttle tanker would be constructed by ASTANO in northern Spain.

- At the same time, a well head protector jacket and platform was to be built in Scotland at UIE's shipyard on the banks of the River Clyde.

Work went on simultaneously to meet the deadlines, with equipment being shipped from all over Europe to the main fabrication centres in Scotland and Spain as soon as it was ready.

The first significant milestone reached was the fabrication yard at UIE in Glasgow. The fast track upon which the Captain project was travelling meant seven horizontal development wells had to be drilled before the platform and FPSO were in place. Accordingly, an 85t drilling template which was to be used to position these wells was quickly fabricated and rolled out of the yard. It was then lowered to the seabed and the drilling rig *John Shaw* began the first phase of development drilling.

The project team assembled offshore on the rig and onshore in Aberdeen demonstrated skills that would become the envy of North Sea horizontal drilling, and well completion proceeded at phenomenal speed. The actual versus predicted number of days for drilling resulted in incredible time savings, finishing well ahead of schedule. Another perceived problem was overcome with regard to drilling through consolidated sandstone. There were concerns over possible collapse of the wells, but some early studies provided information on the way to drill, and the wells stayed open.

Back at UIE the fabrication work on the derrick and jacket had begun in earnest, and major components manufactured in various parts of Europe, such as the accommodation module, platform crane and helideck, began to arrive at the yard. But not everything was plain sailing – a major problem with blistering paint had to be made good. This was done such that the schedule was not impacted.

Meanwhile, in Spain, a similar process was underway to create the FPSO as in Scotland the Captain stopwatch ticked on. But all was not going to plan – industrial action and parallel ASTANO commitments reduced the shipyard personnel available for the Captain project, with the risk of overall schedule slippage. Some redesign of the mooring chains in the central turret of the FPSO was also needed. The project would be doomed if Texaco didn't act quickly. Its solution was simply to beef up the team in ASTANO. Greater Texaco involvement ensured the co-venturers working as a team, and not a moment too soon. Huge oil and water separation units were being loaded onto barges at the Dragados yards in southern Spain. Their journey would take them north to the ASTANO yard where they were lifted onto the FPSO.

Piecing together the jigsaw

Like a jigsaw, the components of the vessel began to take shape. In Scotland, fabrication of the topsides was well advanced as the clock ticked relentlessly on towards the deadline. In a complex roll-up operation, the jacket legs were assembled and linked together to form the support for the platform.

Next the centre-piece of the Captain project was ready to be launched down the slipway in Spain. The Captain FPSO was sent on her way. Further along the coast, the shuttle tanker *Aberdeen* was completed and launched from ASTANOs sister yard in Bilbao. The *Aberdeen* would join a fleet of shuttle tankers that would shuttle oil form the FPSO to its customers around the globe. Next, the Captain jacket and platform deck were ready to be loaded onto barges to carry them to the North Sea. There was indeed a rising tempo for the project. The culture within which such an elaborate project exercise had been undertaken was considered revolutionary by many industry peers and onlookers. The jacket was the first to sail to the site in the outer Moray Firth, and the deck structure then followed to join it.

The sea surface above the Captain field in the Moray Firth then became a cauldron of activity centred on the Seipem installation barge, the *S700* – 600ft from stem to stern. The barge dwarfed the vessels around it. The first major operation installed the jacket, with both cranes and spreader bean being used for maximum control – the *S700* picked up the 500t jacket as though it were a child's toy and lowered the 400ft frame gently to the sea bed, guided by the remote operated underwater vehicles.

After it was secured in place, it was the turn of the Captain deck to be lifted off its barge and into position. Lifting the deck off of the barge is the most critical time, and everyone feels very nervous. However, the operation was completed without a hitch – the deck was lifted 100m from the jacket. The *S700* then slowly repositioned using dynamic satellite positioning and set its 8,000t load gently down on its support. Complex offshore engineering was made to look deceptively easy!

Notwithstanding the euphoria around this, one piece of the jigsaw was still missing – the Captain FPSO in Spain was undergoing a mountain of commissioning work before it could leave the shipyard and join the platform in the North Sea. However, the FPSO finally sailed and reached its destination. The hook-up of all the component parts happened as quickly as possible, albeit slightly past the two-year marker. Lessons learned homed in on the handover from facilities to operations groups.

Finally, some three months later than the self-imposed two-year target the flare on the FPSO burst into life to signal that Captain's first oil was being produced. Within a month the FPSO's sister ship arrived in the field to take charge of its first load of 300,000 barrels of crude oil. Not only was the field producing, it was starting to earn its living. Captain, the impossible project, had finally become a reality. The overall success of this project was extraordinary; a conventional development timeframe had compressed to just over two years – a North Sea record at the time.

Conclusion

By way of some concluding reflections on this case study, it is evident that the success was achieved through a fantastic collaborative effort, embracing many of the principles now being advocated by the new global standard ISO 44001.

One final thought is that that pioneers and visionaries who lead the way always take more risks than those who follow, but only they can be rewarded with the satisfaction of turning an impossibility into a reality. In this case it was the Captain project team who had a vision, and they coupled this with a tenacious dedication to solve the Captain riddle, written in time 150 million years before.

Case study 3 09

Building supply chain functional excellence through collaboration with internal partners

An exemplar of how to engage internally to progress structural and capability building initiatives within an energy sector supply chain function

The compelling case for having the discipline of procurement and supply chain management (PSCM) in organizations has already been made in Chapter 2, along with the role of the PSCM practitioner in helping organizations to be more commercial in managing, planning and obtaining third party goods and services by using robust business processes.

PSCM as a business discipline has grown exponentially over the last three decades. Many organizations across the private, public and third (voluntary/humanitarian) sectors worldwide have elevated PSCM as a core strategic business role and the emergence of PSCM directors and chief procurement officers at board level in forward-looking organizations is a manifest recognition of the rising profile of procurement and supply chain management.

The trend toward collaborative outsourcing of non-core activities has clearly had a positive impact of the discipline, as a large proportion of value creation and addition to organizations comes from the supply base and many organizations have woken up to this fact and manage their PSCM function accordingly. Notwithstanding this, however, the elevation of PSCM to a strategic business function is still a relatively recent development, and unfortunately PSCM remains a low priority for many organizations and businesses. Under such circumstances PSCM most probably remains focused on gaining low prices from suppliers, irrespective of whether the organization or business strategy is focused on low cost or not. So, although in some organizations PSCM has become more intellectual and sophisticated, there remains much scope for improvement of the discipline.

Another interesting development is that an increasing number of people worldwide are choosing careers in PSCM. Twenty years or so ago this was not the case. Professional bodies have been formed, including the Chartered Institute of Procurement and Supply (CIPS) and the International Institute for Advanced Purchasing and Supply (IIAPS). It follows therefore that there is a need to upskill people in the discipline of PSCM because in all likelihood most individuals and organizations are not as competent as they could be, and many individuals and organizations collectively suffer from bounded rationality – they don't know, what they don't know.

This case study explores the 'art of the possible' in terms of building functional supply chain excellence through collaboration with internal partners across an international exploration and production (E&P) operator in Sub-Saharan Africa. We observe the supply chain excellence journey of leading and transitioning an existing PSCM function from 'suboptimal' to 'optimal'.

Background

This case study is based on a historical example of a collaborative business improvement transformation initiative progressed by a major Sub-Saharan African E&P operator. For reasons of confidentiality the organization shall simply be referred to fictitiously as 'ACX'.

By means of some initial background, ACX developed and managed the group's upstream interests in oil and gas exploration and production around the world. ACX was driving the development of the group's upstream business to allow it to meet its overall strategic objective of accelerating the growth of its proprietary gas-to-liquid technology investments in a multitude of ventures.

ACX had already established a supply chain function with a reasonable foundation of functional processes. However, the company had ambitious upstream production growth targets by 2030 which represented an order of magnitude shift from existing production levels.

The company's executive at the time felt that many of the organization's support service functions needed to substantially raise their game to be able to effectively support the new stretch growth targets. The PSCM function was no exception, and indeed, there were already concerns that the existing PSCM function was underperforming in terms of even managing to support existing production levels and challenges, let alone having the capability, capacity, expertise and resource to support the new growth targets. The effectiveness of existing cross-functional relationships across the business had been highlighted as 'suboptimal' in the findings of a previous management consultancy audit and the PSCM function was regarded as being far too reactive, rather than adopting an approach of early engagement.

A new style of leadership

The starting point was the executive board's appointment of a vice president (VP) of PSCM who was to lead and spearhead a supply chain excellence initiative. This was an entirely new position within the company, and the focus of the new role was to drive and implement a major operational excellence initiative from a PSCM perspective to establish a contemporary global upstream supply chain function in terms of organizational structure and capability.

A more collaborative approach was deemed necessary by the executive board in terms of how the PSCM function interacted with its stakeholder both internally within the business and externally with third parties, partners and the general supply chain upon which the company relied. It was a challenging role that entailed:

- supporting a diverse multicultural PSCM team embedded across many international assets and projects;
- integration of contracts and assets;
- managing major capital projects through construction, start-up and into the operational phase;
- transitioning a suboptimal SCM function into a proactive and strategic business partner recognized for its contribution by key business

stakeholders and partners for adding significant value, and managing and reducing risk, reducing the cost base and driving/delivering cost reduction initiatives;

- cross-business synergy capture and engendering a spirit of joined up collaborative thinking between PSCM and its business partners (internally and externally).

Initial diagnostic

The first six months for the new VP PSCM involved significant engagement across all key areas of the ACX business internationally in order to solicit views or opinions with regard to the following four key initial questions:

1 Does the PSCM function have enough gravitas within the business?

2 How mature are the existing PSCM competencies, skill and capabilities?

3 What technology currently exists to support the organization progress its PSCM activities for operations (OPEX) and also major capital projects (CAPEX)?

4 Does PSCM as a function have a supported agenda at executive board level?

The key output finding from the engagement discussion confirmed that the current PSC function was struggling to support the base business and its capabilities were not positioned to support ACX's future growth. Moreover, it was also felt that there was reactive collaboration between ACX's PSCM practitioners and the other stakeholders and disciplines across the business. Additionally, in terms of PSCM governance, there was clear evidence of insufficient focus on high-value, high-risk strategic contracts and low category specific competency of the workforce.

A structured diagnostic was engaged by the new VP PSCM to refresh PSCM's vision, understand capability gaps, and define the journey to reach PSCM functional excellence. In terms of timeframe, a period of three years was indicated to stand a reasonable chance of success with regard to the design and implementation of a supply chain excellence project. The three-year excellence journey was supported by the ACX executive board to address suboptimal practices and complement the overarching corporate growth objectives. The size of the potential prize was simply too big for the company to ignore.

Structured methodology

In terms of structured methodology, the PSCM excellence journey was built by identifying over 100 mitigation activities grouped into seven initiatives across four underpinning strands of capabilities deemed appropriate to drive business improvements, which were then mapped onto a three-year road map. Figure 9.1 highlights the component parts of this.

As can be seen, there were four main '*to be*' capability strands for the journey toward PSCM excellence:

- strategic;
- tactical;
- operational;
- enabling.

Against each of these four main strands current capability and maturity gaps were identified to represent the 'AS–IS' situation. The various PSCM business improvement initiatives can then be captured on the roadmap to the far right along with a realistic and pragmatic timeframe within which to achieve successful transformation:

- Year 1 – Quick wins that can be achieved with relatively little or no 'pain'.
- Year 2 – Establishing a steady state with regarding to new ways for working and different PSCM organizational structures.
- Year 3 – Realizing excellence.

For subsequent years, the focus must be around continuous improvement to position the team as not necessarily a world class PSCM function but certainly one that is 'fit for purpose' delivering value. Various professional bodies such as CIPS and IIAPS run corporate certification programmes that can audit, measure and continuously monitor PSCM organizational capability anchored to their own certification programmes. Certification against ISO 44001 is a further way to help ensure that the organization is embracing collaborative working practices.

So now that we have a better understanding of the structured methodology that was deployed at outset we can build on this by looking at the review areas that were used to determine PSCM maturity and capability to help inform which gaps need to be closed (ie a 'gap analysis').

Figure 9.2 articulates the areas that required focus, with business demand and market supply running across all sub-initiatives.

Figure 9.1 Structured methodology for PSCM excellence journey

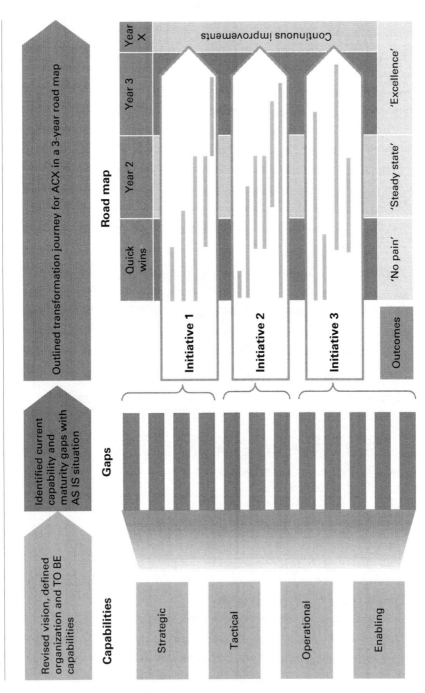

Figure 9.2 Review areas to determine PSCM maturity and capability to inform 'gap analysis'

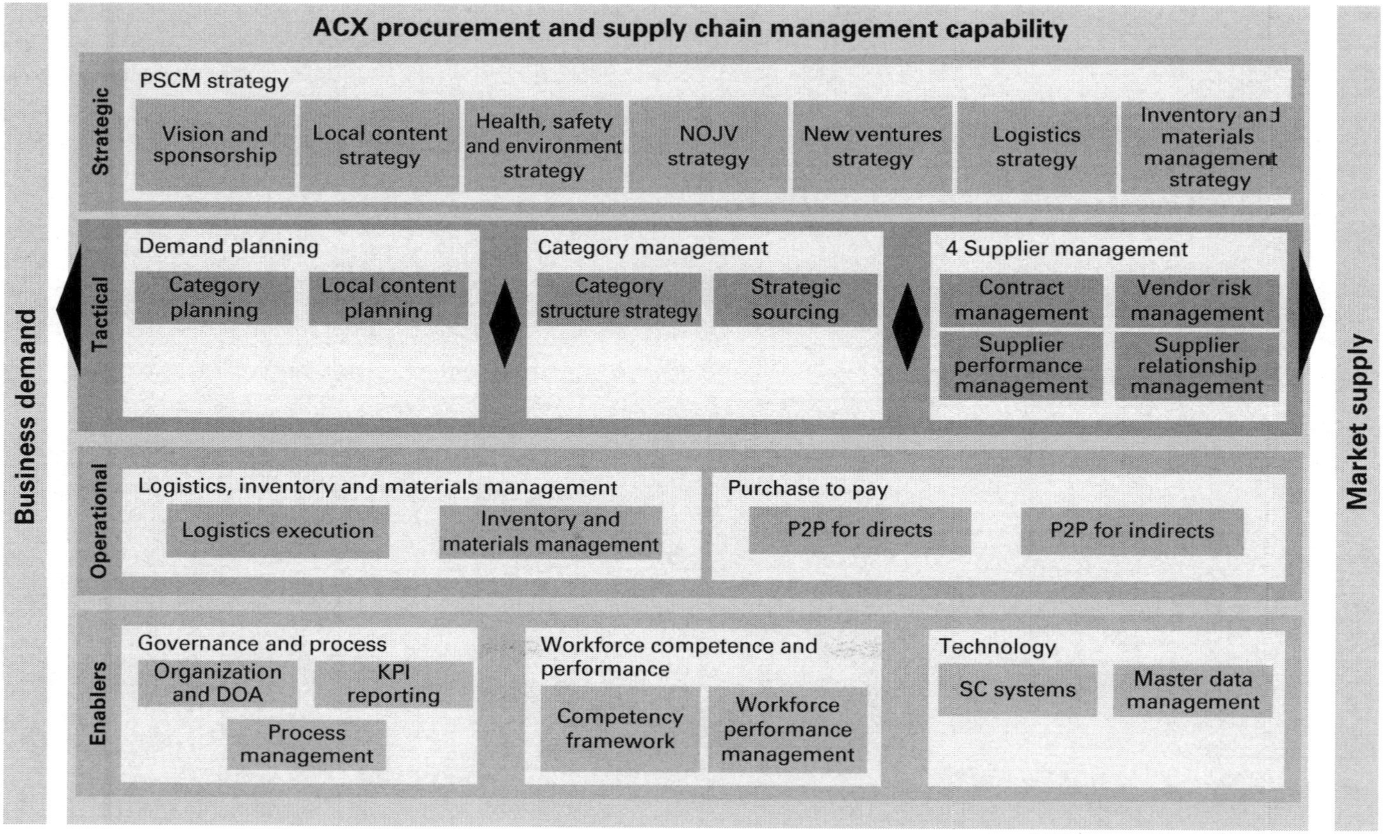

ACX procurement and supply chain management capability

Market supply

Business demand

Strategic

PSCM strategy
- Vision and sponsorship
- Local content strategy
- Health, safety and environment strategy
- NOJV strategy
- New ventures strategy
- Logistics strategy
- Inventory and materials management strategy

Tactical

Demand planning
- Category planning
- Local content planning

Category management
- Category structure strategy
- Strategic sourcing

4 Supplier management
- Contract management
- Vendor risk management
- Supplier performance management
- Supplier relationship management

Operational

Logistics, inventory and materials management
- Logistics execution
- Inventory and materials management

Purchase to pay
- P2P for directs
- P2P for indirects

Enablers

Governance and process
- Organization and DOA
- KPI reporting
- Process management

Workforce competence and performance
- Competency framework
- Workforce performance management

Technology
- SC systems
- Master data management

For **strategic:**

- PSCM strategy;
- vision and sponsorship;
- local content strategy;
- health, safety and environmental strategy;
- non-operated joint venture strategy (NOJV partnerships);
- new ventures strategy;
- logistics strategy;
- inventory and materials management strategy.

For **tactical:**

- demand planning;
- category management;
- supplier management.

For **operational:**

- logistics, inventory and materials management;
- purchase to pay (P2P).

For **enablers:**

- governance and process;
- workforce competence and performance.

A crucial part of collaboration and engaging with others when beginning the process of embarking upon any form of business improvement transformation initiative is to demonstrate that you have engaged with stakeholders and listened to what they had to say. An example of this is shown in Figure 9.3, which captures the output from the new VP PSCM discussion with key stakeholders across the business. The comments made are pretty much self-explanatory, and despite them being critical, they nonetheless represent a huge opportunity for the ACX PSCM transition team.

As can be seen, there were many areas of feedback, much of which was addressed through the PSCM excellence initiative. In particular, however, two stakeholder feedback areas stood out in terms of presenting an opportunity to modify existing suboptimal working practices to create significant value through enhanced collaborative working and joined up thinking. These were ACX's demand planning capability, and the management of ACX's key/high-risk contracts.

Figure 9.3 Captured output from stakeholder engagement discussions

PSCM staff and other key stakeholders (internal & external) had strong views about the key issues with the current PSCM function and their implications on the business.

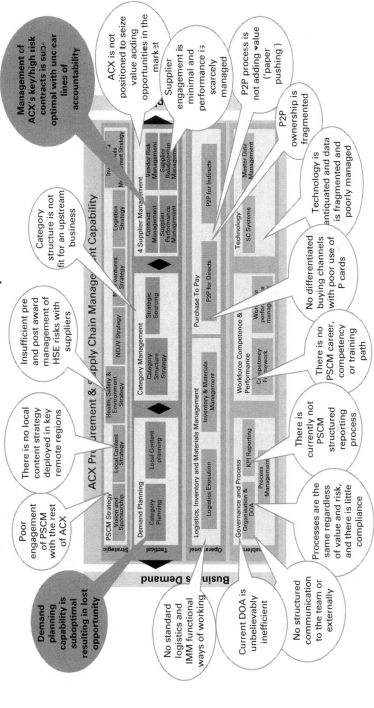

ACX'S demand planning capability

'Demand planning' is the ability of ACX to have 'line of sight' of its forward operations (OPEX) and capital project (CAPEX) activity, looking out, say, two to three years. Effectively, this is the projected *demand* for outsourced third party goods and services, or the degree to which ACX will have to rely on placing contracts with its supply chain.

However, feedback from stakeholders revealed that the relationship between the PSCM function and its technical internal customer groups was suboptimal. Technical teams only tended to inform PSCM of demand requirements at the last minute – very close to the point when the services were needed. This in turn forces the PSCM function to be very reactive and does not allow sufficient time for novel and creative commercial arrangement to be developed and implemented by the function. This is a lost opportunity and is as much the fault of the non-PSCM disciplines as PSCM. The need for a better, more joined up collaborative way of working was indicated.

Management of ACX's key/high-risk contracts

A key contract is defined as a contractual relationship with a particular outsourced third party where ACX:

- spends a significant amount of money on over a longer contract period;
- is reliant upon that particular product/service line in terms of support to a critical part of its business.

An example of this would be an offshore helicopter contractor which transports key offshore worker to/from the manned offshore installations. Without this, offshore installations couldn't operate, and production of oil and gas would cease.

Feedback from stakeholders revealed that the management of key contracts by ACX was also suboptimal:

- Internal ACX contract owners had not been allocated to be responsible for many important contracts.
- Key performance indicators were not in place for many important contracts.
- There was a lack of regular contract performance review meetings with key contractors.
- No contract management plans (CMPs) were in place.

- Many contracts exceeded original budgeted contract sums.

- 'Contract creep' was a frequent occurrence because of weak work scopes outset with many additional works and services simply being bolted onto a contract that was not originally designed for such things.

- There was a lack of general discipline around post-contract administration in terms of variations and contract amendments, resulting in claims being made by contractors, with subsequent higher costs.

- There was maverick spend behaviour, excessive single sourcing, etc.

- There was a lack of interface between PSCM, technical and HSE teams around managing key contracts.

Gap analysis

Figure 9.4 uses a 'spider's web' model to capture the aforementioned gap areas that needed to be closed. By reference to this the reader can observe that the current versus desired state for each area can be mapped onto the web by means of a score of 1 to 4, which represents the assessed level of PSCM capability or maturity on the PSCM excellence journey:

0–1 = Suboptimal capability.

1–2 = Basic capability.

2–3 = Good capability.

3–4 = Optimal capability.

Pareto analysis and 'attacking the tail of inefficiency'

A further consideration from the early diagnostic review was the output from a Pareto analysis of ACX's historical spend on third party goods and services, which showed that some 80 per cent of contracts relate to 10 per cent of spend, whilst 20 per cent of contracts relate to 90 per cent of spend. However, there was no differentiated governance based on level of spend or risk!

Ideally, governance should be fit for purpose, with more enhanced focus and scrutiny on the high-value, high-risk key contracts, deploying already scarce resource on this with less focus on the low-value, low-risk commitments. Better practice dictates that the tail of inefficiency shown in Figure 9.5 needs to be attacked by a prudent PSCM function.

Figure 9.4 'Spider's web' gap analysis capture

ACX's base business and growth agenda will only be supported by a transformed PSCM function ...

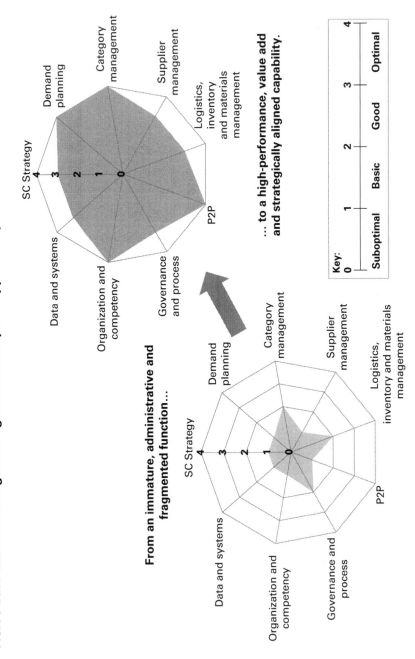

From an immature, administrative and fragmented function...

... to a high-performance, value add and strategically aligned capability.

Key:

0	1	2	3	4
Suboptimal	Basic		Good	Optimal

Figure 9.5 Pareto analysis of spend and 'attacking the tail'

The current PSCM organization was struggling to support the base business

Listed below are key symptoms pointing to a suboptimal PSCM organization

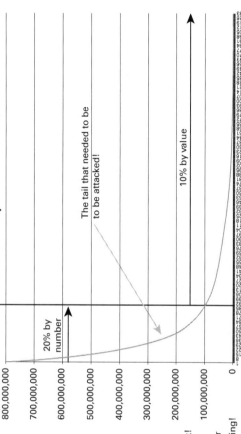

Pareto analysis of ACX contracts

- Historically there had been **no shared PSCM vision** with the Executive Board and the function was perceived by the business as **"paper pushing"** rather than adding value.

- Processes and **Category structure** are not aligned with a typical **Upstream Oil and Gas** Business Operating Model

- Recent Pareto analysis of ACX spend showed some 80% contracts relate to 10% of spend whilst 20% of contracts relate to 90% of spend. However there is no **differentiated governance** based on level of spend or risk!

- **Collaboration** is insufficient between PSCM and the other Business functions, which leads to reactive ways of working!

- **Supplier engagement** is rudimentary and does not allow ACX to leverage market opportunities effectively

- **P2P** governance and regional accountabilities are unclear while long cycle times point to ineffective supporting technologies.

- The ACX PSCM workforce needs **up-skilling as** specific category expertise is lacking to deliver day-to-day activities.

Other noted observations were that:

- Collaboration was insufficient between PSCM and the other business functions, which led to reactive ways of working!

- Supplier engagement was rudimentary and did not allow ACX to leverage market opportunities effectively.

- P2P governance and regional accountabilities were unclear, while long cycle times point to ineffective supporting technologies.

- The ACX PSCM workforce needed upskilling as specific category expertise is lacking to deliver day-to-day activities.

- There was no shared PSCM vision with the executive board, and the function was perceived by the business as 'paper-pushing' rather than adding value.

- Processes and category structure are not aligned with a typical upstream oil and gas business operating model.

PSCM structural and capability building initiatives

Based on the findings of the diagnostic, seven structural and capability building initiatives for the PSCM function were developed. These are shown in Figure 9.6.

The **structural** building initiatives were:

- PSCM leadership and engagement with the rest of the business – collaborative communications structures;

- organization and people development – competency upskilling;

- technology – embed new PSCM databases and systems.

The **capability** building initiatives were:

- design and embed category management;

- enhance supplier and contract management;

- enhance logistics, inventory and materials management;

- enhance P2P systems.

The delivered objectives of the three structural initiatives that will help sustain the value the PSCM function brings to the business are summarized in Figure 9.8.

The delivered objectives of the four capability building initiatives that add high value to the business are summarized in Figure 9.9.

Figure 9.6 Seven structural and capability building initiatives for the PSCM function

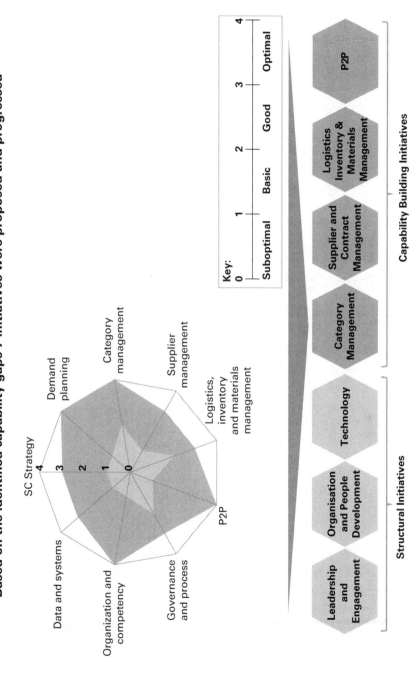

Based on the identified capability gaps 7 initiatives were proposed and progressed

Figure 9.7   Segments discussed by new Collaborative Business Interface Forum

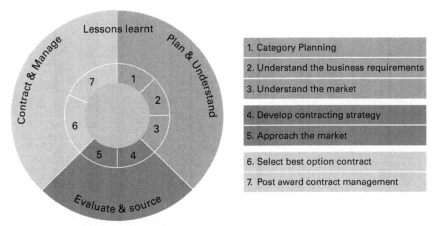

1. Category Planning
2. Understand the business requirements
3. Understand the market
4. Develop contracting strategy
5. Approach the market
6. Select best option contract
7. Post award contract management

A new vision for PSCM excellence through joined up collaborative thinking and business interface

A new vision for PSCM excellence was agreed with the executive board, which read as follows:

> To support ACX's base business and future growth with a flexible and sustainable upstream PSCM organization recognized both internally and externally for its strategic and transactional excellence, for focusing on both value creation as well as a value assurance, and also positioning ACX as a customer and partner of choice, and above all being a great place to work and learn for its people.

The vision was very much supported by a new working approach evolving to contemporary category management. The formation of business interface forums by spend category was crucial in terms of successful collaboration with other stakeholders and align proactively demand and supply plans. Additionally, the business interface fork concept was also essential to ensure ongoing reviews consider how effectively the contract owner/community is managing key or high-risk contracts (again by specific spend category). Figure 9.9 reinforces the key segments of the PSCM category management wheel that business interface forums should be discussing.

Figure 9.8 Delivered *structural* building initiatives as part of the PSCM excellence project

Initiatives	Objectives delivered
Leadership and Engagement	• **A Business Interface Forum was established** by spend management category to ensure engagement with key Business stakeholders to proactively plan and agree forward demand planning with joined up collaborative thinking, and ensure effective regular reviews of business critical contracts, process adherence, lessons learnt, and Logistics/Materials Management challenges • **SC vision, organization and performance was launched** through a structured communication plan with key stakeholder groups. • **A new ACX Procurement & Supply Chain Standard** was developed and embedded, delineating fit for purpose governance dependent on risk and spend threshold including (end to end processes, guidelines, role accountabilities and responsibilities, KPI reporting and structured communication)
Organization and People Development	• **Category Teams** within the new PSCM organization structure were appointed and mobilised with position/competency gaps fulfilled to focus on key/high risk contracts • **Support teams** were recruited and mobilized (including LC teams in remote regions, technology support, contract owners support and Governance and Reporting management embedded) • An ambitious people development plan was developed and rolled out which included the launch of a **structured Competency Framework in alignment with differentiated Career paths** (by speciality and potential) and a progressive **training programme** • **Corporate PSCM certification programmes were embedded** as well as a PSCM Category team rotation programme rolled out to create balanced PSCM practitioner with experience of multiple categories
Technology	• More focus was brought to **Master Data management** to assure quality and accuracy • System functionalities will be installed to **enhance collaboration** such as digital signatures and a communication software • A new tailored version of the **FPAL/ACHILLES** database described in Chapter 4 was embedded for pre qualification and post contract management • A clear **Systems strategy and roadmap** was created to identify and install dedicated systems for Contract Management, Sourcing and Supplier Management

Figure 9.9 Category management segments discussed by business interface

Initiatives	Delivered Objectives
Category Management	• New **ACX Upstream specific supply/demand** process model and category structure was rolled out with absolute clarity on separate accountabilities for SUPPLY and DEMAND. • The design of new PSCM organisation accommodate both **VALUE CREATION** and **VALUE ASSURANCE (GOVERANCE)** • **Proactive collaboration achieved through new BUISNESS INTERFACE FORUMS** which ensure alignment of demand planning with business needs in a joined up collaborative way. • A phased **strategic sourcing programme** of work was introduced thereby addressing key areas of spend to leverage market opportunities and drive more savings

Supplier and Contract Management	• **A local content strategy and engagement** was rolled out for regional specific areas where Local content consideration were needed to fulfill obligations, develop local industries and take advantage of market opportunities
	• **A structured approach to supplier collaboration was developed and embedded** which will included:
	  • Internal capability development (Supplier Performance Management frameworks)
	  • Collaborative external engagement through 'supplier awareness and engagement events'
	• End to end **contract management processes**, RACI, templates and a suite of standard T&Cs were rolled out.

P2P	• **Purchase To Pay excellence was achieved** - through clearly defined buying channels, with ongoing efficiency KPI and cycle time monitoring • **Regional points of accountability** were defined • **Processes** will now be detailed, communicated and adherence against them monitored
Logistics Inventory & Materials Management	• **Global Logistics and Inventory & Materials management** was clearly defined with a new accountability structure • **End to End processes and guidelines** were detailed and rolled out

Figure 9.10 Phased benefits

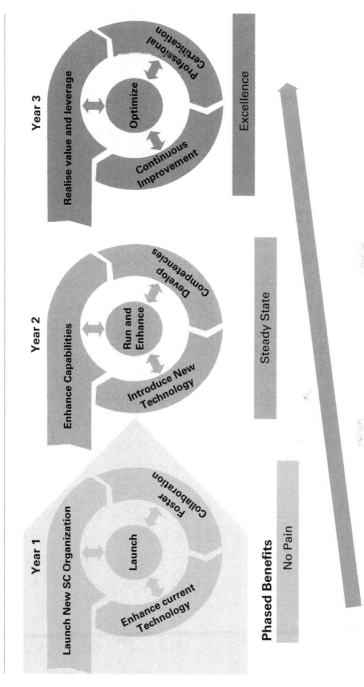

Figure 9.11 Value realization conclusion

Value Realisation through a PSCM Excellence Journey

	Value Description	Value Levers		
		Cost Reduction	Delivery Efficiency	Risk & Control
Leadership and Engagement	• Greater efficiency through alignment of all PSCM stakeholders on vision and performance objectives • Greater efficiency through stronger business collaboration to enable early tracking of demand • Greater efficiency through stronger supplier collaboration to enable visibility of supply • Greater control through visible and standardised reporting leading to better compliance and performance	▨	✓	✓
Organisation and People Development	• Greater efficiency through a contemporary Upstream Supply Chain operating and projects support model • Motivated and highly competent workforce through an aligned career, training and competency plan • Greater control through better workforce planning and leverage.	✓	✓	✓
Technology	• Greater efficiency through installation of digital signature capability and modern communication technology • Greater efficiency of Source to Pay processes through the enhancement of the technology landscape to enhance (contract management, sourcing, supplier performance) • Greater control through process driven master data management which will eliminate errors, redundancies and de-duplication	▨	✓	✓
Category Management	**Savings on Core Spend** • Assimilation and integration of supply and demand on yearly, quarterly, monthly and weekly basis leading to improved planning accuracy • Increased focus on all Core spend by PSCM category experts complemented by fit for purpose governance	✓	✓	✓
Supplier and Contract Management	**Savings: on Core Spend** • Leverage standard Terms & Conditions and master data management for implementing contracts • Standardised ways of managing contracts providing visibility pre and post contracting • Focus on suppliers based on segments for Stronger & deeper collaborative relationships with key suppliers leading to better demand planning, no surprises and trusted relationships	✓	✓	✓
P2P	**Savings: on Total Spend** • Clear buying channels leading to 90% fast track transactions freeing up buyer to focus on critical orders • Error free transactions means fewer duplications, blocks and reconciliations • Automated processes with built in fit for purpose delegated authorities for approval	✓	✓	✓
Logistics Inventory and Materials Management	• **Reduction in logistics cost** through better order planning, scheduling and expediting • **Reduction of inventory cost** through elimination of duplicate and obsolete stock • Greater efficiency of operations and workforce through increased uptime from enhanced Work Planning and Preventive Maintenance	✓	✓	✓

All of the aforementioned key points are embedded within the global standard for collaborative working, ISO 44001, as shown in Figure 9.12.

The 'size of the prize' for organizations such as ACX wrestling with similar challenges is quite simply too great to ignore. For example, to do nothing would means to be prepared to accept ongoing risk, vulnerability and suboptimal practices. Consider the:

- loss of opportunity associated with time delays in starting the SC excellence journey;

- vulnerability to the organization of not securing suppliers of the right quality in the right time and place to meet business critical needs;

- challenges in securing and retaining staff in a burgeoning upstream market because it may not be viewed a good place to work in compared with its peers.

Figure 9.12 CRAFT 8 Stage Life Cycle Model incorporated with ISO 44001

SOURCE Courtesy of Midas Projects Ltd in conjunction with the Institute for Collaborative Working

Ultimately, however, for any organization considering embarking upon a supply chain excellence project of this magnitude (whether it be private, public or third sector), there will need to have been a clear vote of confidence at executive board level that is a credible vision that will benefit the business or organization as a whole.

Conclusion

This case study will hopefully have instilled in the reader's mind a positive sense of the 'art of the possible' in terms of the potential value that can be delivered to a complex multi-cultural organization through embarking upon such a supply chain functional excellence journey.

As Figure 9.11 depicts, phased benefits and value were realized over a sensible three year period through achieving quick wins in year one, showcasing lighthouse examples of value gain, and then building to a position of 'steady state' in year two, and then subsequently positioning the business for excellence in year three and thereafter creating a culture that naturally strives for continuous improvement going forward.

One final note – it must be remembered that there is never a good right time to embark upon such a journey – there will always be excuses not to do something, so the challenge is for the senior decision makers to have vision and foresight and 'grasp the nettle' by committing to action and run with such a transformational business improvement programme in parallel to fluctuating day-to-day activities and challenges.

Case study 4   10

Envoi – value creation through collaborative outsourcing of acquisition and divestment in the upstream E&P sector

A exemplar of collaborative outsourcing to deliver real opportunity and create value across the portfolios of different partner organizations in the international upstream oil and gas industry

Deciding to use specialist consultants is never an easy decision for any director or manager to make in any organization, particularly when outsourcing adds additional cost to often already constrained budgets compared with the use of existing 'in-house' salaried staff. All too often, incumbent staff think they can do the job just as well as a specialist consultant, or are concerned it's a criticism or perception of their own ability, or are simply expected by management to add yet another new specialist task for which they have little specific experience to their already busy workload.

This case study seeks to explore the Challenge around this whole area in the context of value creation through collaborative acquisition and divestment (A&D) in the upstream exploration and production (E&P) industry sector.

So, when and how can 'collaboration' with third party specialists truly work effectively? The key is when the task in hand is indeed a 'specialist task' rather than just more work simply needing more of the same talent one already has in house due to time and/or concurrent activity.

Firstly, by means of a definition for the reader, 'specialist A&D advisory work' is the marketing of upstream (E&P) assets for oil and gas companies to interested parties or future partners. More commonly, this is known in the sectors and financial investment markets as A&D, as opposed to M&A which is more about corporate mergers and acquisitions).

Such A&D activity is indeed a specialist and very niche role in the E&P sector, involving expert assistance to oil and gas companies, both big and small, to manage their portfolio of producing and exploration interests, usually to fulfil strategic goals and/or simply spread and manage risk. This usually involves either assisting companies to 'search for and buy' new assets and opportunities, or to 'sell' interests, either involving non-core appraisal development and producing assets or equity in exploration projects to help share risks and have incoming farm-in partners pay for exploration drilling in exchange for a per cent equity stake in an asset.

Financial organizations will most often be sought to assist with large producing asset package transactions due to the corporate banking and tax implications such deals involve where willing buyers' risk is more linked to value and political risk depending on where in the world the assets are located.

Because of the risk nature of exploration farm-outs, where there is no guarantee that the investment will generate any return with an average of perhaps a one in five or less chance of making a successful discovery, the success of finding an interested party willing to farm-in to such risks is equally not guaranteed. Finding a qualified, specialist A&D advisory with the necessary 'technical' and commercial skills to properly and successfully sell this opportunity and risk, and with the right network of contacts, which improves the chance of success, is highly recommended.

A&D statistics

To put this risk in context, independent statics of 'global deal making' over 18 years sourced by JSI Services, which has screened and tracked all publicly available exploration farm-outs globally (excluding North America) and developed its global upstream deals (GUD) database, shows that an average of only one in three exploration farm-outs identified, reviewed and tracked over nearly two decades have resulted in a successful farm-out deal. Selling the risk of an exploration farm-out is clearly therefore not an easy task at the best of times, and requires a unique set of skills to ensure the maximum chance of success, but such a niche role is perfectly suited to a specialist advisor who spends the entire time engaged in that field.

The keys to successful specialist consultant collaboration

The keys to achieving a successful collaboration in almost any situation where a specialist outsource skill set is needed to complement internal trades are simple, but all too often are not followed. They can be summarized as follows:

- **Plan and prepare** – Plan and prepare properly, including an understanding of the specialist task in hand. Start the assessment process early (remember the 6 6 Ps – prior planning & and preparation prevents poor performance).

- **Consultant selection** – Select the right third party with a proven track record for successfully carrying out the task required. The 6 Ps should ensure that one is properly familiar with what is involved and needed.

- **Timing** – There should be early involvement of a specialist advisor who is more often than not willing to advise on the task and how it should be tackled, even if it does not lead to an immediate involvement. The best agents will offer such advice.

- **Listen** – Be willing to take and progress the specialist advice.

- **Flexibility through process** – As any process progresses, things change, so ensure regular reporting and internal measure of progress as well as any outside influences (which in A&D involves assessment of market conditions and the ability of market to do deals) so keep an open mind to about the actual time involved, allowing for plenty of contingency and cost which may be involved to achieve success rather than simply trying to save money and failing.

- **Plan and manage for success, not failure.**

All of the aforementioned key points are embedded within the global standard for collaborative working, ISO 44001.

Myth and reality

Most experts think they can 'sell', although more often than not incumbent in-house salaried staff, employed for a specific technical or commercial role, only tend to have some of the skills needed to succeed and use cost and time effectively. Not surprisingly, this stems from a lesser understanding of external sales and marketing compared to internal sales to management. The lack of specialist knowledge in turn leads to inadequate planning, failure to properly complete the key tasks and substantially more costs due to inadequate time being budgeted than is realistically needed. Such internal staff should perhaps remain focused on the technical and/or commercial tasks for which they are more qualified, and which in the long term are worth more to their organization.

Taking just time alone as probably the key factor in an asset divestment, it is a fact that organizations often plan for a six-month divestment process that ends up taking 12 or more months. This is clearly supported by the JSI data, which shows that over the last 18 years, even in a buoyant upstream A&D market, asset divestments have on average taken 12–15 months from the time they appear to when they are announced as completed. Many have taken substantially longer (some over three years), particularly if they involve higher risk exploration.

Effective early planning

Proper initial assessment of any task and employment of the 6Ps is essential. This assessment involves three key stages:

1 Consideration of *all* the factors.
2 Review of the obvious options.
3 Deciding on the most effect course of action and execution.

Skip, rush and/or only partially complete the first and second, and more often than not the third is likely to be a guess based on a perception of the best plan, with the decision to outsource often made far too late.

Conversely, early collaboration with specialist advisors can appreciably assist with the early planning process, as they will usually be happy to advise on the key issues that will influences the planning process, which in the long run can save significant costs and you may end up involving them as advisors.

The keys to successful A&D marketing

Effective marketing of an upstream asset is all about the 4Rs:

- right information;
- right way;

- right people;
- right time.

To achieve this in a successful asset divestment, the following key elements all need to be right.

- **Deal psychology** – To understand what information is necessary to include, combining a good understanding of how projects are reviewed by different organizations and are then progressed internally (using perhaps one's own organization as a guide and what causes projects to be rejected) should highlight how clear, positive portrayal of the facts about a project needs to be properly documented so it's less likely to be rejected. Also, knowing how it's more likely to assist the internal organization's champion sponsor relationship is all part of understanding the psychology of not only how to trigger initial interest in a project opportunity but also assist it to variously progress successfully internally through the review and management decision process. Consideration should be made as to how opportunities are often rejected through a lack of the appropriate technical and commercial information for rapid corporate criteria matching.

- **Marketing materials** – In this regard, the way information on a project for divestment is documented in marketing materials is all too often poorly prepared and a disconnected series of facts which that rely upon the reader to fill in the gaps of their existing knowledge or on quick research on a particular country, basin, hydrocarbon play area, asset or regime. A properly prepared marketing summary should be constructed using a connected story that makes it easy for the potential buyer to fully understand the key technical and commercial facts about the asset for sale or farm-out, including its location, hydrocarbon potential, past exploration/production history and value based on the necessary information for the opportunity to be properly understood by anyone reading it, whether they have the background knowledge and experience of the area or not. If they do know a project area, then a project summary needs to overcome any negative perceptions they may have, challenging such perceptions and clearly setting out what is different or new.

- **Global contacts** – Key to contacting enough of the right people, is having access to an up-to-date database of *all* the right global contacts, and at different levels within each potential organization or investor. Most new projects have to first pass rapid initial technical and commercial screening before management will commit the time and budget is spent on detailed due diligence. As a result, each new project is in constant competition with other projects fighting for the same budget funds. Successful projects are more likely to make it through the internal review process if the right information is available and set out in a way that an internal 'champion' can convince a management to 'sponsor'. In this regard, a project is less likely to achieve this if a project introduction is only made to one individual in a company and only a small number of companies. All too often, organizations divesting an asset think they can second-guess a market where, although in the initial phase of a project marketing campaign a shortlist of the more obvious candidates is possible, all too often initial interest does not progress, and the marketing is not expended quickly or widely enough to ensure a potentially interested party with the appetite for a divestment is contacted. The more seriously interested parties that can be found and properly screened, the higher the chance there will be to find several parties that make offers and create the necessary 'competitive tension' which in turn increases the chance of maximizing the value of such offers.

- **Timing** – One has limited, if any, control over the status of an A&D market where the number of E&P deals being completed has historically tracked the oil price. Low oil price means fewer deals being done. The key is to therefore maximize the time a project can be marketed so that as many potentially interested parties as possible can be contacted, and with the time to properly review and even re-review an opportunity as market conditions change and as corporate search criteria, and particularly budgets, change over time. Time is, from experience, the biggest killer of A&D transactions, and particularly those involving exploration risk.

With these key elements in mind, internal seller efforts to market their E&P deals are often half-baked due to the key skills and time being committed. Such poorly prepared efforts can also muddy the waters, which then makes it more difficult if, and when, a specialist consultant is later brought in, as buyer perceptions can be set by the initial contact. Once a potentially interested party has declined an opportunity it is more difficult for them to later reconsider an opportunity it.

The value of specialist consultants

Collaboration with such specialists will more often than not allow all these key elements to be carried out quickly and efficiently, as they have the skills to properly document an opportunity that is more likely to overcome the internal review hurdles. They will efficiently contact more of the right people, and screen the most likely from their experience and regular contact with their network.

Advisors, more often than not, are prepared to work for success-orientated remuneration involving modest fixed up-front fees and expenses (which are usually less than the client's own internal cost) but linked to larger success fees, and this orientates the advisor to the same client aims completely. If the project is a success, the advisors are usually paid a percentage of the deal value, which although bigger than the costs of paying for the up-front work and expertise on the basis of a full corporate day rate, when compared to what it is likely to have cost internally and when double the time originally budgeted is taken to carry out half the effective work, it is probably as much as it realistically costs if carried out by internal staff.

Project development and execution process

We have briefly touched on the need to screen out project opportunities to enable the better ones with a greater chance of success to be selected. A&D activity is a type of project in the same way that major capital projects are. The JSI data referred to earlier is a testament to the need for screening process. To do this screening properly, specialists and/or organizations need a process – a project development and execution process (PDEP), which essentially helps to improve decision making and execution by fostering better planning, collaboration and communication to complement good capital stewardship and organizational capability. The focus of PDEP is to improve two key dimensions associated with a project namely:

1 The decision-making quality on the project.

2 The execution of the project.

If a project team only performs one of those two dimensions well (either decision-making or execution), the project is less likely to provide a successful business outcome. If, however, the opportunity is selected well and executed with excellence, the probability of business success increases dramatically. The PDEP vision therefore is: *the right project choice and then implemented well* (Figure 10.1).

This vision is about selecting the best opportunities through an improved decision-making process and improving the overall outcomes by excelling in the execution of business-driven decisions. An experience A&D advisor can assist greatly in facilitating all of this for organizations.

Figure 10.1   Matrix showing the PDEP vision in terms of decision quality

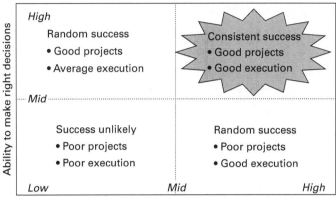

Ability to implement decisions in best way possible

The ultimate goal of such a process is to have all of the organization's projects fall into the top right quadrant in Figure 10.1: in other words, *selecting the right opportunities and doing them well*!

Doing the right project poorly or doing the wrong project well leaves money on the table that an organization could use elsewhere. Without consistent process, projects fall all over the grid.

The PDEP process is nothing new. It is simply a collection of best practices put all together under one umbrella. Common terminology is used to ensure understanding and consistency throughout the organization. Consider, for example, the PDEP impact on asset project value in Figure 10.2.

In the early phase, the value of an opportunity is identified, but not realized until the later phases. Both are important. The curves represent:

- A – Selecting the right project and doing it well.

- B – Selecting the right project, and executing it poorly and eroding value.

- C – Doing the wrong project well.

- D – Doing the wrong project poorly.

Critical to the success of most businesses is to generate the highest earnings and net present value (discounted cash flow technique). This involves the ability to manage the portfolio of opportunities available. Project planning is a critical phase in managing the portfolio because this is where value is identified and created. PDEP provides the core work process that allows collaborative cross-functional teams to collaborate in the generation of well thought-out development plans. This extends to include the use of outsourced specialists.

Figure 10.2 Project definition, value identification, and value realization

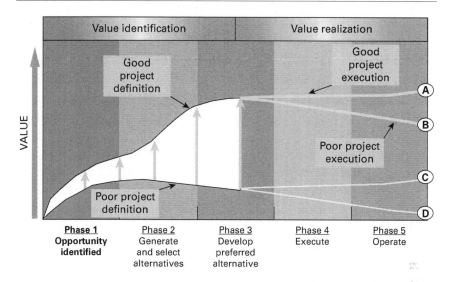

Collaborative innovation and creativity are essential to driving the value of any business and its assets even higher. Generating creative business and technical alternatives, and the use of innovative technology, are examples of value-added activities in the early phases.

A&D outsourcing collaboration: Case studies

Two key examples of historical projects can help demonstrate how effective collaboration can achieve very cost-efficient success. Due to confidentiality, the specific names and places of each project will have been omitted, but even without these, the projects outlines and overview of the collaboration and A&D outsource process will help demonstrate that properly managing the key stages of outsourcing to the right specialists at the right time can be immensely valuable.

Offshore North Sea exploration project

In this instance the project was operated jointly by two major companies and involved an exploration prospect scheduled to be tested by an obligation well within a 12-month period before licence expiry, at a cost of around US$50 million gross. The majors owned a combined 50 per cent equity between them, split 40 per cent and 10 per cent respectively, where a full farm-out would involve their equity cost of the well being paid for by an incoming party (ie US$25 million net to their combined interest), which would earn a majority of their interest with the majors retaining a small carried interest in case of success.

In this project example, the risks were medium to high as the prospect was due to test a new play. Although it had an estimated 2.5 Tcf resource potential in clastic reservoirs, its reliance on the integrity of an up-dip seal meant that the prospect might not have retained the upside reserve potential due to pressure breach.

The majors had initially tried to farm out their project through one of the majors leading a marketing effort on behalf of the two parties using the internal technical and commercial staff. The efforts were targeted at many of the obvious candidates, including partners and other companies already involved within the same play area as the companies. These parties should immediately be able to understand the opportunity; based on their superior knowledge of the play area and the higher scrutiny, they are more likely to carry out a review than companies without the local knowledge.

The joint farm-out effort was initially limited to such candidates and later expanded modestly to others within the North Sea, having been rejected by many of the obvious candidates as too high risk. The joint marketing effort was ceased at that point.

(It is important to highlight that even though specialists could be asked to assist early in a project, it is equally recognized that before rushing immediately to engage third party assistance, some initial contact by a seller with a few of the most obvious candidates but on a less formal basis can act as an 'acid test' where such parties, which are assumed to know a lot about the area in question, particularly if they have exploration budgets, will then be focused on an evaluation of the play risk and, matching this against resource size, can be approached informally and on an exclusive basis. The feedback such carefully targeted companies can also provide can also be very helpful in preparing for more formal project marketing through a third-party specialist. In some cases, the informal contact can result in deals without the need for outsourcing. The key, though, is to limit the time they are given to show interest to a few weeks, where it can be sold as a period of 'exclusive' review ahead of a more formal process.)

In this case history, one of the majors agreed to seek specialist A&D assistance from the specialist A&D advisor, realizing that not only did the project marketing needed to be expanded to a wider audience or global contacts, but also the project documentation needed to be upgraded so that the many companies perhaps less familiar with the project area could be 'queued' into both the technical and commercial aspects of the play area, and which might probably be a new country entry requiring substantially more back ground information.

The specialist A&D advisors' engagement was secured based on fixed upfront fees and a success bonus. A detailed technical and commercial review of the opportunity was subsequently carried out by Envoi and followed by a phase of documentation. The review was able to show that the project could be accurately presented in a more positive light than had been achieved internally by the largely technical staff. They had built the marketing documentation on the internal pitch to management, which had led to the decision to divest the asset showing a potential 'risked' resource of only 70 Bcf for the project rather than the true and combined resource upside, which Envoi was able to highlight as more like 2.5 Tcf.

Not only was the project able to be shown in a far more prospective light, and very much based on the positive technical and commercial facts of the opportunity, but the marketing brochures prepared by Envoi covered not only all the technical regional, play and prospect potential but also country, commercial and fiscal aspects of the opportunity that many companies less familiar with the play area and country would need to know to make it easier to review and match against corporate search criteria.

As important as it is to generate interest, it is equally important to help companies dismiss an opportunity that they might otherwise have wasted time to carry out post-CA (confidentially agreement) project data reviews. Such reviews can be done remotely or physically and managed by the specialist agent.

In this instance, the process relied on access to some remote project information after execution of a CA but ultimately required commitment to attend a physical data room run by the major company. This ensured those most familiar with the asset could explain the technical and commercial aspects of the opportunity but attendance could be limited to the seriously interested parties only after the less serious or so-called 'tyre kickers' (ie potential data gatherers) has been given enough information in the Envoi documentation for them to decline or be declined. As has already been stated above in the outline of the 4Rs, this documentation which provided more than enough detail for interested parties to ascertain the key project criteria and ensured only the few seriously interested parties needed to take their time and the advisor's client's in time-consuming and costly travel and physical data room presentation and data review time.

In the instance of the North Sea project, this ensured that only the seriously interested parties wasted their own, and the seller's, time in detailed data reviews. The upshot was that an acceptable offer from a smaller E&P company for half the first major's smaller equity interest was received and a deal was successfully agreed which covered their full share of the planned well cost.

After the successful farm-out of the first operator major's interest in the project, the second major engaged the specialist advisor, who then ran a second marketing campaign on the same asset which resulted in two more smaller companies farming in to the asset such that the second major's share of the exploration well was also fully funded with a retained carried interest.

The subsequent well resulted in a small discovery that was almost certainly below the major's commercial threshold and so fully justified their reasons for farming out. The outsourcing resulted in three successful farm-outs that would otherwise clearly not have happened, which saved the majors combined US$25 million and was achieved at a fraction of the cost, even including the Envoi bonus, and the internal cost of the initial, but failed, marketing process run before Envoi's involvement.

Comment and the lessons to be learned

Many sellers have the misconception that by not providing all the key information upfront and 'teasing' potentially interested parties into a data room they will be able to 'sell' the project more effectively. In reality this is often not the case and only forces companies to request a data room because the marketing documentation is insufficient to allow proper criteria matching. In turn this wastes huge amounts of time, and expense, that is simply not needed. Envoi's experience is that most projects involving risk will attract in even the most prospective projects a request for no more than 25 to 30 CAs, of which fewer than seven to ten ends up in serious physical data reviews if the pre- and immediate post-CA processes are handled correctly.

To demonstrate this, the same specialist A&D advisor was once asked by another large company why they did not run as many data rooms as the company did, which claimed they regularly ran 50+ data rooms for interested companies on individual projects. When asked by the advisor how many companies had not completed a full day's review after the initial presentation, it turned out that over half had apparently left soon after lunch, having obviously got all they needed in the initial presentation to decline the opportunity, which therefore did not merit a more detailed review. Such initial screening information could have been provided in the pre-CA documentation at substantially lower cost than the many days, manpower cost and expense of running 60+ per cent more physical data rooms than are needed. The internal waste of time and cost of these wasted data rooms almost certainly cost the company more than the equivalent risked upfront cost of engaging a specialist A&D agent for the entire project marketing!

The other very common misconception is the time needed to run and achieve a successful divestment exercise. The independent statistics clearly show this is twice if not three times what most companies budget. When compared to the fixed upfront cost of a specialist outsource agent, the internal costs are usually significantly more, even before the issue of using internal staff is considered. These staff should questionably be preferentially working on the projects that they are more qualified for, and which have the potential to create significantly bigger value than the divestment of a project.

Offshore Africa

In the second project example, the specialist advisor's client was a small independent E&P operator which had originally been a minority partner in a consortium of larger companies in an offshore frontier block in which an unproven play concept had been defined by 3D seismic and required a wildcat well to test the play. The option to progress to the next licence term required commitment to drill a well in what at the time could be described as a hesitant A&D market after a dip in oil prices had resulted in the decline by a major which had a farm-out option, and the subsequent exit of the larger partners. This left the small company holding the entire licence interest. It decided to progress on its own and start a new farm-out process, based on their technical evaluation, and subsequently invited the specialist A&D advisor to assist in attracting new partners based, again, on a modest fixed upfront fee and monthly marketing retainer linked to a success fee. The largely consultant staff and single management team of the client company in this instance was the reason for specialist third party collaboration with the specialist A&D advisor.

The full review and bespoke project marketing documentation was followed by progressive marketing to find one or bigger company partners willing to carry the small operator through a deep offshore frontier well. As the client company was unlikely ever to afford the well, its management recognized the need to budget the involvement of specialist collaboration where the specialist A&D advisor ran the global project marketing whilst the interested parties it generated were managed largely by the company's technical consultant.

The process involved a clear and straightforward collaboration between two parties who clearly understood what such a project required. The key to the ultimate success of the project, and reason for including it here as a case history, is to highlight the main reason for the success which was the small company's willingness to persevere with over three years of marketing whilst the market and interest in frontier exploration projects returned to favour with the E&P sector as oil prices rose. A critical factor was the regular reviews between Envoi and the client about the marketing status, including the analysis of interested party review feedback, and equally if not more important, the willingness to patiently continue marketing with facilitation of more time by negotiation with the authorities, including extensions to allow time for a more buoyant market to return for the right companies to engage. In the end, the small company in question found several partners when the market did inevitably turn positive and several big discoveries were made with deep water wells at substantial cost, which opened a new offshore deep-water play that has since resulted in a very valuable new hydrocarbon province. Not only was the company patient, but it was willing to recognize when the market turned and commit extra resources to targeted roadshows about the opportunity to the seriously interested parties that had been defined to that point. This galvanized new interest and resulted in the farm-outs that fully funded two wells through which the small company was fully carried.

Even though the projects were this smaller company's primary project focus, the important factor was its decision to outsource, albeit spending less risked upfront through Envoi than it would have cost internally for the three years it took to ultimately farm-out. The company showed patience and flexibility, and managed proactivelt when it was needed. Many such companies would not have committed the modest funds to collaborate and would have soldiered on half-cocked or involved an inappropriate third party without the necessary skills, global network or proactivity with a specialist agent. They would almost certainly not have facilitated the extra time through negotiation with Government, which in this instance was instrumental in allowing the project to be available when the market positively turned.

The keys to successful A&D outsource collaboration: Plan and prepare properly

Collaboration on A&D projects can be highly successful, as the aforementioned two general case studies indicate.

The keys to a successful collaboration can be summarized as follows:

- **Start early** – Time is the biggest killer of deals, so starting early and considering collaboration with a specialist advisor is are essential. Even whilst carrying out a short and very targeted internal effort to the most obvious companies known to the farm-out organization, early engage-ment with specialists will enable a rapid expansion of the marketing effort if the informal targeting does not bear fruit quickly. It also ensures those engaged can be a seamless expansion of the effort. All too often the inter-nal effort is extended due to initial enthusiasm by the obvious candidates that then drags on through an internal review where such companies should be best placed to say yes or no quickly. Engagement of a specialist is then far too late, after much damage is done and valuable time is lost.

• **Time extensions** – Although the use and management of a seller's time to market is critical, this is usually defined by the E&P licence obligations and work commitments agreed with the host government or NOC (national oil company) at the time of the award. As E&P cycles progress and the A&D market changes, another key element of time to consider is engag-ing early with such authorities to prepare for licence extensions, to allow for more marketing time in case it's needed. Collaboration should include involvement with the A&D advisor in this regard and they can provide independent specialist marketing status reports to assist with discussions with authorities that more often than not need to be made aware of the A&D climate, which may be the main reason preventing a successful farm-out at that point in time and not the project itself. Collaborative engagement of an agent can also give confidence that the operator is doing all it can to find partners rather than assume the company is stalling for time. In the instance of the African project defined above in the case study, this was critical in enabling the small company to extend their obligations until the market turned and achieve two farm-out wells rather than one and creating the huge success these wells achieved for the country concerned. Arguably, the small company very successfully brought it about and helped the government in a way they had not successful done themselves.

• **Outsource appropriately** – It is imperative to engage the right special-ist third party agent, with the experience, a track record over time and in different A&D market climates that can show its success rate. Some agents say they are specialist deal marketers but do not have the specialist technical marketing skill set and experience to show their worth. Many just list a deal based on what the seller says, which is then sent to lots of contacts or introduced to a few at the so called decision-maker level. Unless it is a corporate transaction and especially if it involves explora-tion risk, this one high-level contact approach has less success than the multifaceted and time-nurturing approach.

Listing services can help expand the target audience if one is very confident about the company's internal marketing abilities, but taking the early advisory group advice will often help demonstrate if the internal approach is hitting all the bells. All too often, listing services are dressed up as a full marketing service and charged at the full advisory rate.

- **Invest less but incentivize to succeed** – In the long run, it usually costs far less to use a specialist agent when the equivalent internal costs are considered and risked that the project marketing will usually take longer than is perceived by management and the project is two of the three that statistics over 18+ years show does not farm out. Be willing to pay enough to the agent and then properly incentivize them if they can demonstrate the value-added services that the top tier of advisors can show.

- **Flexibility** – Regular communication with the advisor is also very important, with regular input as to what more or else could be done to progress the marketing. However, care must be taken not to pressure the agent, due to internal management timelines, to rush tasks that may in fact negatively hinder the marketing rather than progressing it.

  Consider the analogy of being stranded on a desert island with enough food, water and shelter, but a flare gun with only five flares. When do you fire the flares to attract passing ships? Probably not just when it's your birthday or if you think you see a ship on the horizon. When the flares are spent, they are gone, so when the right ship does come close enough, make sure there are flares left!

- **Be patient but time proactivity to market conditions** – Be ready to be more proactive if, and when, the market shows any signs of an uptick when more interested parties are likely to have the appetite and ability to do deals. It's difficult to just market deals by email, on a phone and behind a screen in the office. Pro-activity including progressive travel on marketing trips to the key events and conferences may add to the project marketing expense, but if done correctly and at the right time, led and in league with the specialist advisor through a close collaboration, it is is always worth the modest incremental cost. Targeted company road-shows can also pay dividends if done properly and at the right time, as they did in the African project outlined above.

The reasons for failure: Poor and untimely planning and preparation

The reasons for failure, even when collaboration is sought, should also be summarized:

- **Unrealistic timeline** – Not starting early enough and enabling patience for the appropriate market conditions.

- **Not seeking any specialist third party help** – After a very small targeted initial internal effort, which can also soil the wider market, if and when third party help is sought, which it is often much later than it should have been.

- **Choosing an inappropriate agent** – One that simply does not have the marketing skills.

- **Trying to save money** – and expecting the agent to work for nothing which is a completely disincentivizing, let alone not conducive to commitment. Why should the specialist agent with the right skills make the expertise available and effectively 'pay' to work for the client? The upfront fees should cover back costs and expenses, so the profit is the success fee.

- **Not checking third party track record and credentials** – Many simply do not have the contact network to ensure maximum marketing exposure. Do not expect the agent to let the client have a copy of his contacts but do ask which conferences they attend globally, exhibit and even present at. These are an essential part of keeping contacts and key networks current so the right people can be effectively contacted.

The facts about project marketing failure

As a final note, it must equally be recognized that over the last 18+ years, the independent farm-out statistics from JSI Services Limited show that from some 3,500 or more+ deals tracked during that time, only one in three opportunities was in fact successfully farmed out. This is perhaps not surprising, bearing in mind the inherent risks involved in the E&P business and in particular the exploration sector. This is highlighted by the fact that out of all the farm-outs tracked by JSI that have been drilled, only 15 per cent have been announced as successful discoveries.

The fact that 66 per cent of projects marketed over nearly two decades have not found a buyer or farm-outs further supports the significant benefits of third party collaboration, which should not only cost less for specialist help than is usually available internally but also should be a serious consideration for collaboration. Given that a farm-out has a 70 per cent – 80 per cent chance of failure (which could be the subject of its own chapter), why would a company not want to spend less on reducing failure to 60 per cent to increase the chance of success up to 40 per cent, based on then average success of the few top specialist A&D advisors that E&P companies can collaborate with?

The incentives to the agent are of course the larger success fees, which is in some instances where projects take longer than the seller usually anticipates probably still cost less than a longer internally driven effort. Outsourcing can simply ensure it costs less if the project does not succeed or fails in attracting a partner due to technical merit, high risk, value, politics or a lower oil price market. In the end, projects which have had the right interested party peer group review but which do not get farmed out statistically have half the chance of being declared a discovery.

PART THREE

Case studies of exemplar collaborative practice in play or evolving

Case study 5   11

Humanitarian relief – Food for the Hungry: daring to be different through collaborative innovation

An exemplar of ongoing collaborative practice in the third sector concerning food aid delivery to vulnerable populations

In this case study we review food aid delivery to a vulnerable population in the Democratic Republic of the Congo (DRC) by the humanitarian relief organization Food for the Hungry, who dared to be different through collaborative innovation in their supply chain management.

Background

By means of some background to this third (humanitarian) sector case study, before we get to the collaborative practices that are being used in the DRC it should be noted that these practices are very much a work in progress, and accordingly it is necessary to give a detailed overview of the socio-political-economic landscape within which the organization Food for the Hungry has to try to operate.

The DRC is the second largest country in Africa with an estimated population in the region of 79 million. The country has an estimated $24 trillion worth of untapped mineral reserves, and contains the Congo River, Africa's second largest river, that, if fully harnessed, could supply hydroelectric power to the whole of Africa.

Yet despite all this potential richness, the DRC is a country of missed opportunities. The DRC has been plagued with conflicts and poor governance and faces significant humanitarian challenges. Up to 2.7 million people have been internally displaced due to the continuous armed conflict and ethnic tensions in the east. Low agricultural production and underdeveloped food systems have contributed to food insecurity, with high rates of malnutrition, despite the country's enormous agricultural potential. In 2011 the DRC was ranked the hungriest country in the world and is currently ranked 176 out of 188 countries on the 2015 Human Development Index.

According to the World Bank, the DRC faces possibly the most daunting infrastructure challenge on the African continent. Conflict has seriously damaged most infrastructure networks. Vast geography, low population density, extensive forestlands, and a myriad of 'criss-crossing' rivers complicate the development of new networks. Notwithstanding all of this, some positive progress has been made since the return of peace in 2003. A privately funded GSM network now provides mobile telephone signals to two-thirds of the population. External funding has been secured to rebuild the country's road network, and domestic air traffic has grown. Modest investments could harness inland waterways for low-cost transport. Much more substantial investments in hydropower would enable the DRC to meet its own energy demands cheaply while exporting vast quantities of power. One of the country's most immediate infrastructure challenges is to reform the national power utility and increase power generation and delivery. Capacity needed to increase by 35 per cent over the period 2006–15 to meet domestic demand. The dilapidated condition of both road and rail infrastructure presents another challenge.

Ground transportation and rail needs

The DRC's rail network is of primary importance for shipping mineral commodities out of the DRC to ports in east, west and southern Africa but also to delivering aid in the most impoverished populations living in the most remote villages.

The DRC's road network has fallen into serious disrepair as a result of its extended period of conflict. Sealed roads comprise a mere 3,000 km of the country's total 30,000 km road network. It is estimated that just 42 per cent of the country's roads are in a condition good enough to support freight transport. The World Bank estimates that repairs and maintenance on the DRC's existing road networks will require roughly US$400 million per year.

Ground transport in the DRC has always been difficult. The terrain and climate of the Congo Basin present serious barriers to road and rail construction, and the distances are enormous across this vast country.

Furthermore, chronic economic mismanagement and internal conflict have led to serious under-investment over many years. On the other hand, the DRC has thousands of kilometres of navigable waterways, and traditionally water transport has been the dominant means of moving around approximately two-thirds of the country. During the rainy season, the roads become impassable, making it more complicated to transport commodities from the main warehouses to final distribution points. With the prevailing political situation in the DRC, the Government's efforts are not focused on the infrastructure, but rather on things such as upcoming elections. This means that humanitarian food aid delivery is very complex and there has been a groundswell push for innovative ways of collaborating with different parties, to overcome the problem.

Humanitarian air services are provided by the United Nations (UN), HAS, MONUSCO and ECHO, with flights only for humanitarian staff. Small cargoes can go through this service but not more than 2MT can be taken by air as all the available flights are mostly passengers' flights and small helicopters for MONUSCO.

Governance, compliance and judicial challenges

Corruption and crime in the DRC are high. The DRC is part of the Office of Federal Assets Control and the non-governmental organizations (NGOs) importing goods are mostly exempted, but the exemption process takes around 3 to 12 months to be obtained. This causes delays in commodities delivery and also monetary losses on commodities and demurrage fees.

The Standard Bureau of Control (Office de Control du Congo: OCC) is in charge of controlling the quality before the commodities can be released from the outbound warehouses at the customs point. This service has also been exempted by the Government, and a general exemption has been obtained by Food for the Hungry, but the OCC subsequently cancelled the latter exemption of 2 per cent of the Central Communities Investment Fund (CIF) value to be paid as control fees. This poses a huge handicap for humanitarian aid delivery across all the territories throughout the DRC. A further challenge is that the judiciary system is not as effective as it could be, and Food of the Hungry in the DRC has lost many cases where the transporters or vendors fail to deliver, and when taken to court they cannot be traced throughout the DRC, so there is a lack of transporters and vendors being held to account.

As the level of corruption in the region is high, customer or employer versus supplier or employee matters are mostly resolved in favour of the customer or employer. Notwithstanding this, humanitarian organizations face many legal issues and unsolicited intimidatory actions. Food for the Hungry is no exception, with many issues being procurement or supply chain related. As mentioned, most of such cases are resolved through the courts; however, often the court findings cannot be enforced such that recompense or compensation is forthcoming.

The humanitarian needs situation in the DRC

Humanitarian needs caused by conflict in the DRC have doubled over the last year, the UN Security Council said. According to the UN's Under-Secretary-General, 13 million people are affected by internal conflict gripping the country and require humanitarian aid. More than 4.6 million children are acutely malnourished, including 2.2 million suffering from severe acute malnutrition. Aid organizations in the DRC, among them Food for the Hungry, a US-based Christian non-profit and non-governmental organization founded in 1971, has been providing assistance, with the funding of the US Government through its Agency for International Development (USAID). As can be seen, the organization operates in an exceptionally complex and challenging environment.

Additionally, lack of adequate security has hindered humanitarian partners' ability to reach more than one million people in a single three-month period alone, and limited logistical infrastructure, vast swaths of wilderness, and administrative impediments add further layers of complexity.

Despite these many challenges, humanitarian partners delivered life-saving assistance and protection to close to three million people in 2017. This was still far from the 7.4 million people targeted by the humanitarian response plan. However, funding levels have dropped significantly over the past decade, leaving a significant shortfall against the required $812 million.

Food for the Hungry has been delivering food aid to vulnerable populations both to alleviate immediate food needs in the short term using the method of 'general food distribution' and as food aid for development through its 'food for work and cash for work' approaches. The latter of these two approaches helps particularly with agricultural activities such as drainage, community seeds multiplication centres, feeder roads, or tree planting for preserving biodiversity and natural resources. Food for the Hungry, with the help of USAID funding, is implementing a food security programme (Development Food Security Activities) and is planning to distribute 5,000 MT of food commodities to targeted population in South Kivu, in the territories of Walungu and Kaziba and in the Tanganyika Province in the Territory of Kalemie and Moba.

Collaborative partnering for commodities planning, forecasting and funding

Food for the Hungry has taken the decision to work in collaborative partnership with USAID by embracing the concept of joined up collaborative thinking with the funding organization to better prepare and submit proposals along with the annual estimates of requirements and line of sight of what's in pipeline. Partner selection, internal assessment, working together, sharing knowledge and staying together have all been important for Food for the Hungry in terms of its relationship with USAID.

Coincidentally, these are some of the features advocated in the 8-Stage Life Cycle Model of ISO 44001 (Figure 11.1), albeit that Food for the Hungry had found itself embracing these common-sense principles even before ISO 4400 was launched – so it follows that a degree of common sense has prevailed.

This is a more collaborative approach than has historically been used by humanitarian organizations and it carries the advantage of helping USAID to plan with greater certainty and to ensure they have enough time for sourcing the commodities from farmers and/or from their prepositioned stocks. This brings mutual benefit and is a more effective and efficient way of working. To provide the reader with some awareness of the detail involved in such practices, albeit at a high level, we shall examine ration composition, the commodity management internal cycle, and the commodities order and procurement.

- Ration composition – By means of an indication for the reader, the typical ration for a household of six people for a period of 21 days per month is a total average of 2,168 kcal (Figure 11.2).

- Commodity management internal cycle – In terms of the internal cycle for Food for the Hungry to commodity manage, Figure 11.3 depicts the main areas of activity.

- Commodities order and placement – In terms of how the order and placement process works, after the award has been approved, Food for the Hungry places a sales order at USAID to procure the requested quantities of commodities, through a call forward. The USDA will procure and ship the commodities from the USA or from prepositioned stocks to the port of Dar es Salaam in Tanzania with the mission expediter: shipping from the US/South Africa to Dar es Salaam.

Figure 11.1   CRAFT 8 stage life cycle model incorporated with ISO 44001

SOURCE Courtesy of Midas Projects Ltd in conjunction with the Institute for Collaborative Working

Figure 11.2   Indicative daily and monthly rationing

Food component	Corn meal	Green peas	Vegetable oil
Daily ration (g)	400g	120g	30g
Monthly ration per HH (kg)	50	16	3.7
Kcal	1480	265	422

SOURCE Courtesy of Food for the Hungry

Figure 11.3 Commodities management internal cycle – main areas of activity

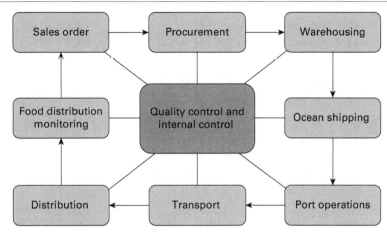

SOURCE Courtesy of Food for the Hungry

Additional collaboration at the level of inland transportation: Daring to be different

To be able get the commodities into the DRC, Food for the Hungry 'dared to be different' from the normal practice adopted by other humanitarian organizations. A decision was taken to enter into an outsource partnership with a third party who offered enhanced expertise to manage transportation and forwarding activities at the port of Dar es Salaam. Additionally, a further decision was taken to commission an independent surveyor to ensure that the commodities were fit to be loaded and met all other mandatory and specified quality standards at the ports of Dar es Salaam and Kigoma. This embraces the 'continuous improvement process' sub-component of the ISO 44001 life cycle model exhibited in Figure 11.1 and is a further example of common-sense collaborative practice in play, placing activities and risk management where it is best handled. Such outsourcing and daring to be different requires a degree of courage as it involves trusting a third party and being prepared to give up control. Trust is another key facet of collaboration.

Magellan Logistics of Tanzania now handles the transportation of over-sized and heavy items or shipments that consist of complex components that must be disassembled, shipped and then re-assembled. Additionally, it offered project cargo manage activities for engineering, procurement and construction which extended to include servicing energy, mining, chemical, petrochemical, pipeline, infrastructure and other sectors with regard to humanitarian commodities cargo which require strict compliance with very specific regulations and requirements.

Due to the specific regulations surrounding the shipping and transport of USAID Commodities, Food for the Hungry, after signing the contract with Magellan, engaged in a series of meetings for proactive planning purposes and to ensure complete alignment amongst all parties such that there was a common understanding of the objectives of the food aid programme and joined up accountabilities in terms of risk/reward shared by the parties to the collaborative arrangement.

One such example of this is the process when commodities are damaged or lost. Under such circumstances, Magellan was charged the value of the commodities, but on the programme side, the number of beneficiaries was reduced, and USAID would not replace the commodities, meaning that Food for the Hungry would have to ultimately pay back the value to the US Government. This type of provision helps to instil a vested interest in all parties involved but also to strive jointly towards a common goal – not just to deliver food to the vulnerable population but also to engender trust in a new contractual relationship, which will hopefully flourish over the longer term.

The decision to outsource and partner was a crucial one for Food for the Hungry and one that involved a degree of due diligence in advance. Indeed, it would be would be difficult for Food for the Hungry to re-advertise and select a replacement third party provider, if ever it is not able to comply, because the commodities would have been already delivered to Dar es Salaam and there would be a corresponding risk of being charged demur-rages fees, that, coupled with heat and frequent unhealthy local climate conditions, would be likely to cause infestation problems. The risk of heavy losses of commodities in such situations is high, especially regarding corn meal, which is very sensitive to infestation. This alone reinforces the decision quality of Food for the Hungry to recruit an independent surveyor consul-tancy at the ports of Dar es Salaam and Kigoma, thereby ensuring quality and strict compliance with all mandatory regulations and law.

Port operations coordination meetings for monitoring progress and measurement

A further consideration for Food for the Hungry in terms of collaborative practice was to ensure frequent regular coordination meetings for monitor-ing progress and measurement. This is a further example of a sub-component of the 8 Stage Life Cycle Model ISO 44001 being adopted by default.

Food for the Hungry organizes port coordination meetings initially with the Magellan team that will be allocated to each specific operation. The commodity manager in the DRC and the regional commodity manager travel to Dar es Salaam and Kigoma to not only coordinate those operations but also to assess the capacity of Magellan and the independent surveyor to execute the given tasks. So, there is a built-in check in the process.

This coordination meeting with Magellan personnel ranges from ensuring alignment with the pertinent regulations to discussing the many common issues related to the clearance and forwarding of USAID food commodities, essentially practising excellent communications and jointly solving problems and challenges that lie ahead. To put this into context, normally these meetings take one full week as they involve travel to KIGOMA port where commodities are transiting to Tanganyika Province (Kalemie and Moba territories) across a very large area of water (Lake Tanganyika).

By means of an example of a typical agenda for a post-operations meeting, the main focus will be on compliance with regard to the reporting requirements of Food for the Hungry and the funding donor USAID, the review and approval of the information required and the documentation that will support or accompany each shipment to destination.

The losses and liabilities for loss or damage or improper distribution of commodities are strictly regulated. Regulation 211.9 specifies the conditions and the guidelines to follow when a loss occurs and lays out and reinforces the responsibilities that come hand-in-hand with loss and damage. This is crucially important, because regular occurrences of such commodity losses can result in the whole programme being suspended, and Food for the Hungry must pay back the value of the lost commodities to the US Government. This is in no one's interest, and is far from being a win–win situation, which of course lies at the heart of collaboration. So essentially the regulation introduces healthy tension to ensure that all parties go forward with the same purpose and objective in mind to avoid non-compliance.

It is important to stress that such non-compliance affects not only Food for the Hungry in DRC, but Food for the Hungry as a wider global organization and has the potential to result in Food for the Hungry not being able to access funding from the US Government on a wide scale. Hence it is imperative for all the parties to work together to jointly mitigate and manage the risks that can result in loss or damage of commodities. Planning is the key to this.

It is paramount that operations ensure that any commodities that are damaged or unfit for human consumption are identified early and interventions made in time to prevent loss of human life. The highest standards of environmental and human protection policies must be adhered to. This is a crucial part of the process to mitigate and prevent such risks by clearly cascading policy expectations across all parties involved in delivering aid into the DRC, regardless whether it's the contractor or the transporter or independent surveyor working in collaboration. Everyone has a shared responsibility in this regard.

Food for the Hungry also practises 'lessons learned' (another key facet of collaboration and ISO 44001). The organization regularly undertakes deep dive reviews of where things have not gone particularly well with previous historical operations. During the joint meetings with partners, Food for the Hungry DRC representatives go through a list of things that can help or bring about continuous improvements to reduce and manage the risk of infestation in the warehouses and thereby help minimize losses.

Examples of risk mitigation strategies discussed during the collaborative coordination meetings are:

- transporting commodities with other non-commodities items;
- offloading when it's raining;
- carelessly unloading or loading the corn meal bags (these are soft paper bags and are easily damaged);
- ensuring the damaged commodities are kept separately from intact ones to avoid the risk of contaminating the whole batch or truck;
- checking to ensure there is no infestation in the commodities and fumigating before loading to destination to avoid more infestations along the way.

After the meeting with the Magellan team, the independent surveyor is also invited to a joint coordination meeting. This meeting with the independent surveyor is to ensure there is smooth collaboration between all the parties.

Information is needed for reports to be submitted to the United States Department of Agriculture regarding any issue that has arisen from the survey of commodities from the marine shipping (missionary expediters) and handling at the port level. These losses are qualified as marine losses and are the responsibility of missionary expediters. Also, the working hours or schedule between the various parties must be harmonized.

Missionary expediters will hand over the commodities at the port of Dar es Salaam after inspection and overseeing the loading and unloading. This helps to establish responsibilities between the marine losses and inland transportation losses. Marine losses are charged to mission expeditors and inland losses are charged at Magellan until handover of commodities to Food for the Hungry at the warehouse in DRC.

Collaboration in warehousing

Historically, DRC has had poor infrastructure, and most NGOs compete for scarce storage space. Apart from the prices being very high because of the scarcity of facilities, the existing warehouses are also very old buildings in a state of disrepair and there are very few good facilities to cope with the overall demand throughout the country. Most of the larger warehouses are owned by the Customs Department, the Breweries Brasserie, the ONC (Office National du Café) in Bukavu and some private business concerns in Kalemie and Moba. Both NGOs and private companies compete for those scarce facilities and resources, with the non-profit organizations struggling to offer better terms than the large private entities can.

DRC also has the challenge of having warehouses located in residential areas that might bring a risk to the wider population when there are fumigation activities being carried out on the commodities being stored. The commodities are fumigated with phosphine gas, which is dangerous. Because of this, USAID lays down strict regulations and procedures to follow and requires a pest management plan that includes both preventive measures and mitigation measures to only fumigate a maximum two times before the commodities are permitted to leave the warehouses.

USAID does not allow NGOs to perform fumigation as they are not ISO licensed to do so in the DRC. Food for the Hungry, then, will hire a third party who will render that service.

Food for the Hungry ensures that all staff who work in the warehouse are trained not on how to do the fumigation, but on integrated pest management practices and techniques before reaching a stage where the fumigation is unavoidable.

Collaboration in commodity distribution

Food for the Hungry has also taken the decision to enter into a collaborative outsourced partnership for 'in-country' transportation services for the transiting of the commodities from the main warehouses to final distribution points.

The commodities distribution in this programme is conditioned by the activities that have been realized in the communities. Most of the activities are agricultural, where the Department of Food Security and Livelihoods will, in collaboration with commodities field monitors, identify or recruit local unskilled labour for the activities of drainage and irrigation, and rehabilitation of feeder roads. This allows greater accessibility to the markets and enhanced communication, and the market linkages thereby ensure that other socio-economic activities are not jeopardized.

The final distribution points will be in very remotes areas where these activities are taking place.

Food for the Hungry, through its programme of food for work, partners with the community to drain and irrigate swamps for improved access to food and rehabilitation of feeder roads to allow the trucks to carry the food commodities but also to help the population in their daily routine movement and access to the markets where they can eventually sell their products from the drained and irrigated swamps or community or individual farms.

The same method of collaboration between Food for the Hungry and the transporters is also required. However, due to poor connectivity, sometimes the transporters are not reachable and are travelling very long distances ranging up to 350 miles. The rate is calculated at 1km per metric ton.

Requirements for food commodities transportation must be respected both by international companies and local companies. However, there are few trucks that do meet those requirements, and it can be very difficult to get enough well-maintained trucks due to lack of garages and proper fuelling stations in the remote areas. The logistics are fraught with many problems.

Despite all these challenges, with proper joined up collaborative thinking and coordination, the commodities are being delivered to the hardest, toughest locations to reach to the most vulnerable populations. This is truly an amazing achievement by all those concerned.

The same measures apply when the transporters incur losses along the way, as the responsibilities are handed over to them until they have offloaded and have received delivery notes duly signed by the Food for the Hungry representatives and the members of committees representing the communities.

The communities also play their part and will contribute by offloading the trucks at the final distribution points and at the same time play an important role in safeguarding the commodities from theft during offloading and during the distribution.

This more collaborative approach has already reaped reward and is now regarded as a better way of dealing with complex situations in the context of the DRC. It should be noted that requests for exemption are required where Food for the Hungry will only provide information regarding the shipment and Magellan, through its clearing agent in DRC, will process the request for an exemption certificate as it has local clearing agents who are very knowledgeable about the local systems and practices.

One of the biggest challenges that has been overcome relates to situations where trucks are detained as the request of the agency of quality control.

Sometimes different government agencies interpret the quality assurance texts differently depending on the province or the ministry concerned. The process to get the trucks released from the customs bonded warehouses requires the Office of Control to perform quality checks and provide a report.

Sometimes relationships with these agencies can be strained because of the personalities involved, and negotiations can take length periods to conclude. OCC sometimes seeks to charge 2 per cent CIF value for quality control, yet this cost is exempted for non-profit organizations. The collaboration relationship that Food for the Hungry has developed with the Government has helped to solve this issue as the Government is aware of the overall humanitarian objective and the plans to be executed in the province that benefit the vulnerable population.

Usually, the trucks are released on the strength of a letter from the governor, who understands that Food for the Hungry, being a non-profit organization, is not obliged to pay taxes and other fees for humanitarian aid that will be directly distributed for direct consumption to the vulnerable needy population of the province.

Additionally, Food for the Hungry, being a non-profit organization and importing food commodities and gifts in kind of deworming medicines and Vitamin A supplement for children, faces a lot of challenges. One example is that of keeping the medicines in bonded warehouses, as the OCC and the Customs Office are permitted to tax those donations, yet they are not for exchange or sale, resulting in higher storage fees, and parking fees having to be paid for times when trucks are detained. There are also reimbursable time charges levied by the transporter.

Under normal circumstances, truck owners provide Food for the Hungry with a three-day period of grace to be able to clear. However, sometimes it can be many weeks, even months, before the shipments are released, leaving Food for Hungry exposed. Attempts to resolve this and reach a palatable compromise are ongoing.

Conclusion

Road infrastructure conditions make it difficult, sometimes impossible, for Food for the Hungry to reach some populations in the very remote areas of DRC, especially during rainy seasons. However, hunger knows no season.

Improved roads and maintenance of the existing roads and an improved rail system would significantly reduce transportation costs for the resources sector and vastly increase general transport efficiency for the entire country, taking trucks off the road system but also significantly contributing to better supply chain services in delivering aid to the most vulnerable. Transportation cost are very high for humanitarian organizations and the cost of maintaining the fleet in the DRC is also very high.

Food for the Hungry is an organization that constantly looks in the mirror to learn lessons while striving for continuous improvement. For example, historical contractual relationships meant that commodities would only be handed over to Food for the Hungry at the discharge port. This resulted in exposure to significant demurrage and detention costs due to lengthy clearance processes coupled with misunderstandings in terms of who bear the costs of such demurrage and detention. This practice was changed under the collaborative outsourced partner arrangement with Magellan, who now takes care of the whole process to deliver door-to-door. As Magellan is based in Tanzania, it also hires a local clearing and forwarding agent to perform the clearance in DRC and deliver the commodities to Food for the Hungry warehouses. Food for the Hungry DRC provides the letter of exemption to Trade Services, who in turn apply to the Department of Customs in Kinshasa because Food for the Hungry does not have permanent staff placed there to follow up on such matters. The while process is streamlined and far more efficient with this new working arrangement.

Finally, it is important in this case study to recognize that information sharing, and effective reliable communication had an important part to play with the revised collaborative working practices now being adopted by Food for the Hungry. In the past, Food for the Hungry operated in a suboptimal fashion because the organization did not know at any point in time exactly how far the delivery trucks or the boats had gone to get the food to vulnerable populations in outlying regions. So jointly with its partners, Food for the Hungry developed a daily tracking sheet, where the information on loading, offloading, clearance, the truck numbers or vessel names, drivers' and captains' names and contacts details are shared daily to all parties and in a dynamic real-time way through enhanced transmission technology that the organization has invested in.

So, in a nutshell, all the key parties have the same information, at the same time and this has helped immensely to solve problems and issues as they arise and in a far more collaborative way than in the past. The value proposition for all concerned is that it helps everyone to plan better, getting ready for delivery receipts, storage, handling, offloading and to anticipate any issues that can arise along the way until the cargo is eventually delivered.

Historically, communication has been suboptimal and there has been lack of clear understanding of what common cause everyone was working towards. For example, once the contract was signed, the transporter would just ensure he delivered the cargo with maybe two or three days' notification. Whatever happened along the way, Food for the Hungry, would not know. Food for the Hungry would be waiting at the delivery point, which would be the first opportunity to find out about problems or issues, by which time it would, of course, have been too late to do anything about it. The transporter would be charged the losses and Food for the Hungry DRC would lose out on the target beneficiaries to be reached. But if the problems and challenges had been collaboratively discussed and resolved along the way, the losses and damages may well have been avoided through mitigating measures. Proper supply chain joint planning, coordination and collaborative information sharing has the potential to improve significantly on aid delivery in the DRC.

Case study 6   12
The Oil and Gas Technology Centre

A dynamic, evolving Government-sponsored collaborative partnership to facilitate technology innovation in the UK upstream oil and gas industry

In this chapter we give the reader a snapshot of a dynamic, evolving, collaborative partnership between industry, Government and academia.

The Oil & Gas Technology Centre (OGTC) was formed in 2017 to help unlock the full potential of the UK North Sea, anchor the supply chain in the north east of Scotland and create a culture of innovation to attract industry and academia to the region. This case study is a fascinating insight into the early workings and delivery successes of the OGTC and also its collaborative interactions with industry, academia and other key stakeholders. The manner in which the OGTC facilitates joined up collaborative thinking and also encourages technology innovation and research in the UK upstream oil and gas sector is already an exemplar of an organization that embraces contemporary collaborative principles and working relationships.

We're experiencing one of the most dramatic, technology-led revolutions that the world has seen and, at the same time, a fundamental energy transition is underway in the UK and globally. For all these reasons, the decision quality around the formation of the OGTC was spot on and all those involved are to be applauded.

Background history to the formation of the OGTC

By means of some background to set the scene, the OGTC was launched in February 2017 as a not-for-profit research and knowledge company, with the aim of becoming the go-to technology centre for the oil and gas industry in the UK and globally.

The OGTC secured £180 million worth of funding from the UK and Scottish Governments, through the Aberdeen City Region Deal, and it inspires and accelerates innovation, co-investing in industry-led projects to take new technologies from concept through to deployment in the oil field. Its goals are to unlock the full potential of the UK North Sea, anchor the supply chain in north east Scotland, and create a culture of innovation that attracts industry and academia to the region.

The year 2017 was one of continued change in the global oil and gas industry, with companies focused on increasing efficiency, reducing costs and improving performance. It was therefore the right time to establish the OGTC to work in partnership with industry to inspire, accelerate and co-fund technologies to drive competitiveness and productivity on the United Kingdom Continental Shelf (UKCS). Strong partnerships are now being created that bring together companies of all sizes to deliver solutions. This has the positive effect of encouraging determination, resilience and, more importantly, a willingness to collaborate.

There is an underpinning sense of need to keep working closely together, being brave about technology and acting as true pioneers. Ultimately, under such circumstances, everyone can be winners and real strides can be made toward transforming the industry through innovative technology, thereby ensuring the UKCS and the north east of Scotland are globally recognized as a thriving technology hub.

Creating value: The OGTC'S first year – one of tangible delivery

The OGTC's first year has seen great progress, identifying hundreds of innovative technologies and co-investing £37 million in more than 70 projects with industry to develop and deploy new technologies. The support of the UK and Scottish Governments, the Oil & Gas Authority, local councils and universities is an excellent example of collaboration and support, as has been the strong involvement of the industry. Figure 12.1 highlights the extent of co-investment in industry-led projects and field trials aimed at creating value.

As can be seen, 10 field trials were approved, identifying, for example, how non-intrusive inspection techniques could deliver annual savings of £244 million and a new thermite well plugging and abandonment solution that could save the industry £100 million each year. Additionally, the OGTC's 'calls for ideas' programme generated more than 180 new technology ideas from inside and outside the oil and gas industry, which helped build strong connections across the UK innovation ecosystem.

Figure 12.1 OGTC year 1 examples of delivery and progress

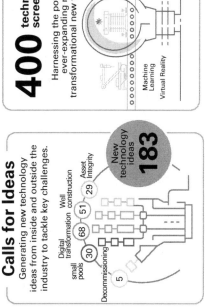

Calls for Ideas
Generating new technology ideas from inside and outside the industry to tackle key challenges.

Digital transformation — small pools **30**
Decommissioning **5**
68
Well construction **51**
Asset Integrity **29**

183 New technology ideas

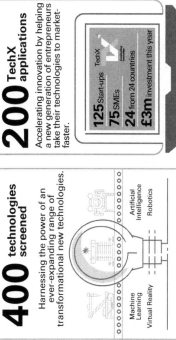

400 technologies screened
Harnessing the power of an ever-expanding range of transformational new technologies.

Machine Learning
Virtual Reality
Artificial Intelligence
Robotics

200 TechX applications
Accelerating innovation by helping a new generation of entrepreneurs take their technologies to market faster.

125 Start-ups TechX
75 SMEs
24 from 24 countries
£3m investment this year

72 projects in total
Delivering technology project to fix today, maximise recovery and transform tomorrow.

Asset Integrity **23**
Small pools **21**
Well Construction **19**
Digital Transformation **7**
Decommissioning **2**

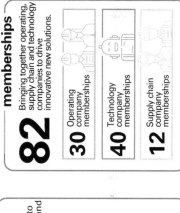

82 memberships
Bringing together operating, supply chain and technology companies to drive innovative new solutions.

30 Operating company memberships
40 Technology company memberships
12 Supply chain company memberships

Government Industry Schools Community

5000 visitors
Creating a culture of innovation in the region through exciting events and workshops.

SOURCE Courtesy of OGTC

Furthermore, some 5,000 people visited the OGTC to take part in events and workshops during the first year and it also opened its innovation hub – a unique, collaborative space that acts as the focal point for activities with schools, colleges and universities. New centres of excellence in the north east of Scotland have also been established: in decommissioning in partnership with the University of Aberdeen; and in sub-sea engineering with the Robert Gordon University, Aberdeen.

Fundamentally, this is all about joined up collaborative re-thinking and re-imagining how the industry collectively produces oil and gas offshore and also embracing an ever-expanding spectrum of new technologies to help stakeholders do so.

Figure 12.2 highlights some of the OGTC year one examples of delivery and progress, which make for impressive reading.

A snapshot of some of the innovative ideas being worked by the OGTC

In terms of work in progress, the following are some of the innovative new ideas being progressed:

- **Field Trial Programme** – Working with technology developers and operating companies to trial new solutions will continue to be a priority in 2018. The OGTC already has more than 30 field trials planned for the year ahead and expect to add more to the programme. Proving new technologies in an operational environment is critical to future commercialization and deployment.

- **TechX accelerator launch** – In December 2017, the OGTC launched TechX, a unique technology accelerator and incubator focused on helping smaller, ambitious technology developers take their solutions into the oil and gas market – faster. There are three tailored programmes – Pioneer, Market Entry and Ventures –and they will help accelerate the future of 100 start-ups and 200 small and medium enterprises. Significant funding, with no equity or payback required, is available to Pioneer companies and also for Market Entry participants. TechX also provides unrivalled access to customers to help companies fast track a route to market. TechX has a strategic partner, BP Ventures, to assist with this, which offers an exclusive group of Pioneers further access to funding, as well as dedicated access to BP's facilities and expertise. The author of this book is a voluntary supply chain business mentor for TechX pioneer start-up companies under this programme.

Figure 12.2 OGTC co-investment in industry-led projects

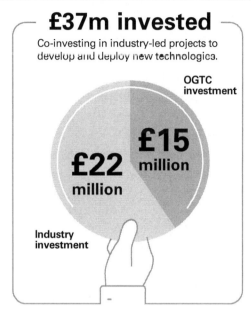

£37m invested

Co-investing in industry-led projects to develop and deploy new technologies.

OGTC investment

£15 million

£22 million

Industry investment

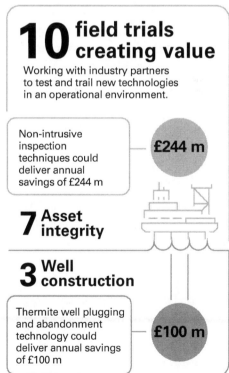

10 field trials creating value

Working with industry partners to test and trail new technologies in an operational environment.

Non-intrusive inspection techniques could deliver annual savings of £244 m

£244 m

7 Asset integrity

3 Well construction

Thermite well plugging and abandonment technology could deliver annual savings of £100 m

£100 m

SOURCE Courtesy of OGTC

- **Robotics: creating opportunity and ideas** – The OGTC facilitated and organized a series of workshops and tech talks at its innovation hub, all designed to accelerate the use of robotics offshore. A team of experts from the oil and gas and robotics industries took part and identified 15 potential solutions for the application of air-, land- and sea-based robotics in the offshore energy industry.

- **Innovative non-intrusive inspection trials create value** –The OGTC partnered with Total E&P UK to organize three early-stage non-intrusive inspection (NII) technology field trials, the results of which demonstrated the potential to deliver significant cost, safety and efficiency benefits compared with traditional intrusive methods. Edify Silvering, MISTRAS and Sonomatic deployed a range of ultrasonic corrosion mapping and time of flight diffraction solutions. Additionally, the OGTC's survey with engineering firm ABB found that adopting NII technology could deliver increased production and lower maintenance costs worth up to £244 million per year on the UKCS.

- **STEM programme** – The OGTC is encouraging more young people to get involved in science, technology, engineering and maths (STEM), which is essential to create a culture of innovation in north east Scotland. The OGTC works with schools, colleges, universities and other partners to deliver a STEM programme using its innovation hub to host events and workshops that inspire the next generation.

- **Transformational technology** – Demand is growing for technologies to help transform the oil and gas industry for the low carbon economy. The OGTC hopes to bring forward new projects in this area, working closely with other parts of the energy sector. At the same time, it is continuing to support the potential UK sector deal for offshore oil and gas in which transformational technology is a key element.

- **Digital transformation 'call for ideas'** –The OGTC's objective here is to tease out ideas on how to harness the power of big data and machine learning to unlock the remaining potential of the UKCS. The OGTC will invest in a portfolio of projects to assess more than 175,000 items of existing data, provided by the Oil & Gas Authority, Common Data Access and the Norwegian Petroleum Directorate, to identify remaining oil and gas reserves in mature fields.

Conclusion

By way of some concluding reflections on this case study, it is evident that great progress has been made to establish the Oil & Gas Technology Centre. Hundreds of initial exciting technologies have been identified and there has been co-investment in many exciting projects with industry partners to develop and deploy new technologies. Overall, there appears to have been a fantastic early response, ranging from SMEs to technology developers to oil majors, along with excellent support from the UK and Scottish Governments, the Oil & Gas Authority, local councils and regional partners. This is a great example of pan-industry collaboration in play.

At the time of publishing this book, we're experiencing one of the most dramatic, technology-led revolutions the world has ever seen, accordingly, we must be brave and seize the moment. The OGTC truly is an exemplar of an organization that embraces many of the principles advocated in the newly launched global standard for collaborative working and relationships (ISO 44001), discussed in the earlier chapters.

One final thought – the OGTC is dynamic, with new ideas around collaboration, research, technology development and knowledge sharing emerging and evolving all the time. This short case study is only a snapshot of good things in play; however, there will be much more to come. Accordingly, the reader may wish to consider regular access to the following links, to be appraised of or indeed contribute to the many new ideas and joint industry initiatives. This extends to include mentoring opportunities through the OGTC and also best practice and lessons learned from the sectors.

Useful links

https://theogtc.com/
https://twitter.com/theogtc
https://www.linkedin.com/company/the-oil-and-gas-technology-centre/
https://theogtc.com/events/

Case study 7   13

All together now – improvements in collaboration in the pharmaceutical and biomedical life science sectors

An insight into the ongoing collaborative 'supply by design for the 21st century' initiative – development of 'good supply practices' in the sector

Historically, pharmaceutical and biomedical life science companies have not tended to embrace collaborative working practices, compared with other industry sectors. However, times are changing and many procurement and supply chain practitioners along with scientists, researchers and academics who work in or alongside the sector now view collaboration as their new 'mantra'.

With the constant emergence of new technology, both for patients and medical/research staff, coupled with the fact that diseases and ailments are becoming more complex, the sector needs to adapt in a far greater way than before. Collaboration is the key to unlocking greater innovation and more effective patient treatments and solutions. This philosophy extends to include different, more joined up collaborative ways of working for the supply chain upon which the industry sector relies.

Many countries have significant assets in terms of health service provision for patients and communities, research universities, large medical charities, pharmaceutical companies and clusters of small to medium sized companies. Such assets have the potential to deliver more by being better-connected. Collaboration allows a better use of resources and improves the capacity for creativity and innovation.

Encompassing pharmaceutical technology, medical technology and medical biotechnology, what we see is a 'high-tech' and highly innovative sector, closely linked to the research excellence of universities. The sector is undergoing a paradigm shift, transitioning from traditional large research and development facilities to more external collaborations, joint ventures and partnerships. Pharmaceutical companies are beginning to change their research and development strategies to new, more outsourced models with greater reliance on specialist supply chains. Additionally, scientific infrastructure is constantly improving, creating opportunities for all stakeholders in the sector to raise their game by building better connections between the assets that are already there and across related supply chains.

This case study is provided courtesy of Dr Marla Phillips, Director, Xavier Health, Xavier University, Cincinnati, Ohio. She is a leader of pharmaceutical and medical device industry initiatives who has a passion for driving industry change.

The case study seeks to explore an exemplar of an evolving initiative within the sector that embraces the very collaborative principles that the sector is moving toward. It focuses on 'supply by design' for the 21st century – the development of good supply practices with an underpinning theme of 'every person, every product, every time'. Additionally, the author captures his own reflections on areas for the pharma/biotech sector that could be improved through further collaboration.

Background, reach and impact of initiative

By means of some initial background, good supply practices are being developed by the USA's Food and Drug Administration (FDA) officials in conjunction with industry professionals across the life sciences industry (pharmaceutical/biotech and medical devices) through a methodical 'supply by design' process that increases the reliability of incoming supply, and therefore reduces the risk to finished product quality, patient safety and business success. This impact has been achieved by determining the source of dysfunction affecting the integrity of supply and implementing sustainable solutions that can be tied to return on investment – such as increased safety, improved quality and enhanced reliability – commensurate with the need.

Perceived forward challenges and formation of a joint industry team

Concerns have been expressed by cross-sector stakeholders for many years regarding not being able to reliably and consistently ensure the supply of incoming materials used in products that are crucial to support and serve the life science arena. As a consequence, because of these concerns, Xavier University formed a pan-industry team comprising FDA officials and a variety of industry practitioners and professionals to investigate root causes and develop meaningful and impactful solutions using the define, measure, analyse, design, verify (DMADV) process.

The composition of that joint industry team included representatives from discipline areas such as: pharmaceutical technology, quality assurance, governance and compliance, life science manufacturers, marketing and business development, supply chain and procurement, strategic global sourcing, microbiology delivery, small molecule operations, research universities risk management, contract manufacturing and product management, security, regulatory affairs and health, safety and the environment.

Scope of work and boundaries

The scope of work and boundaries for the joint industry initiative focused on three principal areas:

1 Incoming material and contracted services procured to support the manufacture of the finished product.

2 The pharmaceutical/biotech and medical device industries.

3 The upstream and downstream supply chain.

Methodology

The methodology applied to capture critical early information for the feasibility study for the 'good supply practices' initiative involved issuing a self-qualification questionnaire to a broad representative sample from across the sector. All information collected was treated with the strictest of confidence such that the output could not be attributed to any one organization.

The self-qualification assessment comprised of the following five distinct sections, with responses resulting in a total score for each section and an overall score:

1 **Choose a finished product** – Respondents had to choose a finished product to assess themselves against. The ideal finished product would be one that fitted as many of the following criteria as possible:

    – on the market and experiencing post-market complaints;

    – on the market and experiencing challenges in production that result in failures, down time, or is requiring changes to the process;

    – a high-risk product from a criticality standpoint (Class III device, sterile, vaccine, etc);

    – one that the company does not have much expertise with (new process technology or equipment, challenging formulation or device design, new therapeutic area, etc).

The assessments were conducted from the standpoint of how well each respondent company is performing with key suppliers related to the chosen finished product.

2 **The assessment** – Respondents had to assess themselves against all questions in the self-qualification questionnaire, using a scoring mechanism.

3 **Mitigation feedback** – Feedback was requested on specific mitigation guidance provided for each section in the self-qualification document relative to the different possible scoring outcomes.

4 **Comparative analysis** – This was essentially a sensitivity check to detect differences in self-risk between two product assessments.

5 **Overall benefit** – Sharing of insights was requested from respondents with regard to what the self-qualification has provided to the organization in terms of insights into risk or potential risk to the product quality. In other words, what benefit did the respondent gain from the self-qualification?

The self-qualification questionnaire referred to in (2) above was based on the premise that prior data has shown that manufacturers in the sector contribute to the overall risk in the supply chain by:

• not understanding their own product and process well enough to be able to scientifically demonstrate what is needed for incoming and final product specifications;

• not having or not following comprehensive supply chain identification and management practices;

- not engaging the right internal and external stakeholders in the discussions at the right time.

The process developed then went on to assess the performance of the manufacturers in a way that could demonstrate the overall risk that is drilled down to individual finished products and suppliers. Specific sections were:

- How well do we understand our own product and process to begin with?
- How well do we engage our suppliers and jointly partner throughout the total product lifecycle to drive high-quality products, robust processes and effective relationships that are commensurate with the need?
- Are we following successful supply chain selection practices?
- Are we operating as good customers in a way that demonstrates respect for our suppliers?
- Do we have the internal resources and processes necessary to protect our business?

Results

It has been, and still is today, widely believed that the perceived lack of reliability of incoming material is based on the poor performance of suppliers and is therefore the basis of many supply chain management practices in the sector. In order to explore the root causes, the life science manufacturers within the joint industry team developed a comprehensive list of failure modes associated with the defined process flow shown in Figure 13.1.

Through the failure mode analysis work that was carried out, a major paradigm shift was recognized in that all of the failure modes were related to risk and vulnerabilities that were either induced by the manufacturers themselves or could have been avoided by the manufacturers. The failure modes were not solely related to the poor performance of suppliers, as

Figure 13.1   Supply chain process flow

SOURCE Courtesy of Dr Maria Phillips, Xavier Health

Figure 13.2   Major paradigm shift revealed through failure mode analysis

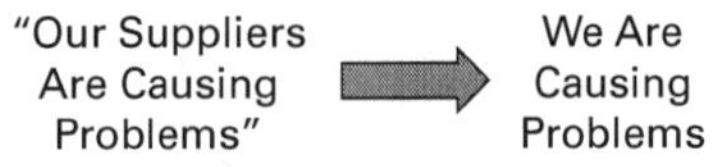

"Our Suppliers
Are Causing
Problems" ➡ We Are
Causing
Problems

SOURCE Courtesy of Dr Maria Phillips, Xavier Health

Figure 13.3   Gap analysis and results – current state versus Xavier approach

Current state	Xavier approach
Risk reduction focus on suppliers	Risk reduction focus on manufacturers
GxP suite: GMP, GCP, GLP, GIP, GDP	Missing: good supply practices (GSP)
Quality by design	Supply by design
Quality focus, risk reduction	Business minded, commensurate with the need, fit for intended purpose

SOURCE Courtesy of Dr Maria Phillips, Xavier Health

originally surmised (Figures 13.2 and 13.3 refers). This critical paradigm shift has enabled the life science industry to focus solutions on reducing risks caused by the manufacturers, and therefore actually reduce risk and vulnerability to the final product.

The identified failure modes were then incorporated into a 'cause and effect' matrix that each of the group participant manufacturers and FDA officials scored against six critical customer criteria. A survey was sent to 162 suppliers who supply the pharmaceutical, medical device, and food and drug industries. In every case, the suppliers corroborated the findings of the manufacturers and, importantly, did not identify an obvious failure missed by the manufacturers.

The direct impact of this paradigm shift is that it:

• shifts resources from trying to improve supplier performance to improving internal performance that affects the ability of the suppliers to perform well;

• enables industry to take ownership of the failure modes impacting supply chain integrity;

• enables industry to develop solutions that will reduce risk to product quality;

• enables global regulators to understand critical root causes to supply chain integrity and therefore product quality risk.

Identified areas of opportunity

A Pareto analysis of the resulting 'cause and effect' scores yielded a rank order of the failure modes in alignment with the critical criteria, and also enabled the team to identify high-level themes of failures present in the data – again, related to risks they themselves introduce into the supply chain management process. These were:

1 Lack of product and process knowledge and development.

2 Poor supply chain development and management.

3 Misaligned and conflicting internal behaviours.

We will reflect on each in turn.

Lack of product and process knowledge and development

The original assumption at the outset of this collaborative supply chain initiative was that suppliers cannot consistently supply what is needed. However, it was discovered through the research that manufacturers often do not know what specifications are actually needed, do not involve suppliers in development discussions at all or at the right time, do not explore the full expertise of suppliers, do not understand their own process well enough to know how the incoming material will impact their process, and do not ask about the process capability of their suppliers. So, this confirms that there is a behavioural and early engagement challenge.

Poor supply chain development and management

Many manufacturers have supplier selection and supplier approval processes in place, yet demands on speed to market often result in the circumvention of these processes. It was found that supply agreements often conflict with the requirements of other agreements and drive the wrong behaviours on both sides of the relationship. Additionally, although supplier qualification is not a new concept, it has been found that the elements of risk assessed are often not representative of key cross-functional requirements, and therefore do not provide a complete representation of risk or vulnerability.

Misaligned and conflicting internal behaviours

Throughout product, process and supply chain development, the data from the participant manufacturers revealed that a lack of internal involvement of cross-functional representatives consistently leads to a lack of alignment that results in increased risk. There is not a harmonized approach to understanding how to align internal objectives, involving the right groups at the right time, delineating roles and responsibilities, and knowing when and how to engage suppliers. There is a perception that manufacturers cannot share important information with their suppliers, and thus the lack of transparency hinders suppliers from being able to perform well for the manufacturers. Additionally, manufacturers historically conduct supplier qualifications to determine the risk level of their suppliers, but do not assess the risk they bring to the relationship, which does not allow them to avoid false starts, delayed timing, poor product performance and increased risk to product quality.

Key aspects of the good supply practices

Mindful of the aforementioned opportunity areas, the following were identified as the key aspects of the good supply practices:

- development of pragmatic (ie 'business smart') supply practices that establish best practices that can be implemented irrespective of company size;
- development of an 'alignment optimization' model for product and process development that guides purpose-driven cross-functional involvement, the goals of each stage to maximize alignment, what to measure to determine the success of each stage of development, who the decision makers are, and when to involve suppliers;
- establishment of a process for manufacturers to conduct a self-assessment to understand and ultimately mitigate risk they introduce into the product, process and supply chain development;
- establishment of key risk elements to assess during supplier qualification, including quality and business success factors;
- clarification for industry of what information truly is confidential, versus what opportunities there are for transparency with suppliers that will enable suppliers to better support the manufacturers;
- examples of how the life science industry can improve scheduling stability with suppliers so as to reduce opportunities for error that are introduced by the manufacturers;
- clear understanding of product, process and supply chain risks for both industry and regulatory authorities.

In terms of project duration for taking this comprehensive pan-industry initiative from concept inception through to successful conclusion of a pilot, it was considered that a five-year period was needed. Figure 13.4 highlights the key activity stages of the initiative throughout this timeframe.

Figure 13.4   Initiative timeframe and key activity stages

Year	Activity	Status
1	• Identify themes – areas of focus • Begin root cause Identification	√
2	• Root cause identification • Root cause verification – supplier focus groups/surveys • Benign solution development – expand team	√
3	• Solution development working teams	√
4	• Further solution development working teams • Solution review and approval – internal and external	√
5	• External review • Solution implementation/pilot	In progress

SOURCE Courtesy of Dr Maria Phillips, Xavier Health

Conclusion

Good supply practices, and the efforts of organizations such as Xavier Health, Xavier University in driving collaborative pan-industry initiatives like 'good supply practices' are to be applauded. Indeed, this is a further example of many of the component parts of the 8 Stage Life Cycle Model of ISO 44001 being applied in practice without those involved in that particular pan-industry initiative having specific knowledge of that new global standard. Yet, the natural collaborative behaviours being exhibited are evident.

Collaboration is key and is very relevant. Pharmaceutical and biotech organizations and the FDA appear to have 'grasped the nettle' and begun to embrace a more collaborative way of working to help overcome some of the challenges the industry is facing. The industry has recognized the expertise that is available, and this will have positive effects on everyone that works in it.

Whilst this case particular case study has predominantly focused on the supply chain that supports the sector and how things can be improved, there are many other obvious areas where the pharmaceutical, biomed and biotech sectors can improve, by the numerous interrelated stakeholders being more receptive to collaboration. For example, consider things such as:

• knowledge transfer partnerships;

• creating the right infrastructure;

• deploying electronic patient records to support research;

• sharing resources and services between institutions;

- opening up access to testing services;
- sharing research data as it is created;
- government reforming fiscal regimes to incentivize and encourage collaboration;
- developing more specialist research support;
- supporting people who move between sectors;
- structuring careers to enable working across boundaries;
- bringing an industry perspective into academia;
- creating organizational structures that support applied work and collaboration;
- getting the right processes in place;
- making university intellectual property policies more consistent to enable successful collaborations.

In terms of a final thought, at the outset the point was made that, traditionally, pharmaceutical, biotech and biomed companies, Government, FDA and the academic research organizations that are linked to the sector may not have embraced collaborative working. Notwithstanding this, however, the reality now is that collaboration has become a necessity for them and, as a consequence, we are likely to see it become more and more commonplace. With new technology for patients and medical staff, and with diseases are evolving to become more complex, the pharmaceutical, biomed and biotech sectors simply have to adapt through collaboration.

Case study 8   14

The emergence of digital procurement technology in the IT sector

A snapshot into the future on how to streamline procurement in the Information Technology (IT) sector with innovative marketplace technology developed through collaboration across different business streams. It is important that we begin to gain insight into SC 4 and future ways for working with technology given the onset of the fourth industrial revolution.

Digital transformation in the field of procurement and supply chain management is a new and emerging business or organizational concept. A confluence of trends – such as consumerization, the 'Cloud' and the ability to process and manage large data volumes – is having a huge impact on the way many organizations in the private, public and third sectors operate. Indeed, the scale of change is gathering pace.

This case study seeks to examine at a high level the recent development of a digital marketplace technology solution called 'Progora' that has the potential to be a game changer in terms of how organizations manage their procurement processes.

The technology offering evolved and developed out of the decision to merge two historical business entities and embrace collaboration with a third from across the same group, namely: Probrand Ltd with Icomm Technologies, and Mercato Solutions Ltd. Additionally, the group's KnowledgeBus and KnowledgeKube helped as part of this journey to provide the basis for an integrated cutting-edge supply chain.

The whole is greater than the sum of its parts

First coined by the philosopher Aristotle, this phrase aptly defines the modern concept of synergy. Heritage across different organizations or company divisions, and the potential for synergy amongst them, is a good starting point for this case study.

It is important to acknowledge at the outset that, combined and in collaboration, the three businesses referred to in the introduction above had already established professional brands in their own right, dedicated to helping customers thrive with relevant and innovative technology. Probrand's IT Index, developed by the group, is Europe's largest business-to-business (B2B) marketplace, coupled with procurement managed services to help customers save time and money buying information technology (IT) products. Icomm Technologies provides IT services to help customers get more from their IT, whilst Mercato Solutions delivers bespoke and branded software platforms and applications for business transformation. The nature of their business and collaborative interdependencies on each other to deliver to their customer base has without question been somewhat unique.

These organizations recently embraced collaboration, merging IT reseller Probrand with IT services business Icomm Technologies, relaunching as Probrand, a new digital marketplace offering IT products and services. The underlying marketplace platform is designed and delivered by software company Mercato Solutions. The objective of this move was to enable customers to choose how they researched and bought IT products and services on their terms, either online or offline, and in the most efficient and transparent way possible and from one single company. As independent companies, Probrand and Mercato Solutions now make up the Probrand Group.

Heritage value proposition

Before discussing the new technology offering, it is important to understand the historical value proposition of each of the three heritage strands of the business prior to merger. They can be described as follows:

- Probrand – Probrand essentially focused on resale of IT hardware and software to business and public sector organizations across the UK. The business branded its historic e-commerce channel as The IT Index. This part of the business undertook substantive research and development work on behalf of many blue-chip clients who cannot be named as they are the subject of exclusive arrangements under strict confidentiality and non-disclosure agreements.

- Mercato – Mercato was the software development house, designing, building and implementing high-end software applications and bespoke software solutions across the globe. Again, many projects were with blue chip clients in respect of server and storage tools rolled out to over 150 countries worldwide.

- Icomm Technologies – Icomm was the service and solutions house, managing end customer IT estates, and offering a complete end-to-end IT solution from consultancy through to deployment and ongoing management. Services ranged from desktop deployment through to managed infrastructure services.

Growth through collaborative innovation and automation

With over two decades of heritage, the Probrand Group has a global outlook and now serves an extensive customer base of thousands of private and public sector organizations as a Crown Commercial Service framework supplier. The business prides itself on investing in great people, putting value into collaborative partnership relationships with its own innovation, commitment and integrity.

Since its inception, Probrand has grown from a small 'value added reseller' to a multi-award winning group. Three years of funding spawned specialist IT services business Icomm Technologies, then the launch of The IT Index, and innovative software business Mercato Solutions. All three have experienced sustained growth and been acknowledged with numerous awards and listings, the pinnacle of which was a Queen's Award for Enterprise Innovation.

The launch of a new digital marketplace achieved through merger has enable the group's customers to choose how they research and buy IT products and services on their terms, either online or offline, in the most efficient and transparent way possible and from one company. The Group has invested in delivering the best possible range of IT products and market leading services available. The rational for this merger was to provide an enhanced offering to the way people research and/or buy business IT, acknowledging the trend that this is changing in line with consumer purchasing and self-service online.

The rise of user-friendly digital marketplaces that offer more choice and make it quick and easy to buy Cloud services and much more is proof of that. Existing supply chain dynamics and manual ways of working can mean that buying IT is a hassle, and customers will dictate the demise of resellers who add no value, just complexity and margin. This has presented an opportunity to deliver on the vision of giving business users the same rich, transparent and personalized digital experience they have come to expect from consumer marketplaces – with additional procurement best practice and benchmarking for those who want it.

Probrand has a mission to automate the supply chain and turn overheads into assets and to eliminate contrived commerce. Empowering people to be more effective in the business and to develop new skills is a priority focus and this harnesses innovation and technology for future growth in domestic and export economies, especially in times of austerity.

The group is a multimillion pound concern that facilitates transformation across a variety of private and public sector organizations right through to global brands operating within hugely volatile worldwide supply chains. It continues to grow its business exponentially, employing a growing mix of specialist developers, web designers, content managers, project managers and senior sales consultants located across the UK and in Calcutta, India.

Fundamentally, the group takes complex problems and solves them with a variable mix of data and algorithms before surfacing the solution into an end user experience or 'tool'. Essentially, their approach is to treat data with priority and tools are then applied to that data to unlock the opportunity within. It is the powerful combination of 'data' and 'tools' that has unlocked the potential or supporting organizations to do more, better and faster, through relentless transaction automation and using creative management of big data as the key driver in supply chain management and procurement. This reduces duplication of effort and releases employee time that can be better deployed in higher-value processes that require human intelligence to further develop and automate.

Probrand has been focusing its efforts on giving IT buyers the most efficient ways of getting competitive deals on IT from across a hugely fragmented, multi-level supply chain globally. It brings a competitive market into one environment where people can buy direct. Probrand, using its developed technology engines, represents the future of collaborative dynamic marketplaces and it has found innovative ways of delivering structured data platforms.

The organizations continuously develop and invest in their technology, for both internal systems and customer-facing innovative big data tools that have been developed. This is driving the business in procurement, process and workflows excellence and supporting their supply chain partners. Their processes also extend to support their customers. Mercato has developed web services and data connectors to enable customer enterprise resource planning (ERP) system integration, allowing them to update previously 'flat' and out of date catalogues with 'live' and dynamic catalogues to ensure efficient procurement, thereby saving time and money checking pricing manually, completing the automated purchase cycle.

The tools developed by the group allow the supply chain to be managed from product manufacturer through to the end user/customer. Data gathering, data cleansing, data aggregators and dynamic catalogue creation are all managed by rules engines that are managed by the procurement team and driven in conjunction with the business strategies and objectives of the group. This roles-based system enables Probrand to be extremely versatile in a fast-changing market, and thanks to the technology it can react much faster to a changing economic environment than its competitors.

KnowledgeBus and KnowledgeKube: The basis for an integrated cutting-edge supply chain

Within Probrand Group itself the procurement and supply chain team has full access to an extensive reporting suite that gives team members real time information on every aspect of the supply chain as well as historical analysis of supplier pricing and stock availability (using the benchmarking solution KnowledgeBus). This allows procurement and supply chain management (PSCM) practitioners the tools and power to manage business contracts and police agreements in far more detail than its suppliers ever could.

These technology developments have resulted in a series of innovative technology toolsets, ww.knowledgekube.co.uk, which are made available on the intranet to encourage all staff to collaborate. These extremely powerful question and ratings engines deliver better-informed decisions formulated by highly complex algorithms and can help to 'de-skill' complex sales cycles or develop an extensive pipeline of opportunities by simply asking the right questions and allowing automated workflow to decipher results and escalate opportunities when required.

This is a fantastic example of a PSCM team making extensive use of advanced technology and highly sophisticated software to create an integrated 'cutting edge' supply chain.

Progora digital procurement solution – a faster, easier digital path to procurement?

Mercato Solutions' 'Progora' solution is a marketplace technology that saves buyers and customers time and money on procurement. It brings buyers and suppliers together in a centralized, Cloud-based purchasing platform configured to their requirements. From a staff and supplier perspective, it feels like a user-friendly consumer shopping experience where it's easy to select and purchase products.

Mercato has created the Progora marketplace/e-procurement platform, and Probrand is a customer using that platform in the IT vertical to deliver marketplace for business IT. However as a system, Progora is so much more. Its innovative technology is designed for complex organizations, adapting to their many business requirements and ensuring each purchase is made in the most economical way. The result, simply put, is lower expenditure, reduced rogue procurement, stronger supplier relationships and better collaboration.

The compelling case for a technology solution like Porgora is:

- A swift return on investment and low total cost of ownership – Users realize the many benefits for a swift return on investment and low total cost of ownership.

- Centralized purchasing platform – Aggregation and automation enable users to save money and reduce rogue procurement.

- Real-time price and stock checks – Algorithms automatically calculate the most economical way to purchase.

- User-friendly experience – Procurement practitioners have said that it feels like home shopping online.

- Fast deployment – Swift deployment of a robust platform that simplifies purchasing and delivers cost savings.

- Enhanced buyer-supplier collaboration – Users can foster strong working relationships across the supplier community, from SMEs to large businesses.

- Flexibility and scalability – New categories, frameworks and functionality, like guided advisors and purchase-to-pay workflows, can easily be added.

Features of the technology

The principal features of the technology are:

1 **Data management** – Progora is built on advanced data management technology capable of processing millions of products and hundreds of prices each day. This means that all a customer's suppliers and catalogues are easily accessible in a central, user-friendly platform, with real time price and stock checks, so that the customer will always know the most economical way to purchase. And with the ability to integrate all the customer's frameworks and procurement rules – and tailor them for user types – it's easy to save money while ensuring compliance.

2 **Product management** – With Progora, customers can manage millions of products while ensuring that everyone is relying on up-to-date, comprehensive and clean data. Enhanced product content improves the customer experience and gives people the information they need to make the right choice:

   – the ability to process millions of products daily;

   – automated aggregation and consistent user experience;

   – rich content drawn from industry-standard sources and suppliers;

   – worldwide supply chain management.

3 **Catalogue management** – Progora's innovative technology turns flat ERP catalogues into dynamic data sources. This means users automatically access the latest product information and are able to eliminate rogue or maverick procurement practices because people only see the products they are allowed to buy. So effectively there is:

   – powerful product/pricing matrices;

   – automatic linking of catalogues and customers;

   – changes published live in minutes;

   – the facility to use the data anywhere.

4 **Price management** – Progora's technology also gives buyers and customers real-time pricing that includes all administration and delivery costs, and stock levels. This empowers users to make informed decisions based on true cost, helping them use budgets more effectively:

   – versatile discount capabilities;

   – rogue, maverick behaviour detection and rules engine;

- able to carry out more than 100 million daily price and stock checks;

- the customer or buyer sees the savings.

5 **Extensibility** – Flexibility is one of Progora's big benefits, and it sets the offering apart from many other market solutions. Not only is it easy to add new categories, products, suppliers and frameworks, but it's also easy to add new functionality to support users, facilitate collaboration, boost efficiency and simplify compliance. The new technology offering also incorporates the following:

- **Virtual product advisors** – These help users purchase the right product without having to pick up the phone. The online virtual advisors ask relevant questions based on the user's needs and respond based on real-life use cases, not just technical feeds. Then they recommend the appropriate products, so it's easy to make the right choice, fast. For example:

  - provides questions and answers to locate the best outcome;

  - simplifies complex business decisions;

  - de-skills product selection;

  - fast, self-serve facilities.

- **Guided experiences** – It helps customers make the right purchasing decisions by making it easy to select the most appropriate products. There is no need to figure out how many lumens you need for a projector, for example – you just need to know how bright the room should be, and the tool does the rest. Salient takeaways here include:

  - a consultative approach;

  - compare without having to get multiple quotes;

  - designed by industry specialists;

  - qualification and signposting.

- **Business process improvement** – The technology makes it easy for departments to collaborate, eliminating inefficiency and duplications that costs money and effects service levels. It makes it easier to integrate organization-specific work flows and automation into organizations' processes, thereby ensuring that everyone is compliant and has the information they need at exactly the right time. Salient takeaways here include:

  - delivers process compliance;

  - automated workflows and actions;

  - event-based automation;

  - simplifies complex decision making.

- **Integration and data sharing** – It connects with multiple data sources and line-of-business applications so the organization can share information and streamline processes across more than 50 products, services, formats and technologies. Salient takeaways here are:
  - customer relationship management and marketing automation;
  - accounting systems;
  - ERP and collaboration;
  - on-premises and Cloud databases;
  - social media;
  - networking.

Transformation and opportunities created by the technology

We turn now to the transformation and opportunities created by this technology.

Digital transformation

Digitalization is creating so many opportunities for both companies and individuals. People are becoming more adaptable in embracing technology and managing digital change. Going forward, it is expected that organizations will increase their digital transformation budgets. Businesses are expected to transform their operational processes, customer experiences and building links between their web, mobile apps and offline engagement. In this time of emerging digital transformation, software organizations will be more and more driven to build smarter solutions that will give them at competitive edge.

Platforms like Progora and KnowledgeKube can create unique marketplaces for both products and services, rapidly build complex enterprise applications to save organizations time and money, increasing operational efficiency. Progora in particular has been designed for complex organizations, adapting to many business requirements and ensuring each purchase is made in an economic way. The result is lower expenditure, reduced maverick or rogue procurement activity, stronger supplier relationships and better collaboration.

Online marketplaces

Online marketplaces are great selling channels that can host large product bases. With the rise of e-commerce, UK online sales have grown exponentially. Nowadays, consumer behaviour depends on how the marketplaces are being built. Modern customers feel empowered when they can shop around at a fast speed and they can make more informed purchasing decisions when it comes to prices. In addition, customers want to self-serve and do not want to be sold to directly over the phone. They will do their own research and reach out if necessary.

The ever-evolving B2B selling space, increasingly complex sales process and buyers' expectations are becoming less effective without an integrated marketplace. B2B online purchasers are looking for a great experience with speed and convenience as two huge factors. An easy search process and seamless check-out will help buyers more easily transition from traditional buying methods to online purchasing.

Progora is essentially a B2B marketplace platform that helps customers reduce time and money on procurement by quickly building bespoke marketplaces using cutting edge technology from an exceptionally powerful and compelling software platform that allows vendors to reach and interact with customers seamlessly. Successful marketplaces rely on creating a community where the customer and the supplier see a mutual benefit. For a supplier it may be access to a larger audience, ease of engagement or lower cost of sale. For a customer or buyer, it may be:

- a centralized location for information;
- a competitive pricing environment;
- ease of engagement;
- lower cost of purchase.

Successful design and automation

The main advantages of automation are increased productivity, time saving, improved search ability and reduced direct human labour costs. A centralized location for all procurement with up-to-date pricing and product catalogues with rich content help with decision making and analytics to review spending and trends.

The Progora web store provides a user-friendly e-commerce experience with plenty of relevant, customized product information and simple price comparisons. Every area of the store's front end is designed to make the purchasing experience as streamlined and intuitive as possible, allowing end users to easily find the products they require, even if they have little to no experience.

How important is the customer journey?

Customer journeys are what drives the user to engage with the content of the platform and be interested in the site's products and services. A well-integrated marketplace brings buyers and suppliers together in an innovative digital environment and creates a space to facilitate both smart purchasing and selling processes. Efficiency, connectivity and integration are Progora's most important features that help businesses achieve a seamless experience for both customers and suppliers.

Public sector practice

The technology developed by Proband has been particularly embraced by the public sector.

The need for better spend management

This sector frequently complains about wanting better spend management information. Fragmented sourcing, unstructured data, incomplete recording systems, and inactive contracted key performance indicators are common challenges, and many public-sector procurement departments struggle with aligning these issues to cash savings targets and capacity objectives. Progora, as an e-procurement platform, helps overcome these challenges by providing structured data to streamline supplier management and enable more informed procurement decisions to help meet objectives

How it works

For users:

- Progora gives users a single marketplace view for buying products and services.
- It enhances searches for what is needed, seeing all compliant suppliers and sorting data by the most appropriate criteria, ie the lowest price.

- It completes the purchase within the system – no more punching out to supplier websites and no more confusion about frameworks.
- It makes purchasing faster and easier while reducing rogue or maverick procurement activity.

For procurement:

- Progora gives more control over procurement processes, and the supply chain.
- With real-time management information and analytics, users have an accurate picture of buying patterns.
- This enables users to monitor compliance, contract KPIs and tail-end spend.
- It allows access to data on market pricing and cost controls, sharing benchmarks, negotiating with suppliers and maximizing savings.
- It assigns suppliers to particular agreements, product categories or service types.
- It provides supplier control at a framework/contract level whilst making it visible online, to allow all users to procure through the correct supply chain.

Governance

Similarly, in the public sector there are constant requests for improved governance and more control over tail-end spend. Managing tail-end spend is difficult if you're struggling with lots of mini-frameworks and you want to trust colleagues to buy appropriately to risk. With so much unstructured procurement-related information available, it's difficult to ensure sufficient oversight, manage risks and deliver compliance. Progora as an e-procurement platform helps streamline governance and monitor spend management decisions. It sits on top of other systems, giving users a central point for making purchases, managing suppliers and accessing data. In terms of how it works for users and procurement the points are similar to spend management above.

Embedding

The demand for procurement as a function to be embedded within the organization is also common in the public sector. Many feel that organizations don't make full use of procurement's market intelligence. If this is wanting or lacking then it is likely that practitioners are unable to make agile responses to rapid changes in supply and demand. Having established purchasing structures and models in place is a good start; however, the next step is to transform procurement into a true enabler, where you're delivering real strategic value by helping stakeholders and suppliers work collaboratively together to achieve the organization's objectives. E-procurement solutions such as Progora again helps to do this. In terms of how it works for users and procurement, the points are similar to spend management above.

Strategic procurement

Many public sector organizations want high-impact, strategic procurement. Indeed, this is the Holy Grail for procurement – to be a true strategic partner in the organization! The reality is that to be able to achieve this level of influence you need the tools to be able to deliver in the following key areas:

- strategic levers for planning and forecasting investment that satisfy taxation authorities;
- market intelligence and insight, the evidence base to enable a strong relationship to be promoted and developed with suppliers and taking a proactive approach to procurement.

E-procurement platforms like Progora provide all of these elements, giving more value to existing processes and systems whilst also providing the extra leverage needed to deliver maximum value to organizations.

University procurement considerations

It is probably also apt to briefly touch on university procurement needs. They tend to look to improve relationships with suppliers, to improve efficiency in finance departments and ultimately to have better procurement spend. Universities strive to provide educational excellence that changes, improves and ensures effectiveness in preparing students for successful careers. Various requirements are needed to help achieve this aim, such as:

- high-quality equipment to support research;
- state of the art facilities;
- better engagement with institutions, stakeholders and suppliers;
- choice and opportunity for students.

Although one of the main priorities is to invest in equipment and innovation, universities are constantly under pressure to cut expenditure and increase service levels. In fact, two of the biggest challenges in education are finding the correct equipment with the right amount of product information, and understanding the pricing structure. A centralized marketplace such as the e-procurement offering outlined in this case study is the ideal solution, connecting different departments of a university together to ensure collaborative research and the purchase of products to meet all requirements.

Conclusion

To conclude this case study, what we have explored is an organization that essentially provides specialist digitalized IT products, managed services and solutions to thousands of clients across small to medium sized businesses and all areas of the public sector, including large blue-chip organizations. Its value proposition has helped customers procure IT more efficiently and deliver IT services that run and transform business operations.

Probrand and Mercato are a great example of overarching unity of two companies working in collaboration. Mercato has created the Progora marketplace/e-procurement platform and Probrand is essentially a customer using that platform in the IT vertical to deliver marketplace for business IT. The tie-in between Probrand (IT selling) and the use of the platform to do so is indeed a very clever synergistic relationship. Indeed, the Proband marketplace has been likened to a business version of Amazon, but better.

Unlike traditional service providers that are sales people heavy or are pure e-shops, this organization has looked to engage customers collaboratively using technology and people in tandem to provide a better experience and more cost-effective service. Probrand was the first organization to use real time price and stock comparison and then auto-attach relevant pricing entitlements to save customers time when purchasing. The combination of digital and physical ensures buyers or clients can choose to engage with the organization at the right time, and in the most effective way, to ensure that they get the best outcome for their business.

In order to share a 'customer eye view' of the technology covered in this case study and show examples of the benefits it delivers, the reader is signposted to the blog links below, which are short case-study endorsements from the housing and government sectors, and which articulate the value proposition of the technology in practice:

https://www.probrand.co.uk/blog/pb/January-2018/Midland-Heart-Housing-Association-streamlines-proc

https://www.probrand.co.uk/blog/pb/November-2017-1/Government-Actuary-s-Department-saves-170-000-with

https://www.probrand.co.uk/blog/pb/November-2017-1/Mears-Group-streamlines-IT-procurement-with-Probra

Probrand is, without question, an early pathfinder in this new and highly exciting field of digitalized procurement, and it is hoped that this case study and the above blog links will have provided the reader with a snapshot into the future.

FURTHER READING AND USEFUL WEBSITES

The author would like to signpost readers to the following further information and reading material, and also to web links to various professional bodies, institutions, industry trade associations that he has made substantive engagement with throughout his career and that he considers strongly embrace a collaborative ethos, with the aim of helping others derive better value.

Further reading

British Standards Institution (BSI) PAS 11000-1 (2010) Collaborative business relationships, The BSI Standards Limited

Chick, G and Handfield, R (2015) *The Procurement Value Proposition: The rise of supply management*, Kogan Page, London

Cox, A (1997) *Business Success: A way of thinking about strategy, critical supply chain assets and operational best practice*, Earlesgate Press, London

Cox, A (2003) *Supply Chain Management: A guide to best practice*, Financial Times/Prentice Hall, London

Cox, A (2004) *Win–Win? The paradox of value and interests in business relationships*, Earlesgate Press, London

Cox, A, Lonsdale, C, Sanderson, J and Watson, G (2004) *Business Relationships for Competitive Advantage: Managing alignment and misalignment in buyer and supplier transactions*, Earlesgate Press, London

Cox, A, Sanderson, J and Watson, G (2000) *Power Regimes: Mapping the DNA of business and supply chain relationships*, Earlesgate Press, London

First Point Assessment, Achilles Information Management Limited website: https://www.fpal.com

Gibbs, R and Humphries, A (2009) *Strategic Alliances and Marketing Partnerships: Gaining competitive advantage through collaboration and partnering*, Kogan Page, London

Goleman, D, Boatzis, R and Hansen, M (2013) *HBR's 10 Must Reads on Collaboration* (with featured article 'Social intelligence and the biology of leadership'), Harvard Business Review Press, Cambridge, MA

Hansen, MT (2009) *Collaboration: How leaders avoid the traps, build common ground, and reap big results*, Harvard Business School Press, Cambridge, MA

Hawkins, DE (2006) *Corporate Social Responsibility: Balancing tomorrow's sustainability and today's profitability*, Palgrave Macmillan, London

Hawkins, DE (2006) *The Bending Moment: Energizing corporate business strategy*, Palgrave Macmillan, London

Hawkins, DE (2013) *Raising the Standard for Collaboration: Harnessing the Benefits of BS 11000 collaborative business relationships*, The BSI Standards Limited

Hawkins, DE and Shan, R (2005) *Sun Tzu and the Project Battleground: Creating project strategy from 'the art of war'*, Palgrave Macmillan, London

Humphries, A and Gibbs, R (2010) *Collaborative Change: Creating high performance partnerships and alliances*, SC: CreateSpace Independent Publishing Platform, Amazon

International Standards Organization (ISO) (nd) ISO 44001: Collaborative business relationships standard, The BSI Standards Limited

Lank, E (2005) *Collaborative Advantage: Organisations win by working together*, Palgrave Macmillan, London

Lipnack, J and Stamps, J (1997) *Virtual Teams: Reaching across space, time, and organizations with technology*, John Wiley & Sons, New York

LOGIC (2018) *Leading Oil and Gas Industry Competitiveness: Part of Oil & Gas UK Industry Association*, Aberdeen and London

Partnership Sourcing. Future Connections.

Partnership Sourcing. Vision 2010.

Springer, ML and de Bock, J (2005) *Sustainable Logistics and Supply Chains: Integral approach*, European Commission, Brussels

Springer, MJS (2014) *Enabling Horizontal Collaboration*, Briefs in Operational Research series, Springer, New York

Tate, W (2009) *The Search for Leadership: An organisational perspective*, Triarchy Press, Devon

Tompkins, JA (2003) *No Boundaries: Break through to supply chain excellence*, Tompkins Press, NC

Waller, A (2018) *Collaboration Across Supply Chains: Case studies on working together for sustainable business performance*, Kogan Page, London

Useful websites

Association for Project Management: https://www.apm.org

Association of Cost Engineers: https://www.acoste.org.uk/

Chartered Institute for Procurement and Supply: https://www.cips.org.uk

East of England Energy Group(contractor trade association): https://eeegr.com/

Energy Industries Council: https://the-eic.com

Institute for Collaborative Working: www.instituteforcollaborativeworking.com/

International Institute for Advanced Purchasing and Supply: www.iiaps.org/
Northern Offshore Federation Energy (contractor trade association):
https://www.nofenergy.co.uk
Oil & Gas Technology Centre: https://theogtc.com/
Oil & Gas UK: https://oilandgasuk.co.uk/
Robert Gordon University, Aberdeen: https://www.rgu.ac.uk/
Royal Institution of Chartered Surveyors: https://www.rics.org/

INDEX